The Book of the WD 2-8-0s and 2-10-0s

By Richard Derry

Irwell Press Ltd.

Acknowledgements

This 'Book Of' varies somewhat from others in that it omits the usual works histories. A lot of the information survives of course though not from the engines' days abroad. But the plain fact of the matter is lack of space. I hope readers will be content with the allocations and that this will be enough of a 'fix' so far as tabulation is concerned. As for 'details and differences' in the case of the WDs these were probably the least pronounced/confusing/maddening of any large BR class (in terms of 'mods per engine' they must be minimal) and I've elected this time to note them in pictures as we go along, in the captions. I hope my fellows in the engine picking fraternity will approve. I owe a debt of gratitude to the following, many of them 'the usual suspects' but in no particular order: Gavin Morrison, George Reeve, Barry Hoper, The Great North of Scotland Railway Association, Allan C. Baker, Brian C. Bailey, Peter Groom, Peter Coster, Eric Youldon, Chris Hawkins, Alec Swain, Andy Foster, Paul Conibeare, Paul Chancellor. The WD remains the only loco that was (at least to us) identifiable *before* you actually saw it...

First published in the United Kingdom in 2008
by Irwell Press Limited, 59A, High Street, Clophill,
Bedfordshire MK45 4BE
Printed by Konway Press

Contents

Just look at the clag! No carbon footprint then, nor any worry about where the coal was coming from. No.77230 (90198 in August 1950) according to the back of this C.R.L. Coles study made into a commercial postcard has a down goods on Ruislip troughs, on the GW and GC joint line. The trough is visible in front of the loco, then on loan to the LNER. It was recalled by the WD in February 1945.

They all started life like this one, 77327 (90239 in May 1951) a North British product which was new in June 1943. The named K2 and the boilers in the background suggest that this is Cowlairs works yard. The same month saw 77320-77331 delivered, not bad at all considering it was all done under war conditions. Although essential the air pump on the right-hand side rather detracts from the smooth lines of the loco. It spent 18 months on loan to the LNER before being returned to the WD.

1. THE CALL OF WAR

Early on these two classes were something of a mystery to me, and to those around me; in the days of one's gilded youth they remained a stubborn, untouched block of endless numbers secreted away near the very end of the Ian Allan ABCs. The 'WD' was also intriguing to a child for, though none of us had even stepped north of the border in generations, the family adapted the old Scottish tradition and bestowed on this son his grandmother's maiden name, in this case Watson, so I was in fact 'Richard WD'. It could of been much worse of course and I think it was Bob Wilson, the Arsenal and Scottish international goalkeeper, who bore the burden of 'Primrose', living for years in mortal terror of the crowd finding out. A time later, during endless wondering gazes at my first Ian Allan *Locoshed Book* (still with me, though largely disintegrated) it was obvious why the chances of finding any in the Weybridge area of Surrey were so few and far between. It might seem obvious now, but it certainly wasn't then, when we all started out. As for the 2-10-0s, they might just as well have been working the Lunar Division of BR. Ronald Wilkinson in *British Railways Illustrated* has recently very amusingly charted his teenage search for similarly obscure engines, in his case, hailing from GN climes, these were the Q1 0-6-0s, engines of course with which we were familiar in the extreme. I hope to repeat his *Q1 Quest* in that esteemed periodical soon; *Austerity Quest* perhaps.

On learning more, it seemed somewhat unfair that fifty-odd of the 2-8-0s had in fact been based at some Southern sheds in very early BR days, including Hither Green, Ashford, Brighton, Bricklayers Arms and Feltham which supplied the local goods engines that worked through our home town, Weybridge. I convinced myself that, sitting in the pram pushed by my sister Jean, I had seen them coming under the local road bridge. Very much later it was gratifying to bag two former Feltham WDs, 90142 and 90578.

My abiding memory of the class is of Friday April 26th 1962 when, with friends, I travelled on an Ian Allan excursion from Waterloo to Southampton Docks and Swindon Works. The cost was a typical 21/- (£1.05p) and did I have to work to raise that guinea. Travel was behind 34094 MORTEHOE and after a good tour of the Docks and a haul of USA 0-6-0Ts we headed for Swindon. Waiting on the station there, a goods train was noted in the distance. Now my camera only took eight shots and printing and developing had to be paid for out of miniscule pocket money; even so I took my one and only shot of a WD at work, 90174, then of Southall shed and destined to be withdrawn in the October and scrapped at Crewe Works the following June. Besides a

2-10-0 3701, later 73701, more or less new on loan to the LMS in April 1944; 'Army green' livery, six inch numbering, tiny WD flanking the vertical arrow on the tender. It went to Rugby shed in April 1944 and was returned to the WD in August for shipping abroad. It ended up in the Netherlands as 5029 and was scrapped in 1951.

No.7071 (numbers increased by 70000 in September 1944) at Hull Springhead shed in 1944 during its loan to the LNER. For some reason it is paired with a tender from C6 Atlantic 532 withdrawn in January 1943. The high running plate allows easy access to the running gear and Riddles perpetuated this sort of feature in his BR Standard designs. The feature behind the chimney was the anti-vacuum, or snifting, valve which in early days was less prominent, as here. See the close-up of 90386 on page 117 for further detail. Photograph B.K.B. Green, Initial Photographics.

couple of visits to Southall shed my best harvesting came on a Sunday visit to Woodford Halse (where from the mid-1950s nearly forty had at times been allocated) thanks to Mr. Potter's London Railfans Club (I believe that was the correct title). This was a red letter day as I saw my only three named B1 4-6-0s (the one I missed was 61011 WATERBUCK – still painful) but the WDs noted were 90040, 90095, 90346, 90433, 90448, 90474, 90504, 90520, 90524, 90563, 90570, 90589, 90667, 90672, 90697 and 90701. Many enthusiasts will find this a piffling amount but from the pauperised remoteness of Surrey it was magical stuff. It was easily the largest number I ever saw at one time, though back then I had no idea of the remarkable story behind these grimy, groaning, clanking beasts, for all the world like rhinos round a water hole...

One thing. The enormous, singular difference in the story of the WDs compared to any other BR class is, of course, their service abroad. This is a hugely complicated story, which I'll hardly even outline in this book; the movements of all these engines in this country before the Invasion of Europe, their subsequent departures from the UK, their movements while in the various countries and then their activities, storage and so on upon

coming back to these shores, is truly daunting in its complexity. Fortunately, with heroics of diligence, scholarship and pure, breathtaking devotion to the task, all this has been authoritatively elaborated, in the following three works that I know of: *The 2-8-0 and 2-10-0 locomotives of the War Department 1939-1945*, RCTS, compiled by D.R. Pollock and D.E. White, 1946.
Allied Military Locomotives of the Second World War by R. Tourret, Tourret Publishing 1976, revised 1995.
Austerity 2-8-0s and 2-10-0s by J.W.P. Rowledge, Ian Allan, 1987.

In such places where the text touches upon the WDs abroad, the references are largely owed to the original work in these three volumes. They have also been consulted for the story before leaving the country and during the period after repatriation but before passing to British Railways, though contemporary journals such as *The Railway Observer*, Stephenson Locomotive Society *Journal* and *The Railway Gazette* have also proved of inestimable value.

WAR COMES
The origins of the two classes lie in the Second World War. It had been accepted that war would come and

Britain eased itself smoothly and soon into the sort of collectivist command economy equipped for total war, the echoes of which are with us still. The only model for the military campaign was the previous one, with the added dismal certainty that air power would prove far more devastating than before, and might well prove conclusive. The British would despatch an Expeditionary Force as before and, as in the previous conflict, the ebbs and flows of territorial gain (though a stalemate was thought the likeliest outcome) would mean a steady attrition in locomotives and stock, that would have to be made up in imports from Britain. Locomotives were *matériel*, just like lorries and tanks. In the Great War, as we all know, the locomotives had been famously the ROD (Railway Operating Division) GC-type O4 2-8-0s along with the GW 0-6-0s and 2-6-0s.

While living in Glasgow in 1939, the LMS man later responsible for the BR Standards, R.A. Riddles (recently returned from the successful tour of the USA with the 'Coronation Scot' which remained trapped over there; the engine was only brought back in 1942) was summoned to London early in September for an appointment at the Ministry of Supply, in its

No.77031 (90128 in June 1949), one of the first that went on loan to the LNER, working past Saughton Junction just west of Edinburgh on the sort of job they were built for, heavy goods. Its home shed THORNTON stencilled on buffer beam, air pump gone of course. It had been loaned to the Netherlands railways – is that a trace of marking on the cab under the number? Photograph W. Hermiston, www.transporttreasury.co.uk

A WD 2-8-0 comes a cropper. There is no information as to the circumstances but the sleepers in the foreground could mean relaying of the track might have been a factor. Whatever the cause the photographer has been quick on the scene - it would take a while to clear this mess up. The engine is 70836, a North British product of May 1944; by now it is on the Great Western, though we could be in BR country by now, for it was not renumbered 90324 until spring 1949. It had been loaned to the GWR at St Philips Marsh since the end of 1946; note the additional GW lamp irons on the buffer beam and smokebox door.

Invaders. Over a thousand of the WD locos went abroad during and after the War in Europe when of course vastly more extensive heavy equipment existed in our docks. This is a group of 2-8-0s being loaded on 'Sea Train Vessel' *Texas* in the docks at Cardiff. This is a later batch then, that went the 'long way' round and not on one of the SR ferries.

One of the 2-10-0s that didn't go abroad. Originally 73797, it was kept at the Longmoor Military Railway in Hampshire and used for training. The location is Polmadie shed, Glasgow which it worked from for a short period in 1957 before a full overhaul by North British. It had been renumbered 601 in 1952 and named KITCHENER after the British General. Jubilee 4-6-0 in background. Photograph B.K.B. Green Collection, Initial Photographics.

Once returned from Europe a number of the 2-8-0s went into store before they could be made serviceable though of course the LNER, chronically short of such power, did purchase 200 of them straight away. The Southern soon ran out of space and the other companies were prevailed upon to find storage sites and this is the dump at Kingham, where the GWR found room for nearly forty WDs. 77006 with its typically Belgian style of numbering was later loaned to the LNER, in March 1947, becoming 90106 in August 1950.

Directorate of Transport Materials, established as the country moved towards the inevitable war. Riddles, like most men his age, had served in the first conflict.

More or less as the British Government's Ultimatum wore away, Riddles was appointed 'Director of Transportation Equipment' as the post soon became, responsible for 'all types of equipment including railways, docks and harbours, inland water transport and the War Department Fleet.' With the British Expeditionary Army soon in France Riddles was going to be kept busy, for locomotives were needed not only over the Channel but elsewhere in the Empire. Despite an offer from the LNER to hand over all its O4s, the idea of sending these older 2-8-0s again was rejected. Things had moved on and the old O4s were a generation or more behind – even though the Eastern Region didn't get rid of the last of them till 1965! As it was, getting on for a hundred of the venerable O4s *did* in fact go abroad in the Second World War. They were consigned to the Middle East and never came back; it is hard not to conclude that the War Department (how many us recall the ever present 'WD blanket' in the 1950s, about an inch thick and feeling like Desperate

Dan's chin, but a weighty comfort when the ice was forming on the *inside* windows of the bedroom?) never cared one way or another if they ever came back.

There had even been a proposal from the LNER (J.W.P. Rowledge, *Austerity 2-8-0s and 2-10-0s*, Ian Allan, 1987) that all its O4s could be handed over if only the company was allowed to build replacement three cylinder O2 2-8-0s. So far as the national picture was concerned, with labour and material at such a premium this, Riddled deemed, could not be countenanced. He had calculated that two engines of a pared-down, simplified design could be produced for every one of Gresley's more complicated engines. The GWR 28XX, while robust and reliable, was out of the general loading gauge. Starting as he would mean to go on one day with the BR Standards, he chose an established LMS type, the 8F. If the need was for a proven, powerful, reliable loco with wide availability which, above all, had to be built quickly, you hardly need the benefit of hindsight to see it as a perfectly sensible decision.

There were 240 Stanier 2-8-0s ordered for the War Department though only 208 were constructed; 50

by Beyer Peacock and 158 by the North British Locomotive Company. The forty ordered from Vulcan Foundry were not built, for by then the switch to Riddles WD 2-8-0s had been made – see below. An earlier 51 Stanier 8Fs built either by Crewe or by Vulcan for the LMS were transferred to the WD and these 8Fs of various origin went on to even more varied careers. Some never left these shores, going in the end back to the LMS, while more than twenty ended up in Davy Jones's Locker (a number of upright Stanier fireboxes loomed into view on the bed of the Red Sea in a Jacque Coustou-esque documentary on the telly some years ago while other 8Fs ended up in the Irish Sea – or was it the Bristol Channel?). Others lived out their lives abroad – most famously the Turkish ones I'd think, chased down by British photographers to the end, while others were repatriated, the last not until 1957, rather after the fashion of those Japanese soldiers who refused to believe that war had ended, emerging blinking into the modern world after decades in hiding.

But back to our WD 2-8-0s. As is famously well known, the WD is the 8F pared of materials and practices which were either scarce or protracted; it was rather if, had you

One of the lower numbered LNER locos, 3017; it had carried WD 77360 and was obtained by the LNER in December 1946. It is running light engine, tender first somewhere, it is assumed, in LNER territory, the footplate crew quite intent on the photographer. Or maybe they're holding on tight; tender first running with a WD could be perilous... This loco later became BR 90017, in June 1951. Photograph J. Robertson, www.transporttreasury.co.uk

Although looking like it still might be working for the WD 77456 is at Aberdeen Ferryhill shed on 16 June 1949, when based at Dundee Tay Bridge shed. Its scruffy condition ('start as you mean to go on' as it were) belies the fact that internally it is in good nick. It was renumbered 90600 in July 1950. Photograph H.C. Casserley, courtesy R.M. Casserley.

LNER days with 3069 (90069 from September 1950) working a goods train through Doncaster. Just look at the condition of the boiler and the cabside; the conventional number has disappeared and someone has helpfully chalked it high on the cabside. The number is far clearer on the front buffer beam. Photograph J. Davenport, Initial Photographics.

been designing an Austerity version of some grand marque of car, you'd substituted a four cylinder mass produced engine for the six cylinder turbo, simpler gearbox, folding instead of wind-down window, no chrome; all that sort of thing. You end up with something like the American Jeep. E.S. Cox in *British Railways Standard Steam Locomotives* (Ian Allan, 1966) put it all down very carefully. Riddles determined upon the 'pared down 8F' with much of the drawing work, Cox relates (he knew them all of course) done in consultation with T.F. Coleman, Chief Draughtsman of the LMS. In addition, the Drawing offices of various private builders were at his disposal.

In the stark balance sheet of wartime, every day of labour and every ton of metal (some were more scarce than others but all were at a premium) saved was precious. The figures, again, are well known, and are summarised from *British Railways Standard Steam Locomotives*:
Round top parallel boiler instead of Belpaire taper boiler
Fabricated/cast iron instead of steel castings and, so far as possible, forgings
Cast iron instead of steel wheel centres
A bare cab instead of Stanier cab

There were a lot of detail simplifications too which reduced the

time and complexity required in the construction of the engines. These largely concerned lubrication; given the expected foreshortened lifetime of the WDs, this did not need to be so sophisticated as in normal practice, where engines were expected to last forty years or more. As it was, of course, there were still substantial studs of WDs gasping away on coal trains in the north of England even till 1966. An interesting alteration was the substitution of a 'Laird' crosshead above the piston rod, reminiscent of that on Bulleid Pacifics, for instance. This was a 'modification' rather than a 'simplification' in anticipation of extra wear from sand and neglect in various desert theatres.

The efforts made under Riddles' direction, along with the manufacturers' ingenuity in coming up with quicker procedures for existing components, made for a saving of 20% in the man hours required to complete each loco, or about 6,000 hours! The importance of this, in the middle of total war, can be gauged from the fact that production was eventually ratcheted up to about seven *per week*. With the work closely overseen by a constantly-visiting Riddles, wielding all the authority and, if necessary, menace, of 'The Ministry', there were no real teething troubles and those that did arise were quickly remedied.

Colonel Rogers, the biographer of Riddles (*The Last Steam Locomotive Engineer: R.A. Riddles,* Allen & Unwin, 1970) tells the story (well, *a* story anyway – there seem to be others) of the oddly diminutive WD chimney. Criticism of his 2-8-0s was expected and Charles Lake, a respected railway journalist and a good friend had observed that, as the first thing anybody noticed about an engine was the chimney then the best way to deflect criticism was to design one that was ridiculous. The critics would then concentrate on that and forget about the rest of the thing! It certainly attracted attention (it was three inches lower than the rest of the boiler mountings) and continued to do so; Cox called it 'a squat little chimney' while Brian Haresnape considered it a 'very plain ...stumpy'. By the 1950s of course we merely accepted it as just one more of their foibles.

Production of the locomotives was carried out at private builders because the works of the 'Big Four' were occupied with their own repairs and the production of armaments. The North British Locomotive Company and the Vulcan Foundry built all of the British Austerity tender locomotives. The first one, 7000, came from NBL and was handed over in a ceremony in Glasgow on Saturday January 16th 1943, in the presence of the Minister of Supply, Sir Andrew Duncan. It had been hoped that the

The 'E' prefix on 3119 in August 1948; it became 90440 in March 1949. A perfect portrait of an engine on a turntable, in this instance at Eastfield. Turning is complete or about to begin. A good profile shows the squat chimney, clack valves, steam dome with safety valves behind, and good access to oiling points. Photograph J. Davenport, Initial Photographics.

A few of the LNER locos had 60000 added to their running numbers before BR re-cast all 733 in the 90000-90732 sequence. 63120, later 90441, is working west of Edinburgh on 11 June 1948, in what was now the Scottish Region of BR. Running number on front buffer beam and early BRITISH RAILWAYS on the tender. Photograph J. Robertson, www.transporttreasury.co.uk

St Rollox shed on 3 August 1959 with 90765 of Grangemouth partnering a Kingmoor Jubilee. The eight wheel tender was an impressive thing, 5000 gallons and 9 tons capacity but no water scoop, a thoroughly unnecessary complication for an 'Austerity' on war work in Europe. Two breathing tubes, lifting brackets at the corners, four rung ladder for access to the tender top but relatively poor footstep access from ground level. Photograph B. Hilton, www.transporttreasury.co.uk

first one would be ready before the American S160s began arriving (to much fanfare) but it was not to be, the first US locos coming in December 1942. The British locomotives were called 'Austerities' from the first, in keeping with so much else in British life at the time; Riddles himself is said to have suggested it but you can't help feeling it is the name they inevitably would have got anyway. The central specification was that they should haul 1,000 ton loads at 40 mph; here is the official wartime description:

The locomotive conforms fairly closely to the standards usually adopted on British railways for this class of engine. It has two outside cylinders driving the third pair of coupled wheels, and Walschaerts motion is employed for actuating piston valves working above the cylinders; these valves are arranged for inside admission. The control of the valve gear is effected by hand-screw reversing gear arranged for left-hand drive. The constructional details of the locomotive have been reduced in number to the lowest limit consistent with efficient working, and as far as possible renewal parts are duplicate with those of LMS standard locomotives.

The main frames are manufactured of steel-plates with stretchers formed of flanged plates and fabrications; the smoke-box saddle is of cast iron. The

boiler barrel and firebox casing are built up from steel plates of boiler quality, with longitudinal seams jointed with outside and inside butt straps. The boiler barrel is parallel and the firebox casing is of the round top type. The inner firebox is of copper. The two cylinders are of 19in. diameter and the coupled wheels are 4ft 8½in. diameter; the wheels of the leading truck are 3ft. 2in. diameter. The coupled wheelbase is 16ft. 3in. and the total wheelbase 24ft. 10in. Boiler pressure is 225lb per sq.in and the tractive effort at 85 per cent boiler pressure is 34,215lb. Weight of the engine in working order is 72 tons and of the tender 56 tons giving a total of 128 tons; of this 62 tons is available for adhesion.

The tender is of the eight wheel non-bogie pattern like that of the LNER Pacifics, with disc wheels incorporating the tyre section. All the wheels of the tender are braked by steam and hand brakes, Westinghouse and vacuum automatic brake apparatus is fitted for train working. The tender tank is formed of steel plates and is of welded construction throughout. The tank, framing, stretchers and so forth are so designed that water pick up gear may be fitted.

Interestingly, so closely were the 'Austerities' based on the 8F that *The Railway Magazine* in comparing

them with the other 'standard war locomotive' (that is, the LNER O4 2-8-0) called the design a 'modified LMSR 2-8-0'. The first few had drop grates of a sort, though it is said they usually jammed and were soon useless. All of the class, however, had some system of drop bars, whether it was this arrangement as fitted to the first few or a modified version, though it remained something of a trial; see LNER wartime experiences, later.

There were two live steam injectors below the cab and feed water for the boiler passed along pipes either side of the engine under the running plate, angling up through the running plate to curve around the boiler to clacks on the top, between the chimney and the dome. These were very prominent on the first 2-8-0s, and actually passed *outside* the vacuum ejector pipe but *underneath* the handrail which was bent around them to suit. Soon after, they were run inside the boiler cladding. This should mean that only the first few were so arranged but... The 2-8-0s, remarkably, did not have boiler lagging, except of course for the firebox backplate. Riddles relied on the insulation qualities of air between the boiler and the cladding. For a machine about to be hurled into war service, with the possibility/ probability of its total loss, the economic/running advantages of cladding seemed small beer. When

LNER 'loanee' 3170 (90491 from September 1949) on a heavy goods somewhere on the LNER. The loco still has the air brake gear fitted but it wouldn't find any use back in England. Loaned to the LNER in March 1946 it was taken over in the December. The 'lock' on the smokebox door looks pretty basic and what is that piece of metal seemingly hanging down? Photograph T.G. Hepburn, Rail Archive Stephenson.

63182 passing St Margarets, Edinburgh with, unusually, a local passenger train (made up of a set of Gresley coaches) on 13 August 1948. This was quite possibly an outcome of the Border floods the day before, which had left locomotives stranded here and there. Photograph B.W.L. Brooksbank, Initial Photographics.

Between March 1946 and December 1947 fifty of the 2-8-0s went on loan to the Southern Railway, distributed among half a dozen sheds. This is Eastbourne shed on 3 August 1947, which suffered bomb damage in the War and more or less closed as an independent shed in the 1950s. WD 77205 (later 90181) has worked down on duty no.541 from Bricklayers Arms, then its base. Photograph J.J. Smith.

questioned as to the post-hostilities value that might be placed on the engines, Riddles had famously, after all, declared himself indifferent; so far as he was concerned they could push them off the side of the ship!

Between them, North British and the Vulcan Foundry produced 935 2-8-0s, the second largest class of British steam locomotives ever built and exceeded in numbers only, as is often pointed out, by Ramsbottom's DX goods 0-6-0s.

The 2-8-0s were built as below:-

Order No.L943 Nos.7000-7049 North British. January-May 1943.
Order No.2289 Nos.7050-7059 Vulcan Foundry. May-June 1943.
Order No.2290 Nos.7060-7109 Vulcan Foundry. June-October 1943.
Order No.2291 Nos.7110-7149 Vulcan Foundry. October to
Order No.2291 Nos.7450-7459 Vulcan Foundry. December 1943.
Order No.L943 Nos.7150-7449 North British. May 1943-March 1944.
Order No.2292 Nos.7460-7509 Vulcan Foundry. December 1943-March 1944.
Order No.L943 Nos.800-879* North British. March-September 1944.
Order No.L943 Nos.8510-8624 North British. September 1944-January 1945
Order No.2299 Nos.8625-8671 Vulcan Foundry. March-June 1944.
Order No.2300 Nos.8672-8718 Vulcan Foundry. June-September 1944.
Order No.2307 Nos.9177-9219 Vulcan Foundry. September-November 1944.
Order No.2308 Nos.9220-9262 Vulcan Foundry. November 1944-February 1945
Order No.2313 Nos.9263-9312 Vulcan Foundry. February-May 1945.
*Evidently the original order (no.L940 of March 1942) was for LMS Stanier 8Fs; when this was changed to an order for Austerities it was easy enough to keep the same running numbers.
The NBL ones were divided between the firm's Hyde Park and Queens Park factories as follows:
Hyde Park: Nos.7000-7049; 7150-7262 (then Nos.3650-3749 2-10-0s) 7263-7299; 8560-8624.
Queens Park: Nos.800-879; 7300-7449; 8510-8559.

In September 1944 it was decided to add 70,000 to the WD running numbers as a good many of the existing engines were still being used on the railways in Britain and their existing number often clashed with 'native' engines; 8510-8624, for instance, could have easily been confused with some Stanier 8Fs. So, NBL's first five-figure WD tender engines were 78518, 78560 and the first 2-10-0 73750 while Vulcan turned out 78715 as their first five-figure 2-8-0.

The War still had nearly three years to run when the first engines appeared though of course the builders and operators didn't know that; the new engines were to be used by the home companies (just as the new American S160 2-8-0s) until they were advised otherwise. There would be landings in North Africa in 1943 and the Americans had only reluctantly agreed to the Invasion of Europe in 1944 rather then the preceding year.

E.S. Cox in *British Railways Standard Locomotives* writes that Stanier was 'a bit restive' about the treatment of his 8F, but saw the point of it as it were. He was incensed, however, by publicity ('spin' as we'd call it now) which hinted that the men from the Ministry had somehow 'sorted out' the design. Cox was put to the task of preparing a detailed rebuttal, though it was never sent.

2-8-0 DIMENSIONS
Cylinders (2) = 19" diameter X 28" stroke
Total wheelbase = 24' 10"
Heating surfaces
tubes = 1,512 sq ft
firebox = 168 sq ft
Superheating = 338 sq ft
Total = 2,018 sq ft
Grate area = 28.5 sq ft
Working pressure = 225 lbs psi

Tractive effort = 34,215 lb (at 85%)
Adhesion weight = 62 tons
Total engine weight = 72 tons
Water capacity = 5,000 gallons
Coal capacity = 9 tons
Tender and engine weight = 128 tons
(As published at the time in The Railway Magazine)

THE 2-10-0s APPEAR
One of the most interesting and important locomotive designs of recent years

The 2-8-0s were a success and it is easy to forget that Riddles designed *two* classes of Austerity tender engines. The War office deemed that a more wide-ranging engine would be necessary for use in ever more remote climes, one indeed with the same tractive effort but with only 13½ ton axle loading instead of 15½ tons. The four sets of driving axles on the 2-8-0s were as follows, starting with the leading pair: 15 tons 1 cwt; 15 tons 10 cwt; 15 tons 12 cwt and 15 tons 2 cwt. So how to spread the axle loading? Once more foreshadowing later BR Standard developments, Riddles thought about a 2-8-2 but settled for a 2-10-0. This enabled a longer boiler barrel, 15ft 8in compared with the 11ft 7½in of the 2-8-0 and a larger, wide, firebox resulting in the grate area being 40 sq ft. It was able to run through a 4½ chain radius as the middle pair of driving wheels were flangeless, a feature that appeared in the very popular BR 9F of the 1950s.

There were still concerns over the long wheelbase but tests at Longmoor and the first demonstration of one in yards likely to prove problematic revealed such fears to be baseless.

The type had long been familiar across large parts of the world but this was Britain's first 2-10-0; it employed all the techniques for cost savings perfected on the 2-8-0s but was of course a 'new' design and not a modified version of a pre-existing type, as was the case with the 2-8-0. But the lesson had been well learned; 'for all their size and power, these new engines are remarkably light' the Ministry of Supply information sheet helpfully advised. They had rocking grates operated by hand from the footplate, an arrangement that functioned, more or less, it seems, unlike the apparatus on the 2-8-0s. Along with the more successful drop grate the 2-10-0s had steel rather than copper fireboxes. Unlike the 2-8-0s, they had the feed water pipes leading to the clacks on the boiler top (between the chimney and the dome) out of sight inside the boiler cladding from the first. Unlike the 2-8-0s the 2-10-0s had a cover on the clacks. The 2-10-0s had boiler lagging, for it was anticipated that they would serve in areas where temperature extremes were greater than the expected sphere of operation of the 2-8-0s, though how this could be foreseen is hard to imagine. It was possibly a case of having decided to do without lagging on the 2-8-0s, but

with second thoughts it might be better to use it after all. It was bitterly freezing in North West Europe in 1944-45. The 2-8-0s began to get fibre glass insulation from 1955, when it was clear none would be 'tipped in the sea' for a while yet.

The ample boiler was another of the features which prefigured the 9Fs; as with the 2-8-0s a round top was chosen for ease of construction compared to a belpaire arrangement. They boasted 'a most generous steam space', the firebox provided with three arch tubes. With the class intended for work abroad the boiler was built so that it could be converted for oil burning without removal from the engine; it was necessary 'only to add a false bottom in the ashpan and fit front oil burners. The slides normally occupied by the two halves of the firedoor serve to hold in position a firehole blanking plate which is provided with a firedoor having a small opening for furnace observation'. The tender too was 'so designed so that conversion to carry fuel oil was easy'; it is not known to what extent this was the case on the 2-8-0s, if at all, though you'd assume it to be so.

The 2-10-0 tenders had the same self trimming bunker as the 2-8-0s, inset so that a reasonable view was allowed when running tender first. The marked platform was wide enough to form a convenient resting place for the fire irons; as on the

SOME PIPES: 1. 90576 fresh out of Darlington Works, March 1962. The curiously sagging pipe (about 2in diameter) running along the boiler not quite half way up, fed steam to the blower (the 'jet', on the LMR at least), entering the smokebox just ahead of the steam pipe. That hand valve close by diverted the steam to that forward extension of the pipe which ended in a valve to which the tube steam cleaning lance cuold be attached when servicing was underway. The vacuum ejector exhaust pipe, as is often seen, is 'dog legged' to accommodate those large washout plug caps on this side. See 90274 page 21. Photograph J. Davenport, Initial Photographics.

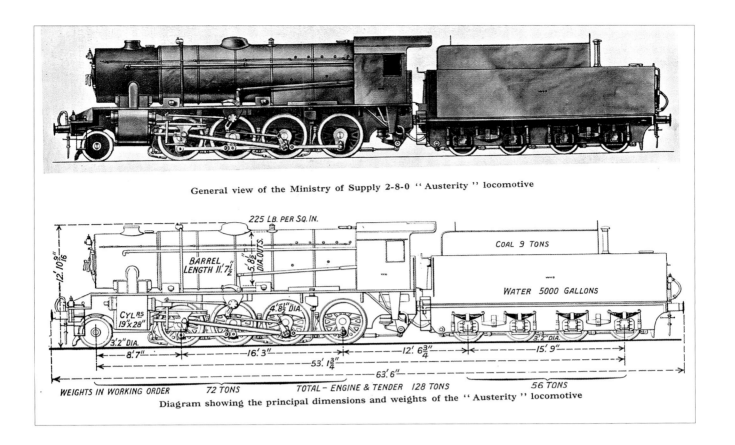

General view of the Ministry of Supply 2-8-0 '' Austerity '' locomotive

Diagram showing the principal dimensions and weights of the '' Austerity '' locomotive

Facsimiles from the railway press of the time.

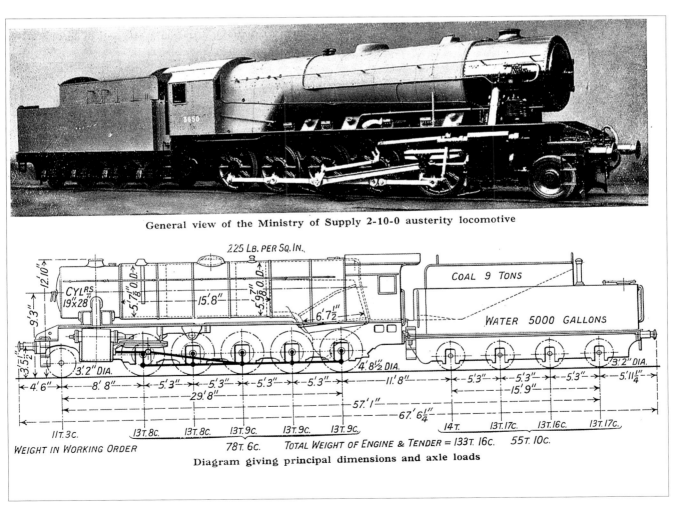

General view of the Ministry of Supply 2-10-0 austerity locomotive

Diagram giving principal dimensions and axle loads

SOME PIPES: 2. 90606 in standard nick, covered in priming deposit at Colwick shed in May 1965. This was another ER shed that had a good many of the class, with 44 on stock in 1950 and this number hardly varied for a decade or more. It was down to 23 by 1965. What looks like hastily-assembled cabling running down the WD boilers on this side carries oil from the 4-feed Detroit hydrostatic sight feed lubricator in the cab to the cylinders and valves. Photograph J. Davenport, Initial Photographics.

2-8-0s suitably placed 'loops' were sufficient to keep them on board. We next saw the 'inset tender' when BRITANNIA appeared in 1951.

All 150 of the 2-10-0s were completed by NBL at its Hyde Park works as follows:
Order No.L945 Nos.3650-3749 December 1943-June 1944.
Order No.L948 Nos.3750-3799 March-September 1945.

2-10-0 DIMENSIONS
Cylinders X 2 = 19" diameter by 28" stroke
Piston valves = 10" diameter
Driving wheels = 4' 8½" diameter
Bogie wheels = 3' 2" diameter
Coupled wheelbase = 21'
Total wheelbase = 29' 8"
Heating surfaces
Large tubes = 589 sq ft
Small tubes = 1170 sq ft
Firebox = 192 sq ft
Total = 1951 sq ft
Superheater = 423 sq ft
Overall total = 2374 sq ft
Grate area = 40 sq ft
Boiler pressure = 225 lb psi
Tractive effort = 34,215 lb. (At 85%)
Adhesion weight = 67.25 tons
Engine in working order = 78.5 tons
Tender in working order = 55.5 tons
Total = 134 tons
Axle loading
Leading drivers = 13 tons 8 cwt
Second pair = 13 tons 8 cwt
Middle pair = 13 tons 9 cwt
Fourth pair = 13 tons 9 cwt
Rear pair = 13 tons 9 cwt
Total = 67 tons 3 cwt

A subject that can fascinate and mystify today is that of makers plates and North British was famous for producing theirs in the shape of a diamond. Rowledge, naturally, in his excellent *Austerity 2-8-0s & 2-10-0s* untangled a very tangled situation, the bare outline of which is that the five digit works numbers in the 24000-25000 series were not put on the locos strictly in the order they were allotted, or were not used at all or were duplicated! To summarise from *Austerity 2-8-0s & 2-10-0s*:

reveals that four engines had duplicated plates, due to mix-ups. 8556-8559 got 25411-25414 and so did 868, 870, 8510 and 8515. The whole thing was a muddle and a half but fortunately the Vulcan Foundry threw up no such problems with its own works numbers; these were strictly adhered to with Nos.4866-5255, so engine no.77050 had works no.4866 and engine no.79312 had works no.5255. These were the 390 2-8-0s built by the Vulcan Foundry, Newton-le-Willows.

The NBL works numbers for the 2-10-0s were 25436-25535 for 3650-3749; for the second batch of fifty

Works Nos	Allotted to	Used on
24891-24970	800-879	813-82, 829-841, 851, 853, 842, 854, 843-848, 850, 849, 852, 855-867, 869, 871-879, 8511-8514, 7281-7299
24971-25020	7000-7049	7000-7018, 7300, 7020-7049
25021-25170	7150-7299	7150-7280, 7424-7427, 7429-7435 821-828
25171-25320	7300-7449	7301-7305, 7311-7320, 7306-7310, 7321-7329, 7332-7339, 7330, 7331, 7340-7351, 7357, 7353, 7354, 7358-7362, 7355, 7363, 7356, 7388, 7428, 7364-7380, 7383, 7381, 7382, 7384-7387, 7390-7407, 7417, 7408-7416, 7418-7423, 7436-7449, 800-812
25321-25385	8560-8624	8560-8624
25386-25435	8510-8559	8531-8555, 868, 870, 8510, 8515, 8516, 8518-8526, 8517, 8527-8530

Works numbers 25246 and 25430-25435 were not used, while engines 7019, 7352 and 7389 were 'unplated'. One can only gawp at the determination needed to track all this down; furthermore, Peter Rowledge

2-10-0s the works numbers allotted were 25596 to 25645.

LULL BEFORE THE STORM
The first 2-8-0, 7000, after official

18

LUBRICATORS: 1. This side on view shows well the three lubricators (along with the sanding gear and fillers) which used worsted trimmings to feed by capillary action. There are four lubricators, one for each axle box, the one for the trailing box being in the cab, the other three visible as here, on the running plate. This pattern was repeated on the right-hand side. Each lubricator had feeds for the axle and the horn guides. Sanding is to front of leading wheel and front of 'third' wheel with conventional LM-style fillers; sand to rear of 'third' wheel for rear running is gravity, with a different filler. Dairycoates' 90078 (77279) is at Stockport Edgeley, partly in the 'coal hole' with one of the local 'jockos', 47601, behind, about 1961. Photograph D. Forsyth, Paul Chancellor Collection.

LUBRICATORS: 2. On the 2-10-0s, logically enough, there were four axle box lubricators on the running plate with the hindmost in the cab, as was the case with the 2-8-0. Painted smokebox number familiar from other 2-10-0s in the early BR period; a local foundry shortage perhaps. 90756 has instead some neatly painted digits. It stands at Eastfield shed on 12 September 1953 awaiting a return in the general direction of Motherwell. '8F' and 'RA6' on the cabside, as per the 2-8-0s; yet to get some of the recommended alterations such as gangway doors or sliding cab side windows; as for the cab roof ventilators, these are almost impossible to spot from anywhere near ground level. Note also difference in sanding from the 2-8-0s, to leading and trailing side of the intermediate (flangeless) drivers and to front of leading wheel but steam operated in all three cases. The main principle of sanding was to apply it to the leading and the driven coupled wheelset (i.e. the one with the connecting rod) which was the best way to reduce the risk of bent side rods. Photograph J. Robertson, www.transporttreasury.co.uk

Newly overhauled and now numbered E3131 the former 78634 is outside the Vickers Armstrong Works at Scotswood, Newcastle, next to the River Tyne on 3 February 1948. Having purchased 200 of the WD 2-8-0s in November 1946 (190 already on loan) at £4,500 each and reclassifying them O7 the LNER needed somewhere to overhaul them as their own workshops were fully occupied with arrears. So 167 of the O7s received 'General' repairs at these Scotswood Works; once outshopped the locos had trial runs from the nearby Blaydon shed before going into traffic. E3131 later became 90452 but there can't be many of us who can remember the WDs in this sort of condition.

handing over (given as 16 January 1943) went to work on the LMS in Glasgow for a few weeks before moving to the LNER. In fact the great majority of the 2-8-0s that were lent to the four British railways went to the LNER, for there the need was greatest. Many of the new locomotives constructed by NBL went initially to Eastfield shed, *The Railway Observer* reporting that they worked at first between Edinburgh and Glasgow. They were soon distributed all around the system, south to York, New England, March and Stratford among many other sheds. They were soon on the GN in the sort of numbers that were familiar under BR in the 1950s, *The Railway Observer* reporting that 'large numbers of WD 2-8-0s are in evidence on all kinds of goods and coal trains and even the shortest visit to the Main Line north of Hornsey will usually produce at least one within a very few minutes; 7304 passed New Barnet light about 4pm on 22/5/43'. The LMS had only a seventh (50) of the LNER's 350 2-8-0s but they too penetrated every corner of the system; they were at Kingmoor, Shrewsbury and even the far end of the Central Wales line at Swansea Victoria. On 21 May 1943 7313 was piloting 8F 8164 over Beattock while Kingmoor examples were to be found at Leeds Holbeck and even Cricklewood. Others were on Springs Branch turns, probably running in from Vulcan Foundry.

The first Southern 2-8-0s arrived at the beginning of 1944, with 7422 at Bricklayers Arms; the Southern too got 50, like the LMS and soon there were allocations at New Cross, Eastleigh, Hither Green and Feltham. They must have been quite a sight amid the 0-6-0s and moguls on, say, London-Brighton goods, like 7435 on 6 March 1944. The Feltham ones were often on the exchange traffic between Feltham, Old Oak Junction, Neasden and Cricklewood. One that was eventually to be Dutch-owned, 7495, had even been noted at my home town, Weybridge (they were regulars on the 12.54pm Feltham-Hither Green goods) while I had yet to be even a twinkle in an eye. Eastleigh Austerities would have worked everywhere with the mountainous traffic in and out of Southampton and all over the south coast; on 22 April 1944 one was noted light on the Southampton via Netley to Fareham line, an unusual event as even SR 4-6-0s weren't allowed on this line.

The GWR's Austerities came with previous service on the other three companies including 7042-7044, 7048 and 7050 which had arrived at Oxley via Bushbury. It was suggested that 174 Austerities would be allocated to the GW, though eventually only 95 came, from 1944-45, replacing the US S160 2-8-0s. They were based mainly at the London, Midlands and South Wales sheds, none going to the West Country. The GW ones were soon

recalled by the War Department; rather true to form, one dares to say, it was GWR crews who found reason to complain about the Austerities, while crews everywhere else seem to have taken them more or less in their stride. On the Great Western, to be fair, there were rather fewer of them and they were more scattered so crews only got them now and again; in such circumstances the verdict was nearly always a poor one.

This outpouring of new engines, joining the ranks of the 'natives' and destined for war service, made for a remarkable procession and it was a shame that so few (either in the Forces or unable to travel far) were around. Photography of course was forbidden. Fortunately *The Railway Observer* did just that, observed it all; its 'spies', now in uniform around the country, kept it informed. On the LNER (and presumably elsewhere) it was generally agreed that they suffered one major defect, the system and manner in which the drop fire-bars were operated. 7026 and 7027, both of York shed, were noted at Harrogate in the spring of 1943 with the bars collapsed. 'The ashpans on these engines' the *RO* continued, *are set on a very steep slope, no back damper is fitted as the bottom of the pan nearly touches the bars at the rear and slopes steeply forward towards the front damper. The drop bars, contrary to LNER standard practice, drop inwards when down and are operated*

Official record of ex-works 90274 which was at Rose Grove shed for a number of years before ending its days on the ER at Frodingham. The rods are 'down' in conventional fashion with the background 'whited out' as was customary. Doncaster fitted its own pattern of washout 'doors' in place of the ordinary plugs on the firebox sides and in the end, with the work carried out also at Darlington (as well as Gorton and Crewe in would seem) about a third were so dealt with. The alteration was quite distinctive, for the boiler hand rail each side had to be split, leaving a short separate section either side of the smokebox; additionally, on the left-hand side, the ejector pipe had to be altered too, to a 'dog leg'. See 90576 on page 16.

70843 (90327 from March 1952) retains its WD running number even though BR is over three years old. The year is 1951 and it has got a shed plate 26A which means it was then at Newton Heath, though it is stabled 'round the back' at Lostock Hall, a shed which itself had an allocation of WD 2-8-0s. It had spent time on the Great Western – witness the lamp irons and even the 'spare' ones on the running plate ahead of the steam pipe. Photograph J. Davenport, Initial Photographics.

Aftermath of a bit of a heavy shunt; 77115 is at home on 84K Chester (WR) shed and certainly needs some attention to the right-hand end of the buffer beam. This was one of three of the class then allocated to 84K in 1950 the other two being 90214 and 90286 which were still there in 1959. Note the GW-style fire iron 'tunnel'; the GW men did not like (among several other features) the way the irons were stashed on the tender side and this was one of the means by which the authorities sought to sooth their concerns. Photograph J. Davenport, Initial Photographics.

by cranks and a bridle rod through the ashpan itself. Therefore when cleaning and dropping takes place the whole of the fire and hot clinker is deposited on the bridle rod to the drop grate, and in a short time warps it and even burns it through as it is just under the bars. On LNER locos, if the front damper is opened prior to dropping the grate the fire, etc., will of course fall out of harms way, but on Austerity locos is imprisoned in the ashpan, if in large quantities.

Newcomers and strangers to the districts they worked in, the Austerities (once back from war) would nevertheless become a common sight in many areas for some twenty years. Official figures show 450 of the production engines were lent to the 'Big Four' with 350 working on the LNER, 50 on the LMS and 50 on the SR with some of these going to the GWR from October 1944 before returning to the War Department. York, unsurprisingly, saw the 2-8-0s all the time and O.S. Nock wrote that a high ranking LNER officer there 'who loved N.E. engines' thought that the Austerities were 'by far the best they had ever had'.

ACTIVE SERVICE

We are only really concerned here with the WDs in Britain and though they ventured far and wide, lending an exotic air to engines we nevertheless thought humdrum in the extreme, their work in Britain was telescoped into a relatively short period of time. A few of course never left these shores, for they were retained at military railways and ports/depots for work and training.

The engines for Europe post-Invasion went over in two specially adapted Southern Railway ferries but the US S160s went first. The first WDs, 2-8-0s and 2-10-0s, seem to have gone to Dieppe in late September/early October 1944. They came both from store and from work in Britain, and a good number passed straight to the Americans. At this point we have Colonel H.C.B. Rogers' memoir (*The Last Steam Locomotive Engineer: R.A.Riddles*) of General D.J. McMullen, Director of Transportation, writing to Riddles in February 1945 to let him know how excellently the Austerity 2-8-0s and 2-10-0s were doing. It has of course been quoted before but is too good not to repeat here: 'Everyone' he wrote *loves the 2-10-0. It is quite the best goods engine*

ever turned out in Great Britain and does well on even Belgian 'duff', which is more like porridge than coal. The 2-8-0s by contrast did not cope nearly as well on the said 'muck' (demonstrating the advantage of the bigger wider firebox on the 2-10-0s) but got along fairly well if some decent coal was mixed in with it. He added that it was amazing to trundle along on a 2-8-0 Austerity only three miles from the German front line. In Nijmegen station the shell bursts in the battle area could be seen from the footplate, so the Austerities were close by the action, 'often ahead of the medium artillery positions'. The General again wrote to Riddles declaring that he had yet to come across any engine in Europe to touch the British 2-10-0, 'weight for weight'.

Over 1000 of the Austerities were shipped from the UK to be used in the expanding territory liberated by the Allies, frequently close enough to be damaged by shellfire. The very 1000th one was a 2-10-0, 73755, appropriately carrying the name LONGMOOR. For this reason alone it still survives and is kept in a railway museum in Utrecht, Holland, where I was much puzzled to see it on a school holiday in 1962. Some engines were lost. First

A WD on the Southern. Pictures are not plentiful of WDs on the Southern for their departure took place early on, in 1950-1951. The exact date of these pictures is not known; when 77296 was on loan to the SR it had gone first to Ashford shed and we see it at Hither Green in line with a Q1 0-6-0, another 'austerity' loco if you like and again (below) in Woking Yard. The engine later became 90360 and was moved to Newton Heath in August 1951 when the Southern Region was getting rid of all its WDs. Photographs John Davenport, www.transporttreasury.co.uk

Sideways scrape on 90392, dumped at Cambridge shed in February 1950. The WD was then based at March shed; it ended its days at Gorton in Manchester. Photograph M.N. Bland, www.transporttreasury.co.uk

was 78678, used by the Americans in Belgium, in June 1945; it was withdrawn on 26 June 1945 at Mechelen Works, 'damaged beyond repair'. On 16 August 1945 at Philsdorf in Germany 77125 and 77238 were involved in a head on collision and met their fate accordingly at the same works. Of 79189, Rowledge notes that there is no record after January 1946. Missing in action?

The Netherlands State Railways came to own and operate as many WDs – more probably – than any BR Region and once the dust had settled on that country's truly painful liberation nearly 200 2-8-0s and over a hundred 2-10-0s were purchased to get the smashed system running again. They were familiar even on passenger trains for several years but suffered a withering withdrawal rate as the Dutch took the expendability of the engines literally. As it was, Dutch railway electrification and the elimination of steam proceeded like no other western European nation while a number of 'native' steam locos came home for repair. Dozens of the 2-8-0s were withdrawn as early as 1949; the 2-10-0s had all but gone by 1951 and the last 2-8-0 went with the end of steam in the Netherlands in January 1958.

Other theatres saw our North British and Vulcan Austerities, before and after Western Europe. First to go abroad in fact had been twenty 2-10-0s in early 1944, to Egypt, where they were hardly used, if at all. Four of them went on to Palestine/Syria and the other sixteen to post-war Greece, in 1946. Like many systems after the War, Hong Kong's railway was much in need of refurbishment and it duly got a dozen 2-8-0s from Longmoor 'stock' in 1946. Though LNER 'rejects' they were not in too bad a shape, it seems and one or two even worked into the early 1960s.

The most unexpected development was the sale of two of Holland's 2-8-0s to Sweden in 1953. There had been alterations to the Austerities before, such as extra cab roofs in Greece and tall chimneys in Holland, but the most marked changes of all were made to the Swedish pair, with the shortening of the tenders to six wheels to fit the country's standard turntables.

REPATRIATION

As the chaos in Europe subsided with the end of the War, it was clear that many of the locos would be coming home and as early as October 1945 a total of 460 was determined, 310 to the LNER, 100 to the GWR (allowing

them to pass their Stanier 8Fs back to the LMS) and 50 to the Southern. They went home largely on the SR ferries which had taken them across the Channel the year before, the process taking more than six months. The immediate problem was where to store so many locomotives in need of repair and overhaul. With the LNER in particular short of heavy freight power, further repatriations were arranged through 1946 and 1947. The LNER, for instance, had purchased 200 of the 2-8-0s but then took another 210, these 'further locos being reconditioned for service on the LNER to be merely on loan.'

So, as will be seen, a great number of the 2-8-0s returned home, though many remained in store well into BR days. The allocation lists show some of the BR ones had four different running numbers thanks to the LNER's purchase of 200 of them and subsequent renumbering; indeed some had 60000 added in early BR days and thus carried *five* running numbers at different times. And that's without the E prefix... This could be a British record. Although the 2-10-0s had proved themselves superior to the 2-8-0s on various counts only 25 returned to work in this country. The hosts, perhaps, were happier to hand back the 2-8-0s, most of the 2-10-0s

York station has always been impressive and this WD (note damaged cab window) certainly doesn't spoil it. 77395 (later 90276) is running light through the station. The outside piping, thick outside steam pipes and reversing gear are shown in good detail. The shed code denotes it was then allocated to Staveley (ex-GC) shed which in 1950 had ten of the class on the books. Photograph J. Davenport, Initial Photographics.

A grainy picture but an unusual one, of 78531 and 77259 at Eastbourne shed with the water softener tower in the background. Good study of the tender rear, demonstrating the excellent view when working tender first, the access handles and ladder on the back. But why has one tender only got a single breather pipe? Photograph J.J. Smith.

having been sold abroad. Rowledge makes reference to the Railway Executive Committee, meeting in May 1947, rejecting the 2-10-0s on mechanical and operating grounds and, much more intriguingly, the US S160s too. Where might they have worked, and in what number series?

It was at this period that the abortive scheme to convert a number of engines nationwide to oil burning was introduced and *The Railway Observer* reported that two of the LNER 2-8-0s by now classified O7, 3012 and 3143, were undergoing conversion in the Vickers Armstrong Scotswood works. This work was not complete when the oil firing scheme was cancelled though 63152 had managed to get converted, at Doncaster. It went for trials at March (see, in particular, Richard Hardy's battles with it in *Burning the Midnight Oil, British Railways Illustrated*, Vol.4 No.4, January 1995). After some 16,000 miles of testing it went to Old Oak on the Western Region in exchange for 78522 in March 1948. It was returned to March shed at the end of October 1948, 'its oil burning equipment having been removed earlier in that month', *The*

Railway Observer reported.

1948 saw the birth of British Railways so the LNER class O7 came under national ownership, joined by another 533 2-8-0s on loan (many to the LNER) now classified 'WD' by the new owners (definitely not 'Austerity' – an unpleasant recent association, after all) with a power rating of 8F. Apart from the 200 sold to the LNER, 558 WDs (533 2-8-0s and 25 2-10-0s) were on loan, working on BR or stored awaiting BR service by October 1948 and an official sale was conducted, the locos passing to the Railway Executive for a sum of £1,500,000. BR numbering saw them as 90000-90732. Some of the former LNER locos had 60000 added to their running numbers (Rowledge even notes one that got a Regional 'E' prefix – E63197!) and these can be located in the allocation lists elsewhere in the book. Also under this heading can be found the fate of the Austerities not taken over by BR including the large number of 2-8-0s purchased by Dutch Railways. In the new BR sequence 90000-90732 the

422 North British engines came first, followed by the 311 Vulcans. Within two groupings, the LNER engines came first, so that the WD numbering did not follow, at all, really, the sequence of construction but, instead, the works of origin. This was odd for the time but of course we saw lots more of this in subsequent BR Standard classes. The 2-10-0s merely followed on at the end with their own

Number series 2-8-0s	Builder
90000-90100	NBL (LNER O7 3000-3100)
90101-90421	NBL
90422-90520	Vulcan (LNER O7 3101-3199)
90521-90732	Vulcan

Number series 2-10-0s	Builder
90750-90774	NBL

series. They are neatly tabulated thus: The tenders were renumbered simply 1-758 in sequence 90000-90774 and the 2-8-0 boilers renumbered (from already renumbered Regional series) 1-757 more or less in sequence with 90000-90732 with twenty-four additional spares. There were odd exceptions, omissions and downright mysteries, the Byzantine style complexities heroically unravelled by Rowledge in his book. Crewe built a number of further spares for both 2-8-0s and 2-10-0s in the early 1950s.

1948 AND ALL THAT

Amid the sound and fury of the different Pacifics and the Kings it is often forgotten that a WD 2-8-0 and a 2-10-0 took part in the 1948 Locomotive Exchanges. Along with the other freight locomotives, Stanier 8F, ER O1 and WR 28XX, they were tried, with the dynamometer car, on major routes as selected by four Regions. These were Bristol-Eastleigh via Salisbury, London-South Wales with the great test of the Severn Tunnel and the two great coal plodding grounds, Hornsey-New England and Toton-Brent. 2-8-0 77000 (90101) was tried on the WR and SR routes and 63169 (90490) on the ER and LMR routes. The 2-10-0s used were 73774 (90750) and 73775 (90751), the latter running Toton-Brent and the former on the other routes. They were manned by local crews unlike the other Exchange engines which took their own crews with them, which certainly should have led to 63169 shining on the New England jobs. Results for the 2-8-0s saw 3.77lb of coal per horsepower hour and 28.75lb of water per horsepower hour. For the 2-10-0s they were 3.52lb and 28.05lb respectively.

Transfers from all over to the LMR during 1948-1949 were followed by a hundred or more WDs coming out of store in 1949 and through to the summer of 1950. *The Railway*

Boiler washout underway at March shed on 3 March 1960 reveals some interesting close up detail. In truth boiler washing was widely neglected so far as the WDs were concerned; see notes under *Eastern Region Memories* later in the book. The shed had 50 of the class allocated in 1950, by now reduced to 18. This is one of the residents, 90522.

78675, formerly working in Belgium, at Stratford shed on 21 March 1948, connecting rod secured on the running plate for its journey back to Blighty. The backing plate on the running plate was for a name, SAPPER. Air brakes and small circular plate fixed under cab window. Photograph R.J. Buckley, Initial Photographics.

2-8-0 No.7001 (90102) in that rather pleasing 'as new' style of matt body and gloss smokebox/cylinders. Visible as little more than white marks are the tiny two inch cab numbers and tender WD lettering.

Observer gave the position at mid-January 1949 as:

Region	Ex-LNE class O7	already on loan	Stored
LMR	2*	1*	-
WR	-	94	75
SR	-	50	-
ER (Eastern Section)	37	23	33
ER (Western Section)	54	118	-
NER	80	72	-
ScR	31	67	-
Totals	200	425	108

*63063, 63126, 77089 at Carlisle Canal
25 2-10-0s have also been acquired giving a total of 558 engines purchased.
Location of these is: ScR 1, Rugby Test Station 1, SR (stored) 23

'digging and flying up under certain conditions of curvature and cant'. The regulator handles 'required lengthening to make observation easier while shunting'. Alterations were made to the coupled

'Performance and Efficiency Tests', enacted principally to examine the performance of the live steam injector and to 'afford a direct comparison between the two distinctive boiler designs', took place in August 1952. Two engines were involved, 2-8-0 90464 and 2-10-0 90772 both run in for approximately 500 miles since General repairs; each covered nearly 3,000 miles during the trials, carried out between Carlisle and Hurlford near Kilmarnock using the LMR

ALLOCATION OF W.D. LOCOMOTIVES PURCHASED NOVEMBER, 1948.

NOTED that, following intimation from C.F.O. that transfer to the Regions concerned of their portions of the first cost involved in the purchase in November, 1948 of 558 W.D. locomotives may now be carried out, allocation to book stock has been made as follows (effective date to be advised) :-

Type	L.M.	W.	S.	E.	N.E.	Sc.	Total
2-8-0	252	57	-	127	52	45	533
2-10-0	-	-	-	-	-	25	25
Total	252	57	-	127	52	70	558

It is not intended that this book stock change shall make any difference to the operating position for the time being, but the foregoing will enable Regions to draw up correctly their loan statements on which the operating stock is based.

The necessity for doing everything possible to increase the availability of these large type locomotives was STRESSED. Mr. Chrimes was also REQUESTED to try out the West Country class locomotives on the work W.D. locomotives are at present doing, with a view to making the best use of the former type.

Extract from the BR Motive Power Committee, 31 March 1950. There is no record of any comparisons with Bulleid light Pacifics.

The WD population did not become stable until the Southern allocation went to the LMR and ScR in 1950-1951. This was presaged by a bizarre rumour in the enthusiast press that, in exchange, the LMR and ScR would provide 4F and J39 0-6-0s. How might the view have changed from that bridge at Weybridge, with these two types alternating with US S160s!

Early detail changes included improvements to the cab by the fitting of sliding windows (photographs of these in use are rare – though look at 90271 on page 90 for instance) and gangway doors; see the M.P. Committee extract. Tender platforms were altered to prevent fall-plates

axlebox lubrication along with some re-staying of the boiler and firebox, the original plate gusset stays for the smokebox tubeplate and firebox doorplate having proved troublesome. The water gauges were 'absolute fiends' according to '45671' writing in *Trains Illustrated*, November 1958: 'If the left-hand gauge broke it was next door to impossible to shut off the cocks unless you were wearing asbestos gloves!' They were largely replaced by LM or BR standard fittings. Crossheads, too, were modified to take nutted gudgeon pins, the earlier pins having shown 'a marked tendency to part company from the crosshead, usually with disastrous results...'

Mobile Test Plant working out of Durran Hill shed.

The engines were tested over a range of constant speeds, and cut offs. Both engines were tested using two coals, Blidworth Cobbles grade 2B hard coal, regarded as a good quality for the work undertaken; steaming was satisfactory with this coal with a high rate of evaporation. Blackwell B, a grade 3B soft coal was also tried; normally used for shunting and local goods it produced a considerable amount of non-porous clinker on the firebars. The 2-10-0 steamed relatively freely on the Blackwell coal and the 2-8-0 poorly. Most of the tests at the lower speeds were conducted

Modifications to W.D. Type 2-8-0 and 2-10-0 Freight Locomotives.

No.	Detail.	Approximate No. of engines to be dealt with.	
		2-8-0	2-10-0
1.	Increased clearance at top of front damper, and ashpan stiffened	439	- ∅
2.	Removal of drop grate.	292	- ∅
3.	Injector overflow valves modified.	325 (L.M.& Sc. Regs. only)	25
4.	Crossheads modified and new type gudgeon pins fitted.	728	25
5.	Gangway doors fitted.	302	25
6.	Cab roof ventilators fitted.	300	25
7.	Sliding cab side windows fitted.	302	25
8.	Tender front dragbox stiffened.	600 ✚	25 ✚
9.	Cylinder relief valves fitted.	50 ✚	- ∅
10.	Additional clip fitted for axlebox oilpipes.	50 ✚	- ∅
11.	Improved type water gauges to be fitted.	597	25

∅ Not applicable to 2-10-0 locomotives.

✚ Estimated number of engines affected.

Chairman STATED, it is realised that this list does not include the whole of the items embodied in applications and proposals received, but the modifications will go a long way towards making these locomotives more satisfactory from a Motive Power Department viewpoint.

Extract from the BR Motive Power Committee, 29 December 1950. Complaints had been collated from all the Regions and work authorised under authority of 'Minute 5132 of 7.12.50'.

for a period of 60-70 minutes but due to temporary and permanent pw checks it was only practicable to test for 40-50 minutes at the higher speeds. The 2-10-0 was run at constant speeds, approximately 10, 20, 30, 40 and 46 mph and at a range of cut offs. It was found impracticable to conduct tests over 40 mph with the 2-8-0 due (it will come as no surprise) to rough riding. With the 2-8-0 not only did higher speeds cause rough riding but low speed at 60% cut off resulted in excessive slipping. The 2-10-0 was more satisfactory in both respects.

If the 2-10-0 was proved superior to the 2-8-0 in economy of operation the results for both types showed them inferior to, say, the Stanier 8F. Deficiencies in steaming, draughting and cylinder efficiency were laid at the door of wartime cheapness and economy. The testers concluded somewhat blandly: *The main purpose of these tests was to provide data on which the most economical working of the locomotive could be based, consistent with meeting traffic requirements. There is no reason to think that in general, present day schedules and trainloads, based upon* *longstanding practice and experience, do not allow economical locomotive operation. But since in the testing equipment now available to the Railway Executive there is means of finding accurately the coal rate range, it will clearly be of some value to examine present schedules and loads to check that they are in fact within the most economical range in their entirety, and if not, whether by adjustments over particular sections acceptable to the Operating Department, they could not be so modified as to bring about a reduction in coal consumption. Similarly, proposals for new or accelerated timings can be examined in relation to their cost in coal.*

In the rough and tumble real world of working a fleet of WDs, you get the distinct feeling that these 'Performance and Efficiency Tests' had very little part to play...

Somewhat unloved by authority and enthusiasts alike, little appeared in the railway periodicals though in one edition of the monthly *Trains Illustrated* (November 1958) the author '45671' wrote kindly of the WDs: *In a number of respects the design improved on the LMS model. The Midland brake valve was discarded for a 'Dreadnought' valve with separate graduable steam brake valve. The exhaust steam injector and Midland live steam injector were replaced by two 'Monitor', injectors, really first class devices. The LMS reversing rod from the cab, a flat-section rod with a lot of 'whip', which needed a steadying bracket, was passed over for a stiff tubular rod.*

'45671' considered the WDs, for all that were built for a short life, to be 'basically excellent machines'. They steamed well (particularly since the blastpipe caps had been reduced slightly) and the injectors were most reliable; tellingly, they had 'real brute pulling power'. This was everything the engineman could ask for, in fact, except the ability to coast in comfort.

Unpleasant fore and aft forces could build up over about 40 mph and above when the engine was coasting downhill, as the load 'leaned' on the engine. '45671' claimed that just one WD was not subject to this, 90527. It had been rebalanced (like the 'starred' 8Fs) and the fore and aft motion when coasting eliminated. *The enginemen were quite amazed and wondered what we had done to the intermediate drawgear to effect such an improvement (the answer was nothing). Would that the powers that be could be persuaded to modify the rest.*

The balancing and the tendency of the eight wheel tenders to derail when running light in reverse, remained the principal failings of the WDs. '45671' revealed that the tender derailments arose directly from the effects of the partially equalised spring gear and were officially acknowledged to be so serious that engines going on to Crewe Works for repair 'had their tender tanks filled with water and then emptied again when they were safely in the works yard'. Apparently spring modification to the third and fourth tender wheels to 90184 and 90473 at Crewe in 1953 and 1954 proved encouraging and the LMR even got authority to so modify its WDs but the work does not seem to have proceeded. For the WDs, it was the same old story!

'The 1000th and 1001st locomotives' being loaded (the former, No.73755, was named LONGMOOR) at Dover, 9 May 1945. Two of the SR's train ferries, the HAMPTON FERRY and the TWICKENHAM FERRY were adapted so that they could transport locomotives to the European theatre.

This WD (90003) is described as 'Utility Loco No.7300', in contemporary officialese, 'somewhere in England' in March 1943. This looks a lot like the GN to me.

77181 (90165) at Brighton after return and, from its condition, overhaul locally; it was loaned to the LNER in September 1947. It had been agreed from July 1946 that the air pumps should be removed and this was accomplished over the next year of so, though some ran with the brackets for a while. Sometimes the rearmost lubricator on the right-hand side appears to be set at a right angle to the others, as here – see also 90457 late on, for instance, on page 130.

Austerities assembled at Dover in March 1945, ready to go. Note the removal of the cab roof extensions to accommodate the lifting gear.

77388 (90271) on the Western, 2 June 1949 with one of the 'local' modifications, the fire irons compartment, though the other main WR modification - covered top feed - has not yet appeared. The train is a Class 'C' up potato express utilising all manner of requisitioned stock, including near life-expired cattle wagons, near Parsons Tunnel Signalbox on the Teignmouth sea wall. Photograph E.D. Bruton.

90048 up-ended in the North East in 1953. A V2, already disconnected from its tender, was also involved. Washout plugs/hand rail already altered, pony truck missing and a NOT TO BE MOVED disc helpfully fixed to the tender, just in case. The WD appears to have run up against a portion of platform. Photograph A.N. Bowman.

Late period WD. 90448 at Woodford Halse shed in good shape for the time; even the electrification flashes are visible! Photograph J. Davenport, Initial Photographics.

One *on* BR but not *of* BR! Longmoor Military Railway WD 2-10-0 601 KITCHENER, previously 73797, at Polmadie on 8 June 1957. It worked from the big old Caley shed for a while before overhaul at North British. Note two air compressors. It emerged from NB as an oil burner in October 1958 and spent some months working from Kingmoor (including various trials with the dynamometer car) before returning to the LMR in February 1959. Photograph James Stevenson, courtesy Hamish Stevenson.

90774 (73799) had acquired an official wartime name; in fact it was one of two called NORTH BRITISH, the other being 73798 (90773). The names stayed on, oddly, after purchase and painting into BR garb; witness this well-known picture at Eastfield on 21 June 1949. The plates seem to have been quietly done away with later that year. Photograph H.C. Casserley, courtesy R.M. Casserley.

NORTH BRITISH not yet officially BR and still lettered WD, as 73799, at Motherwell shed on 10 April 1948; compare it in thoroughly overhauled condition as 90774 the following year, below opposite. Photograph James Stevenson, courtesy Hamish Stevenson.

Motherwell again and 73783, later 90759, on 7 May 1949. In these years a big do-anything machine like this was just what sheds like Motherwell needed. Photograph James Stevenson, courtesy Hamish Stevenson.

70811 (90317) home from the war on the Southern; this *might* be Guildford...

NORTH BRITISH (73799) again, this time with a down goods at Beattock, while on loan to Kingmoor, 22 July 1947. Photograph James Stevenson, courtesy Hamish Stevenson.

Austerities at Nijmegen shed, 77043 (NS 4325) in front, 1 August 1946. It was purchased by the Netherlands State Railway that year and scrapped in 1954-55 and never, of course, got back to Britain and BR. The WD behind has the curious NSR chimney extension to overcome the problem of drifting smoke. The 'EHV' on the cabside is presumably the shed allocation; Eindhoven at a guess.

Popular post card of the period.

2.10.0 M.O.S. Austerity Freight Loco

90000 10/50 3000 3/47 63000 6/48
77009: Eastfield 13/2/43; Tay Bridge 4/12/43;
WD 12/44; New England 25/5/46; Annesley 26/4/47;
Colwick 29/11/47; New England 7/2/59;
Frodingham 22/9/62
WITHDRAWN 6/65; Cox and Danks,
Wadsley Bridge 11/65

90001 4/49 3001 2/47 63001 4/48
77002: Heaton 28/5/47; Tweedmouth 29/11/47;
Dairycoates 1/51; Annesley 4/51; Immingham 8/51;
Colwick 29/12/51; March 10/8/57; Doncaster 10/9/60;
Colwick 9/10/65; Doncaster 27/11/65
WITHDRAWN 4/66; Drapers, Hull 8/66

90002 6/50 3002 3/47 63002 5/48
77021: New England 3/43; WD 1/45; Annesley 26/4/47;
Colwick 29/11/47; Staveley 1/51; Colwick 8/51;
Doncaster 4/12/65
WITHDRAWN 4/66; Drapers, Hull 8/66

90003 12/49 3003 2/47
77300: Eastfield 3/43; WD 1/45; March 20/3/46;
Immingham 3/10/53; Retford 15/7/61;
Doncaster 16/12/61; Langwith Jct 23/3/63
WITHDRAWN 6/64; Wards, Beighton, Sheffield 8/64

90004 3/49 3004 2/47
77033: Eastfield 4/43; York 4/43; WD 12/44;
Eastfield 3/46; Thornton Jct 4/46; Polmadie 4/6/60;
Thornton Jct 27/1/62
WITHDRAWN 12/63; Wards, Inverkeithing 5/64

90005 4/49 3005 2/47
77046: Kingmoor 5/43; Wellingborough 11/11/44;
WD 27/1/45; Immingham 1/47; March 7/50; Colwick
31/10/53; Mexborough 22/6/54; Colwick 28/1/56;
Retford 5/10/63
WITHDRAWN 4/65; Drapers, Hull 7/65

90006 5/49 3006 2/47
77316: Kingmoor 6/43; Wellingborough 11/4/44;
WD 2/45; Heaton 28/5/47; Tweedmouth 29/11/47;
Dairycoates 27/8/49; York 8/10/49; Dairycoates 11/49
WITHDRAWN 9/63 Darlington Works 9/63

90007 9/49 3007 2/47 63007 10/48
77318: Wellingborough 6/43; WD 1/45; Woodford Halse
20/3/46; Gorton 28/9/46; Mexborough 28/5/47;
Springhead 23/10/48; Dairycoates 2/50;
Mold Jct 16/1/52; Colwick 17/5/52; Staveley 28/1/56;
Frodingham 20/2/60
WITHDRAWN 7/65; Cox and Danks,
Wadsley Bridge 2/66

90008 3/49 3008 3/47
77322: Wellingborough 7/43; WD 1/45; Woodford Halse
20/4/46; Gorton 28/9/46; Colwick 26/10/46; Springhead
23/10/48; Dairycoates 12/2/49; York 10/49;
Dairycoates 11/49; Tweedmouth 1/51; Dairycoates 4/51
WITHDRAWN 4/67; Drapers, Hull 6/67

90009 10/50 3009 2/47 63009 3/48
77336: Eastfield 7/43; St Margarets 12/43; WD 1/45;
Woodford Halse 20/3/6; Mexborough 28/5/47; Colwick
8/48; Springhead 23/10/48; Dairycoates 12/2/49; York
8/10/49; Dairycoates 24/12/49; Sunderland 17/6/67
WITHDRAWN 9/67; Hughes, Bolckows, North Blyth
11/67

90010 7/49 3010 4/47 63010 5/48
77339: Eastfield 7/43; Dairycoates 9/43; WD 1/45;
Woodford Halse 20/3/46; Annesley 23/8/47; Colwick
29/11/47; Springhead 23/10/48; Dairycoates 2/50;
Immingham 8/51; Oxley 6/10/51; Leamington
3/11/51; Shrewsbury 3/10/53; Leamington 27/3/54;
Shrewsbury 14/7/56; St Philips Marsh
28/12/57; Westhouses 8/8/59; Gorton 30/6/62
WITHDRAWN 2/65; Wards, Beighton, Sheffield 8/65

90011 5/51 3011 2/47 63011 6/48
77343: Eastfield 9/43; Dairycoates 9/43; Springhead
4/44; WD 1/45; Woodford Halse 20/3/46; Gorton
28/9/46; Mexborough 28/5/47; Colwick 8/48;
Springhead 23/10/48; Dairycoates 12/2/49; York
8/10/49; Dairycoates 24/12/49; Springhead 17/6/50;
Dairycoates 13/12/58; Darlington 11/7/59;
West Hartlepool 26/3/66
WITHDRAWN 6/66; Drapers, Hull 10/66

90012 3/50 3012 2/47 63012 4/48
77211: Eastfield 9/43; Tyne Dock 9/43; WD 1/45;
Springhead 20/3/46; Heaton 28/5/47; Stockton on Tees
12/2/49; West Hartlepool 13/8/55; York 15/6/57;
Normanton 7/9/57
WITHDRAWN 2/64; Darlington Works 4/64

90013 4/49 3013 2/47 63013 4/48
77213: Eastfield 9/43; March 9/43; WD 2/45; March
8/12/45; Frodingham 4/51; Doncaster 26/3/66
WITHDRAWN 4/66; Drapers, Hull 8/66

90014 12/50 3014 2/47
77220: Eastfield 9/43; Thornton Jct 11/43; WD 2/45; New
England 28/12/45; Annesley 26/4/47; Colwick
29/11/47; Dairycoates 23/10/48; Neville Hill 14/5/49;
Newport 8/10/49; Thornaby 14/6/58;
Darlington 18/6/60; West Hartlepool 26/3/66
WITHDRAWN 4/67; Arnott Young, Dinsdale 7/67

90015 1/50 3015 2/47 63015 7/48
77354: Eastfield then Thornton Jct 9/43; Banbury
23/11/44; WD 2/45; March 8/12/45; Mexborough
14/2/53; Colwick 28/1/56; New England 7/2/59
WITHDRAWN 5/63; Doncaster Works 7/63

90016 9/50 3016 2/47 63016 4/48
77357: Eastfield 9/43; St Margarets 12/43; WD 2/45;
Newport 8/12/45; Wakefield 4/4/59; Thornaby
14/6/58; Darlington 18/6/60; Tyne Dock 29/12/62;
Wakefield 28/12/63; West Hartlepool 27/2/65;
Immingham 26/3/66; Goole 3/12/66
WITHDRAWN 6/67; Drapers, Hull 1/68

90017 6/51 3017 2/47 63017 9/48
77360: Eastfield then March 9/43; WD 1/45; Dunfermline
Upper 20/3/46; Thornton Jct 27/7/46; Tay Bridge
8/10/49; Dunfermline Upper 9/51
WITHDRAWN 9/63; Campbells, Airdrie 12/63

90018 4/51 3018 2/47 63018 3/48
77363: Eastfield 9/43; Dunfermline Upper 10/43; WD
2/45; March 20/3/46; Stratford 25/2/61; March
15/7/61; Doncaster 7/10/61
WITHDRAWN 4/66; Drapers, Hull 8/66

90019 2/50 3019 2/47 63019 4/48
77367: Eastfield 9/43; Tay Bridge 11/43; March 2/12/44;
WD 1/45; Thornton Jct 8/12/45;
WITHDRAWN 12/63 Inverurie Works 12/63

90020 9/50 3020 2/47 63020 12/48
77223: Eastfield then to WD 10/43; Eastfield 25/5/46;
Aberdeen Ferryhill 23/2/52; Thornton Jct 16/5/53
WITHDRAWN 4/67; Motherwell Machinery and Scrap
Co, Wishaw 9/67

2-8-0s
90000 to VULCAN

In March 1962 a rather weary 90000 (77009) is passing Welwyn Garden City working what looks like a cattle train, a traffic long since lost to road. The engine was based at New England but finished its days at Frodingham. Now this was one we spotters really wanted... Photograph A.G. Forsyth, Initial Photographics.

Timeless scene. A Doncaster WD, 90001, heading a long rake of coal wagons, all in a day's work, near Scunthorpe on 9 September 1964 and presumably on its way to feed the steel works at Scunthorpe, or perhaps a local power station? Another WD banks at the rear; this was 90714 pictured on the same job later in the book, page 178. Photograph Stephen Gradidge.

Early BR days for 90004; BRITISH RAILWAYS on the tender and a good view of the metal hoops where the firing irons were kept. Note the pipe leading up to the clack valves; the first few had these pipes outside the boiler clothing, resulting in a hoop in the handrail. Other shots show this pipe incorporated in the boiler sides and the shape of the handrail straightened out as the pipes were altered in shape to pass under the boiler clothing on later builds. The angle of light, and the depth of grime, sometimes throw up features that are otherwise invisible, though they might be absent anyway, whatever the level of light or grime (the joys of engine picking). Take the six rivet/bolt heads on the smokebox side and the four up by the hand rail. You'll search in vain for these in many cases; presumably they are relics of the air pump days and disappeared when new smokeboxes were fitted. The linkage from the cab to running-plate I believe to be the old type blowdown which gradually disappeared. You can often see the blanking off plate. See also 2-10-0 73744 on page 207.

90009 has just taken water at Ryhope Grange, on the coast just south of Sunderland, on 23 August 1967. These were colliery trips; note the shunter's pole on the front, also the AWS shield and the conduit on the running plate. Once a Hull Dairycoates engine this WD had come to Sunderland just two months before, hence the lack of any shed plate; it was late on and no one bothered. The engine was amongst the last to go, the next month and was later broken up in North Blyth. Photograph A.G. Forsyth, Initial Photographics.

Filthy of course, 90010 (77339) at Gorton shed in April 1965. Although transferred here in June 1962 there is no sign of a shed plate. You can hardly make the running numbers out; electrification flashes barely visible, no AWS. 'USA' gnomically chalked high on cabside! Photograph J. Davenport, Initial Photographics.

90011 dwarfed by the cooling towers over the other side of the main line from Darlington (its home shed for a number of years) in April 1961. A good profile showing the arrangement of sanding which, we have observed earlier from the angle of the downpipes, are steam operated to the front of the leading and third wheels for forward running and gravity (note the 'straight down' pipe) to the rear of third wheel for rear running. The filler caps (the 'gravity' one is different from the usual simple cap, flush with the running plate) stand out well too, though the BR totem on the tender side is, as usual, barely visible. The cab footsteps and those giving access to the fall plate in front of the loco are pretty basic adding to the austere (that word again) look of the things. Photograph J. Robertson, www.transporttreasury.co.uk

A good view of the tender back, showing how good the lookout was when running tender first, despite the inevitable trepidation on the part of the crew. Prominent overhead electric warning signs, though this NER WD would hardly have worked anywhere near 'the juice'. 90011 is at the late lamented Darlington Works, where the bulk of the ER/NER WDs were overhauled, in 1963. Photograph Paul Chancellor Collection.

An extremely clean WD, AWS fitted; the shed code 51L is Thornaby, the loco having moved from the now-closed Newport. All coaled up at home, 90014 awaits her next duty. The hand rail runs the length of boiler and firebox, the washout plugs are unaltered. The one little flourish to be found on the dear old WD was that extra hand loop on the right of the smokebox. Photograph Paul Chancellor Collection.

NER WD 90014 hard at work in May 1954 with a heavy goods in tow at Ouston. Once past, the photographer only had a short wait for a working on the line above. Photograph J. Robertson, www.transporttreasury.co.uk

An ex-works butterfly emerges from its chrysalis of everyday grime at Eastfield shed in September 1953. 90020 (77223) should feel at home for all the NBL WDs started off here during the War. The WD is being shunted by the J83, 68447, and though it has acquired a 62A shed plate (it was indeed a Thornton loco for a few years) the smokebox number is merely painted on for the present, until a plate becomes available. Photograph J. Robertson, www.transporttreasury.co.uk

90021 6/49 3021 3/47
77233: Eastfield 10/43; Worcester 23/11/44; WD 2/45; New England 28/12/45; Colwick 6/4/47; Annesley 20/2/48; Colwick 20/3/48; Dairycoates 23/10/48; York 10/49; Dairycoates 11/49; York 19/11/55; Darlington 16/6/56; York 15/6/57; Normanton 7/9/57
WITHDRAWN 10/62; Crewe Works 6/63

90022 8/50 3022 3/47
77236; Eastfield 10/43; Heaton 9/44; WD 12/44; Colwick 8/12/45; Gorton 28/9/46; Colwick 26/10/46; Dairycoates 23/10/48; York 8/10/49; Dairycoates 24/12/49; Darlington 1/51; D'coates 8/9/51; Thornaby 20/2/60
WITHDRAWN 10/62; Darlington Works 12/62

90023 11/50 3023 2/47 63023 8/48
77369: Eastfield then WD 10/43; Eastfield 25/5/46; March 30/11/46; Spital Bridge 19/12/59; Tilbury 20/2/60
WITHDRAWN 9/62; Stratford Works 12/62

90024 7/50 3024 2/47 63024 12/48
77370: Eastfield 10/43; Tyne Dock 10/43; WD 1/45; March; 20/3/46; Colwick 31/10/53; Mexborough 21/5/55; Colwick 28/1/56; New England 20/2/60; Frodingham 22/9/62
WITHDRAWN 2/66; Drapers, Hull 6/66

90025 10/49 3025 3/47
77373: Eastfield then Parkhead 10/43; WD 2/45; New England 8/12/45; Colwick 26/4/47; Annesley 20/2/48; Colwick 15/5/48; Annesley 1/51; Immingham 8/51; Colwick 8/8/53; Frodingham 8/10/60
WITHDRAWN 8/65; Arnott Young, Parkgate and Rawmarsh 10/65

90026 6/49 3026 3/47 63026 7/48
77382: Eastfield 10/43; Springhead 4/44; WD 12/44; Woodford Halse 20/3/46; Annesley 23/8/47; Colwick 29/11/47; Dairycoates 23/10/48; Springhead 10/49; Dairycoates 11/49; Tyne Dock 2/50; Neville Hill 15/6/57; York 19/12/59
WITHDRAWN 12/63; Darlington Works 1/64

90027 6/50 3027 2/47
77243: Eastfield then Parkhead 11/43; Worcester 23/11/44; WD 12/44; New England 8/12/45; Colwick 26/4/47; Annesley 20/2/48; Colwick 20/3/48; Neville Hill 23/10/48; Newport 8/10/49; Thornaby 14/6/58
WITHDRAWN 5/63; Darlington Works 6/63

90028 4/49 3028 2/47 63028 3/48
77250: Eastfield 11/43; St Margarets 12/43; WD 1/45; Springhead 20/3/46; March 30/11/46; Stratford 9/49; New England 2/50; March 5/10/57; Stratford 4/4/59; Mexborough 21/5/60; Canklow 1/12/62
WITHDRAWN 12/62; Arnott Young, Bilston 4/63

90029 5/50 3029 2/47 63029 9/48
77251: Eastfield 11/43; St Margarets 12/43; WD 1/45; York 20/3/46; Gorton 28/9/46; March 30/11/46; Colchester 15/5/48; March 10/51; Immingham 3/10/53
WITHDRAWN 7/65; Drapers, Hull 11/65

90030 9/50 3030 2/47 63030
77254: Eastfield 11/43; Canal 12/43; WD 1/45; Heaton 26/10/46; Springhead 25/1/47; Heaton 28/5/47; Tweedmouth 29/11/47; Dairycoates 4/51; York 23/9/61; Dairycoates 27/3/65; Goole 9/10/65
WITHDRAWN 4/67; Drapers, Hull 8/67

90031 7/50 3031 3/47
77385: Eastfield 11/43; Bath Road 23/11/44; WD 2/45; New England 27/7/46; Frodingham 6/51; New England 18/11/61. WITHDRAWN 5/63; Doncaster Works 7/63

90032 3/49 3032 2/47
77391: Eastfield 11/43; Haymarket 12/43; WD 1/45; Immingham 1/47; March 10/50; Frodingham 4/51
WITHDRAWN 2/66; Drapers, Hull 6/66

90033 10/50 3033 3/47 63033 8/48
77397: Eastfield 11/43; Canal 12/43; WD 2/45; Woodford Halse 20/3/46; Gorton 28/9/46; Woodford Halse 26/10/46
WITHDRAWN 5/63; Crewe Works 9/63

90034 9/49 3034 3/47 63034 5/48
77410: Eastfield 12/43; Colwick 29/1/44; WD 1/45; New England 27/7/46; Plaistow 19/4/58;
WITHDRAWN 9/62; Stratford Works 1/63

90035 2/51 3035 2/47 63035 8/48
77412: Eastfield 12/43; Newport 29/1/44; Westbury 23/11/44; WD 12/44; Eastfield then Dunfermline Upper 20/3/46; Thornton Jct 27/7/46; March 28/12/46; Immingham 3/10/53; Frodingham 9/10/65
WITHDRAWN 2/66; Drapers, Hull 7/66

90036 10/49 3036 3/47
77420: Eastfield 29/1/44; Banbury 23/11/44; WD 2/45; New England 25/5/46; Colwick 26/4/47; Annesley 20/2/48; Colwick 15/5/48; Staveley 1/51; Colwick 4/51; Immingham 20/9/58; Colwick 8/10/60
WITHDRAWN 12/65; Drapers, Hull 4/66

90037 10/50 3037 2/47 63037 5/48
77422: Eastfield 29/1/44; Bricklayers Arms 29/1/44; WD 12/44; March 1/47; Doncaster 31/10/53; Colwick 28/1/56; Doncaster 26/2/60; Immingham 4/12/65; Doncaster 26/2/66
WITHDRAWN 4/66; Drapers, Hull 8/66

90038 7/50 3038 2/47 63038 7/48
77423: Eastfield 29/1/44; Stewarts Lane 26/2/44; Bricklayers Arms 25/3/44; WD 11/44; Ferryhill 26/1/46; St Margarets 1/3/47; Colwick 3/10/53
WITHDRAWN 8/65; Arnott Young, Parkgate and Rawmarsh 11/65

90039 10/49 3039 3/47
77427: Eastfield 29/1/44; Stewarts Lane 26/2/44; Bricklayers Arms 25/3/44; WD 12/44; Woodford Halse 20/3/46; Dawsholm 23/3/57; Grangemouth 18/5/57; Dawsholm 19/4/58; Polmadie 9/8/58; Dunfermline 7/9/63
WITHDRAWN 9/66; McWilliams, Shettleston 12/66

90040 7/50 3040 4/47
77430: Eastfield 29/1/44; Bricklayers Arms 25/3/44; WD 11/44; Woodford Halse 26/1/46; Gorton 28/9/46; Woodford Halse 30/1/47; Nottingham 28/12/63; Woodford Halse 18/4/64; Rose Grove 16/5/64
WITHDRAWN 7/65; Cashmores, Great Bridge 12/65

90041 4/49 3041 2/47 63041 12/48
77435: Eastfield 26/2/44; New Cross 25/3/44; WD 12/44; Eastfield then Dunfermline Upper 20/3/46; Thornton Jct 27/7/46; Aberdeen Ferryhill 28/9/46
WITHDRAWN 12/66; McWilliams, Shettleston 4/67

90042 10/50 3042 2/47 63042 9/48
77437: Eastfield 26/2/44; Eastleigh 25/3/44; WD 11/44; York 26/1/46; Heaton 28/9/46; March 28/12/46; Colwick 31/10/53; March 6/10/56; Tilbury 20/2/60; Doncaster 15/7/61
WITHDRAWN 1/65; Drapers, Hull 4/65

90043 3/51 3043 2/47 63043 7/48
77448: WD 3/44; Woodford Halse 26/1/46; Gorton 28/9/46; Woodford Halse 30/11/46; Annesley 26/3/49; Colwick 18/6/49; Woodford Halse 8/51; Colwick 17/5/52; Langwith Jct 22/6/54
WITHDRAWN 12/65; Drapers, Hull 4/66

90021 of 51A Darlington shed on home soil, under the footbridge built for the new diesel depot on the other side of the main line. Like most Darlington locos this one would have been overhauled at the local works, though it moved on from 51A in May 1957. Photograph Paul Chancellor Collection.

Beautifully ex-works and never to be clean again until the next General, 90027 is on a goods train making slow progress through the sharp curves of Newcastle Central in May 1954. The chalk/paint markings around the smokebox door catch probably indicate a minor leak, for the engine to go back to works, maybe, for 'rectification'. Photograph J. Robertson, www.transporttreasury.co.uk

Greenwood on the GN, 4 September 1952 with 90028 (77250) working an up goods through one of the old Hadley Wood tunnels, under a smart signal gantry. The engine was one of the New England 'plodders' that worked coal up the GN to London and empties back for a number of years until 9Fs partly displaced them. See *Eastern Region Memories* later on. The train is a grand mixture of mineral and wooden bodied wagons and who knows how far back into the tunnel that goods train goes? 90028 later migrated to March shed and even had a short period at Stratford, a shed that only ever had a few WDs. Photograph J. Davenport, Initial Photographics.

90028 at March, its home after spending most of the 1950s at New England, on 26 August 1958; note the Fenland flying saucer about to land... Photograph Peter Groom

90031, surely ex-works, working tender first (gingerly, one presumes) past the exotic and ancient York South in May 1955; at least that is believed to be the location. Suggestions to the contrary on a postcard, as Mr Coster would say. Rearranged washout plugs; in that 'inset bunker' tender we see so much of the form adopted for the BR Standards. Photograph J. Robertson, www.transporttreasury.co.uk

90032 comes through Lincoln Central with a train of flats on 20 June 1960, in the days when the citizenry did not regard a footbridge that was not secured like a U.S. penitentiary as an invitation to chuck something off of it. You can almost hear that clank-clonk; compare the washout plugs to the ones on 90031 above. Photograph Paul Chancellor Collection.

90035 (77412) working through Barnetby on 17 April 1961, not far from its home shed of Immingham on a train of those bolsters we associate with steel workings. After a move to Frodingham this was one of the class scrapped at Draper's Hull; this proved something of graveyard for the WDs which were of course concentrated in its hinterland; it accounted for 205 of the class. Look at the separate hand rail and the 'dog's leg' of the ejector pipe; compare with 90031 and 90032 we've just seen... Photograph B.W.L. Brooksbank, Initial Photographics.

Clean WDs attracted photographers, at some subconscious level, is my theory. This is Darlington shed on 20 April 1958; it received locomotives ex-works, of course, so 'clean ones' could be found here more than at most sheds. The plate 31B shows 90042 to be going home to March; in February 1960 it moved to Tilbury with a final move, to Doncaster, in July 1961. After withdrawal in January 1965 it was stored at Dairycoates before becoming one of the Drapers '205'. A clear view of the reversing gear shows the use of steel tubes for the bridle rod and weigh shaft, both famously 'needing end pieces to be welded on.' Photograph J. Davenport, Initial Photographics.

90044 6/49 3044 2/47
70800: WD 3/44; Newport 29/12/45; Motherwell
11/3/50; Hamilton 11/2/50; Newport 8/50; York
20/8/54; Starbeck 19/11/55; Goole 3/10/59;
Dairycoates 30/11/63
WITHDRAWN 12/66; Drapers, Hull 2/67

90045 11/50 3045 2/47 63045 6/48
70804: WD 3/44; Springhead 20/3/46; Heaton 28/5/47;
Newport 12/2/49; Consett 18/4/53; Tyne Dock
29/1/55; Neville Hill 15/6/57; York 19/12/59
WITHDRAWN 10/65; Drapers, Hull 2/66

90046 7/49 3046 4/47
70810: WD 3/44; Woodford Halse 26/1/46;
Westhouses 8/10/60; Gorton 30/6/6
WITHDRAWN 3/63; Crewe Works 6/63

90047 8/50 3047 2/47 63047 7/48
70813: WD 3/44; Colwick 29/12/45; Gorton 28/9/46;
Mexborough 28/5/47; Colwick 8/48; Springhead
23/10/48; Dairycoates 12/50; York 18/4/53; Darlington
16/6/56; Wakefield 20/9/58
WITHDRAWN 6/67; Drapers, Hull 2/68

90048 10/50 3048 2/47 63048 5/48
70815: WD 3/44; York 29/12/45; Heaton 28/9/46;
Stockton on Tees 12/2/49; West Hartlepool 8/10/55;
Thornaby 8/8/59; Colwick 9/10/65
WITHDRAWN 5/63; Darlington Works 6/63

90049 11/49 3049 2/47
70816: to WD 4/44; Colwick 1/12/45; Thornton Jct
29/12/45; St Margarets 18/11/50; Kingmoor 22/5/54;
Eastfield 6/11/54; Dawsholm 16/12/61;
Dunfermline 7/4/62
WITHDRAWN 9/63; Campbells, Airdrie 12/63

90050 5/50 3050 2/47 63050 6/48
70818: to WD 4/44; Colwick 26/10/46; March 1/11/52;
Mexborough 14/2/53; Colwick 7/3/53; New England
20/2/60
WITHDRAWN 5/63; Doncaster Works 7/63

90051 4/49 3051 2/47 63051 3/48
70821: WD 4/44; Colwick 29/12/45; Gorton 28/9/46;
Colwick 26/10/46; Woodford Halse 7/50; Colwick
10/50; Langwith Jct 22/6/54; Canklow 11/7/59;
Colwick 5/9/59
WITHDRAWN 10/65; Drapers, Hull 1/66

90052 4/50 3052 2/47 63052 5/48
70822: WD 4/44; Woodford Halse 26/1/46; Gorton
28/9/46; Mexborough 28/5/47; Colwick 8/48;
Springhead 23/10/48; Dairycoates 11/2/50; Springhead
6/50; Annesley 4/51; Immingham 8/51; Staveley
29/12/51; Colwick 26/1/52; Barnsley 16/5/59;
Mexborough 11/7/59; Doncaster 6/10/62;
Canklow 26/1/63
WITHDRAWN 3/64; Wards, Beighton, Sheffield 4/64

90053 5/49 3053 2/47 63053 6/48
70823: WD 4/44; March 1/12/45; Colwick 31/10/53;
Mexborough 22/6/54; Colwick 28/1/56;
Immingham 26/3/60; Frodingham 8/10/60
WITHDRAWN 7/65; Cox and Danks,
Wadsley Bridge 2/66

90054 5/49 3054 2/47
70824: WD 4/44; Newport 1/12/45; Consett 18/4/53;
Tyne Dock 29/1/55; Starbeck 15/6/57; Wakefield
3/10/59; Low Moor 29/12/62; Wakefield 25/1/64;
Royston 18/6/66; Normanton 8/10/66
WITHDRAWN 1/67; Wards, Killamarsh 3/67

90055 6/51 3055 2/47 63055 3/48
70826: WD 5/44; New England 29/12/45; Immingham
15/5/48; March 17/6/50; Immingham 3/10/53;
Langwith Jct 13/8/55; Staveley Central 14/6/58;
Langwith Jct 27/2/60; New England 21/5/60;
Immingham 22/9/62
WITHDRAWN 3/65; Drapers, Hull 6/65

90056 11/49 3056 2/47
70827: WD 5/44; Colwick 29/12/45; Gorton 28/9/46;
Colwick 26/10/46; Woodford Halse 29/11/47; Colwick
20/2/48; Neville Hill 23/10/48; York 8/10/49; Darlington
16/6/56; Wakefield 20/9/58; Ardsley 6/10/62; Wakefield
11/9/65; Sunderland 3/12/66
WITHDRAWN 5/67; Drapers, Hull 8/67

90057 9/50 3057 3/47 63057 3/48
70828: WD 5/44; Colwick 1/12/45; Gorton 28/9/46;
Mexborough 28/5/47; Colwick 8/48; Springhead
23/10/48; Dairycoates 12/2/49; York 8/10/49;
Dairycoates 24/12/49; Darlington 11/7/59; Tyne Dock
29/12/62; Dairycoates 28/12/63; Goole 3/12/66
WITHDRAWN 6/67; Drapers, Hull 1/68

90058 2/50 3058 2/47
70830: WD 5/44; Thornton Jct 26/1/46
WITHDRAWN 12/63; Inverurie Works 2/64

90059 9/50 3059 2/47
70831: WD 5/44; Mexborough 28/5/47; New England
12/47; Doncaster 26/1/52; Frodingham 22/3/52
WITHDRAWN 4/65; Arnott Young, Dinsdale 10/65

90060 11/50 3060 2/47
70832: WD 5/44; New England 29/12/45; March
23/10/48; Colwick 31/10/53; March 6/10/56; Polmadie
23/3/57; Dawsholm 13/7/57; Polmadie 25/1/58
WITHDRAWN 6/62; Cowlairs Works 8/63

90061 1/50 3061 2/47 63061 7/48
70837: WD 5/44; Newport 29/12/45; Heaton 28/5/47;
Darlington 12/2/49; Dairycoates 8/51; Springhead
19/3/54; Darlington 14/6/58; Wakefield 20/9/58;
West Hartlepool 3/12/66
WITHDRAWN 6/67; Drapers, Hull 10/67

90062 10/50 3062 2/47 63062 6/48
70840: WD 5/44; March 29/12/45; New England 1/3/47;
Stratford 29/1/55
WITHDRAWN 12/59; Stratford Works 2/60

90063 3/50 3063 2/47 63063 9/48
70841: WD 5/44; St Margarets 29/12/45; Canal 9/48;
Peterborough (LMR) 8/50; March 20/2/60;
Doncaster 10/9/60
WITHDRAWN 4/66; Drapers, Hull 8/66

90064 1/51 3064 3/47 63064 4/48
70842: WD 5/44; New England 29/12/45; Immingham
15/5/48; March 17/6/50; Colwick 31/10/53; Doncaster
11/9/54; Colwick 28/1/56; Barnsley 16/5/59;
Mexborough 11/7/59; Canklow 29/12/62
WITHDRAWN 1/64; Doncaster Works 3/64

90065 6/50 3065 2/47 63065 8/48
70844: WD 6/44; Woodford Halse 26/1/46;
Gorton 28/9/46; Woodford Halse 26/10/46
WITHDRAWN 4/64; Crewe Works 5/64

90066 7/51 3066 2/47 63066 11/48
70846: WD 6/44; New England 1/47; Immingham
15/5/48; March 17/6/50; Colwick 31/10/53;
Mexborough 22/6/54; Colwick 28/1/56;
Woodford Halse 23/2/57
WITHDRAWN 5/63; Crewe Works 9/63

Now I would not like to have to clean this one, well not on my own. 90044 (70800) then of Neville Hill shed is at Normanton in September 1955. The shed had been taken over by the North Eastern Region that year and recoded 55E. Although dirty the cast iron cylinder covers show up well here. Photograph J. Davenport, Initial Photographics.

Thornaby shed (closed only recently, by EWS) on 23 September 1962 with one of its resident WDs, 90048. Opened in June 1958 it replaced the ancient and decrepit sheds at Middlesbrough and Newport, inheriting most of their locos, including thirty WD 2-8-0s, though 90048 did not arrive until August 1959. Behind it is one of its replacements, a Type 2 diesel. Photograph J. Davenport, Initial Photographics.

This one has certainly seen better days, though this description applies to every WD through most of their lives. That almost looks like a WR fire iron 'tunnel' on the tender inset, definitely not in its proper place on the right-hand running plate! Local initiative? No.90051 (70821) is at home on Langwith shed, carrying the correct shed plate 40E, so the period is before February 1958 when it was recoded 41J. Photograph J. Davenport, Initial Photographics.

90054 at Starbeck on 24 May 1958; at the uttermost end of utilitarian need, only in Britain could the resulting design be so 'smooth' and largely devoid of domes, cylinders, pipework and all the rest found in foreign practice. Photograph M. Mitchell.

90056 surrounded by spilt coal at Lees (Oldham) shed in April 1952 and a good way from its home at York. The fellow in the background is one of the legendary Lees coalmen, watering down a wagon of coal to reduce dust in the coal 'shelter'. Photograph J. Davenport, Initial Photographics.

Now a WD in its dotage in the North East, 12 May 1967, 90056 a month before withdrawal. This is its home shed of Sunderland where the class saw little action in their final days and the shed was hardly in better condition than the locos. Tender fully coaled for the next duty; inevitably, by this time, a colliery pick-up. Photograph Stephen Gradidge.

That spotter's delight, two for the price of one. A pair of WDs run light through Retford, between shed(s) and yards, on 7 October 1964. AWS-fitted 90057 (70828) hails from Dairycoates. Photograph J. Davenport, Initial Photographics.

90058 was a highly unusual WD; it got to Thornton Junction in 1946 and stayed there, rarely straying out of the coalfield or the Kingdom of Fife apart from visits to works. It sits proudly on a brand new 'Mundt' type turntable (note how shallow the pit is) which we can only presume is at Thornton Junction shed itself. See opposite too.

90058 on that turntable again. Thornton Junction suffered from mining subsidence and was rebuilt and re-equipped in the 1930s. It had been provided with a 70ft turntable but by the 1950s further subsidence made its operation difficult and it was resolved to 'equip it for electric operation'. If we *are* looking at Thornton Junction, then the proposal evolved into an entirely new 'table.

A New England WD makes for a dramatically powerful passage with a down freight through Hadley Wood in the early 1950s. New England obviously started as it meant to go on, so far as the engine's condition is concerned. The train is fascinating with huge logs (North London was not famous for its forests) followed by a tanker and various covered wagons. Wonderful! Photograph Paul Chancellor Collection.

90065 of Woodford Halse, passing Denham on 28 October 1961 on an inter-regional working - what looks like empties returning to pick up more cars from Oxford. Photograph Stephen Gradidge.

90070 was an old-time LNER WD, one that got to carry five running numbers. The New England plate means the period is quite early, 1949-1950 and the engine, doubtless, is sitting in one of the endless yards along the length of the GN; ancient brake van in background. 90070 still has the original outside pipe for the top feed and the required loop in the 'one length' hand rail. One's attention is drawn to the flimsy footsteps on the buffer beam and the solid pony wheels, a unique feature of these locos. Photograph Paul Chancellor Collection.

90067 7/49 3067 2/47 63067 5/48
70847: WD 6/44; Newport 29/12/45; Heaton 28/5/47;
Stockton on Tees 12/2/49; West Hartlepool 13/8/55
WITHDRAWN 10/64; Thompsons, Stockton on Tees 1/65

90068 11/50 3068 2/47 63068 7/48
70848: WD 6/44; Colwick 1/12/45; Gorton 28/9/46;
Colwick 26/10/46; Annesley 20/2/48; Colwick 15/5/48;
Neville Hill 23/10/48; Newport 8/10/49; York 15/6/57;
Wakefield then to Low Moor 14/11/59; Mirfield 23/9/61;
Wakefield 25/1/64
WITHDRAWN 7/66; King's, Norwich 10/66

90069 9/50 3069 2/47
70854: WD 6/44; Woodford Halse 26/1/46; Annesley
23/8/47; Colwick 27/12/47; Annesley 20/2/48; Colwick
15/5/48; Neville Hill 23/10/48; York 8/10/49; Immingham
8/51; Oxley 6/10/51; Shrewsbury 21/2/53; Pontypool Road
6/11/54; Ebbw Jct 1/1/55; Canton 31/10/59; Southall
6/10/62; Canklow 26/1/63; Barrow Hill 24/6/65;
Langwith Jct 19/6/65
WITHDRAWN 1/66; Drapers, Hull 5/66

90070 8/50 3070 2/47 63070 4/48
77265: WD 6/44; New England 8/12/45; Colwick
27/11/48; New England 12/2/49; March 10/50;
Frodingham 4/51
WITHDRAWN 2/65; Drapers, Hull 5/65

90071 11/49 3071 2/47 63071 5/48
70852: WD 6/44; Tay Bridge 26/1/46; St Margarets
18/11/50; Motherwell 3/51; Hamilton 11/8/56; Motherwell
6/9/58; Dunfermline 13/7/63
WITHDRAWN 4/67; Motherwell Machinery and Scrap
Co, Wishaw 9/67

90072 7/50 3072 2/47 63072 5/48
70858: WD 7/44; March 25/5/46; Heaton 23/8/47;
Tweedmouth 29/11/47; Dairycoates 1/51; Thornaby
20/2/60; Goole 7/9/63
WITHDRAWN 12/65; Drapers, Hull 4/66

90073 10/49 3073 2/47 63073 6/48
70870: WD 8/44; March 25/5/46; New England 1/3/47;
Annesley 26/4/47; Colwick 27/12/47; Annesley 20/2/48;
Colwick 10/7/48; New England 19/12/59; Doncaster
20/4/63
WITHDRAWN 2/66; W. George, Station Steel, Wath 8/66

90074 9/49 3074 3/47 63074 4/48
70872: WD 8/44; Newport 29/12/45; Thornaby 14/6/58;
Tyne Dock 29/12/62; Wakefield 28/12/63; Sunderland
8/10/66; West Hartlepool 25/3/67
WITHDRAWN 9/67; Arnott Young, Dinsdale 11/67

90075 1/50 3075 2/47 63075 11/48
77272: WD 8/44; New England 8/12/45; Immingham
15/5/48; March 10/50; Colwick 3/10/53; New England
20/2/60; Immingham 22/9/62; Wakefield 21/12/63;
Frodingham 11/9/65; Doncaster 26/3/66
WITHDRAWN 4/66; Drapers, Hull 9/66

90076 7/50 3076 2/47 63076 7/48
77276: WD 8/44; Newport 8/12/45; Heaton 28/5/47;
Darlington 12/2/49; Newport 17/6/50; Thornaby
14/6/58; Normanton 17/6/67; West Harlepool 15/7/67
WITHDRAWN 9/67; Arnott Young, Dinsdale 11/67

90077 6/50 3077 2/47 63077 6/48
77277: WD 8/44; Tay Bridge 8/12/45; Dawsholm 10/8/57;
Polmadie 9/8/58; Carstairs 25/2/61;
Aberdeen Ferryhill 17/6/61
WITHDRAWN 5/63; Inverurie Works 7/63

90078 9/50 3078 2/47 63078 8/48
77279: WD 8/44; March 8/12/45; Heaton 23/8/47;
Darlington 12/2/49; Dairycoates 8/9/51; York 23/9/61;
Sunderland 8/10/66
WITHDRAWN 11/66; Willoughby's, Morpeth 7/67

90079 10/50 3079 2/47 63079 6/48
77281: WD 8/44; March 8/12/45; New England 1/3/47;
Annesley 26/4/47; Colwick 29/11/47; New England
18/6/49; March 16/1/54; Doncaster 10/9/60;
Frodingham 16/12/61
WITHDRAWN 1/64; Doncaster Works 2/64

90080 10/49 3080 3/47
77284: WD 8/44; Woodford Halse 20/3/46; Gorton
6/10/62; Rose Grove 2/1/65; Colwick 19/6/65;
Frodingham 4/12/65
WITHDRAWN 2/66; Drapers, Hull 7/66

90081 1/50 3081 2/47 63081 3/48
77290: WD 8/44; Newport 8/12/45; Thornaby 14/6/58;
Goole 7/9/63
WITHDRAWN 6/67; Drapers, Hull 12/67

90082 11/50 3082 3/47 63082 4/48
77298: WD 9/44; York 8/12/45; Gorton 28/9/46; Heaton
1/47; Stockton on Tees 12/2/49; Springhead 17/5/52; Neville
Hill 10/9/55; Stockton 2/11/57; Darlington 11/7/59;
Polmadie 23/3/63; Darlington 15/6/63;
Thornaby 25/1/64; West Hartlepool 16/5/64
WITHDRAWN 7/66; Thompsons, Stockton on Tees, 10/66

90083 5/49 3083 2/47 63083 7/48
78513: WD 9/44; March 29/12/45; Stockton on Tees 2/49;
Immingham 31/10/53; March 6/10/56
WITHDRAWN 12/59; Darlington Works 2/60

90084 3/51 3084 2/47 63084 9/48
78515: WD 9/44; Colwick 29/12/45; Gorton 28/9/46;
Colwick 30/11/46; Barrow Hill 2/1/65
WITHDRAWN 6/65; Cox and Danks,
Wadsley Bridge 11/65

90085 2/49 3085 2/47
78516: WD 9/44; March 8/46; Colchester 15/5/48; March
10/51; Mexborough 7/3/53; Colwick 28/1/56; Staveley
10/11/56; Langwith Jct then to Canklow 27/2/60;
Barrow Hill 25/1/64
WITHDRAWN 5/65; Cashmores, Great Bridge 8/65

90086 8/49 3086 2/47
78520: WD 9/44; Newport 26/1/46; Heaton 28/5/47;
Stockton on Tees 12/2/49; Haverton Hill 20/9/58; Thornaby
11/7/59; Tyne Dock 23/3/63
WITHDRAWN 8/63; Darlington Works 10/63

90087 12/50 3087 2/47 63087 9/48
78562: WD 9/44; March 29/12/45; Immingham 3/10/53;
Langwith Jct 26/2/55; Staveley Central 14/6/58;
Frodingham 20/2/60
WITHDRAWN 10/62; Doncaster Works 11/62

90088 8/50 3088 3/47
78565: WD 9/44; New England 29/12/45; Colwick 8/48;
New England 23/10/48; Immingham then to Langwith Jct
5/10/57
WITHDRAWN 7/65; Wards, Beighton, Sheffield 11/65

90089 5/49 3089 2/47 63089 4/48
78527: WD 10/44; St Margarets 29/12/45; Newport
29/1/49; Haverton Hill 10/50; Dairycoates 8/9/51;
Wakefield 7/9/57
WITHDRAWN 1/67; Cox and Danks, Wadsley Bridge 6/67

Motherwell's 90071 (without smokebox plate as yet) going very steady with a loose-coupled freight crests the summit at Beattock, early on in the 1950s. What a place to stand and watch Bridge No.260 must have been. The train is heading south; on the left is the headshunt of the down summit loop. Photograph W. Hermiston, www.transporttreasury.co.uk

90071 during one of its two periods at Motherwell. Smokebox number plate has received typical Scottish Region attention. Good close-up of the AWS conduit clipped to the buffer beam; diesel tanks on left. Photograph Paul Chancellor Collection.

90076 hard at work somewhere in the Pennines. What is also interesting in this unusual view is the presence of an extra tank inlet, offset from the original fitting on the tender rear. Also revealed is a disadvantage of the 'inset' tender; it allowed better visibility when running backwards but coal and dust accumulated on the flat surface and flew back in your face. That's why the BR Standard tender 'insets' had a pronounced slope and the fire irons went in a separate enclosed 'tunnel'.

A WD line-up at Thornaby, headed by 90081 with what looks like 90132 behind. A number of them came here from nearby Newport in June 1958. In the background is Q6 63411, also a 'local'. All three WDs have the ER/NER altered washout plugs, hand rail and vacuum ejector. Photograph Paul Chancellor Collection.

Local 90087 of March shed (31B) on a local up goods from March at Ely North Junction. Footplateman caught for a moment in his working life at 10.57am on 30th July 1953. The WD finished its time at Frodingham and was broken up at Doncaster Works. Photograph A.R. Carpenter, www.transporttreasury.co.uk

90088, during its eight years as a Langwith engine, in line at a shed somewhere. But where exactly? The locos are on one of the LNER wet ash pits, installed at various major sheds such as York, Gorton, Darnall and New England. Fires were simply dropped into concrete 'ponds' and the sludge then scooped out by grab cranes later, for taking away in wagons. The gantries in the background suggests we are in Manchester-Sheffield DC country which means Darnall or Gorton. The somewhat ex-works look of the WD and the presence of both a J94 0-6-0ST and a 4F 0-6-0 clinches it as Gorton, to my mind. Photograph Paul Chancellor Collection.

Darlington shed on 23 September 1962 with Thornaby's 90090 ex-works and awaiting return home to 51L. Accumulated ash in the foreground. Darlington overhauled a good number of WDs and also scrapped 47 of them. They were a short term investment which proved doggedly long-lived; 'in their last days, affection turned to contempt, or regret as deteriorating mechanical condition did not endear these essentially short life locomotives to enginemen or operating staff.' Photograph J. Davenport, Initial Photographics.

90090 10/50 3090 2/47
78528: WD 10/44; St Margarets 29/12/45; Newport 29/1/49; Thornaby 14/6/58; Tyne Dock 23/3/63
WITHDRAWN 6/63; Doncaster Works 11/63

90091 10/50 3091 3/47
78570: WD 10/44; Newport 29/12/45; Thornaby 14/6/58; Dairycoates 7/9/63; Goole 30/11/63
WITHDRAWN 6/67; Drapers, Hull 12/67

90092 10/50 3092 2/47 63092 4/48
78577: WD 10/44; York 29/12/45; Heaton 28/9/46; Stockton on Tees 12/2/49; West Hartlepool 13/8/55; Polmadie 23/3/63; Stockton 15/6/63; Dairycoates 7/9/63; Goole 30/11/63; Dairycoates 8/8/64
WITHDRAWN 10/65; Drapers, Hull 1/66

90093 12/50 3093 2/47 63093 7/48
78582: WD 11/44; New England 20/4/46; Plaistow 19/4/58; March 11/7/59; Plaistow 3/10/59; Tilbury 14/11/59
WITHDRAWN 8/62; Stratford Works 11/62

90094 5/50 3094 2/47 63094 6/48
78584: WD 11/44; Colwick 29/12/45; Gorton 28/9/46; Mexborough 28/5/47; Colwick 8/48; Springhead 23/10/48; Goole 15/11/58
WITHDRAWN 6/67; Drapers, Hull 1/68

90095 10/49 3095 2/47
78591: WD 11/44; Colwick 9/12/45; Gorton 28/9/46; Woodford Halse 30/11/46
WITHDRAWN 6/63; Crewe Works 9/63

90096 12/51 3096 2/47
78603: WD 12/44; Heaton 31/8/46; March 28/12/46; Stratford 8/10/49; New England 4/2/50; Doncaster 20/4/63
WITHDRAWN 9/65; Drapers, Hull 12/65

90097 3/49 3097 2/47 63097 6/48
78608: WD 12/44; Aberdeen Ferryhill 26/1/46; Cambridge 9/48; Aberdeen Ferryhill 27/11/48
WITHDRAWN 8/63; Cowlair Works 9/63

90098 7/49 3098 2/47
78534: WD 1/45; Newport 1/12/45; Thornaby 14/6/58; Darlington 15/6/63
WITHDRAWN 11/64; Thompsons, Stockton on Tees 2/65

90099 4/49 3099 2/47 63099 3/48
78540: WD 2/45; Springhead 20/3/46; Heaton 28/5/47; York 12/2/49; Dairycoates 8/9/51; Goole 30/11/63
WITHDRAWN 6/67; Drapers, Hull 1/68

A perfectly disgraceful Tilbury WD at Stratford, 90093 on 1 September 1962 and what a state it is in though there is a good reason, to be fair, for it had been withdrawn the previous month and was awaiting scrapping at Stratford Works. It was among a group of former Tilbury WDs stored at Plaistow shed at times in 1962 and where on Sunday afternoon in the same year a group of tired and rather dirty oiks led by yours truly trespassed all over the closed shed. We made play with 90023, 90034, 90093, 90196, 90244, 90256, 90298 and 90653 (all later scrapped at Stratford Works) followed by a long ride home along the District Line to Richmond and the third rail to Weybridge. The fact that, along with another Plaistow withdrawal, it is dumped on the western turntable at Stratford emhasises the fact that, with closure a few weeks away, only a handful of steam workings remained at 30A, once the biggest steam shed in the country, and maybe the world. Photograph Stephen Gradidge.

90097 of Aberdeen Ferryhill shed illustrates how the spotter certainly had to travel to get numbers in sequential order in his ABCs, if I can venture such a Weybridge-centric view. The next three, 90098-90100, were in the NER. A timeless scene in Scotland, the enchanting station at Glenfarg, on the NB line to Perth. At Glenfarg the line ran roughly north by east/south by west which puts the time at early afternoon; the 7.42am Class 9 train ex-Craiginches was due to pass at 1.18pm which makes it the likely candidate. It is here that we first come across (with any clarity anyway) the question of 'the Scottish clacks'. Note that the good old Austerity top feeds have gone, replaced by these very 9F-like clack valves lower down. The Scottish Region made a concerted effort to thus 'convert' its WDs from about 1957, and all but a handful were dealt with. The reasons are unknown, but presumably the ScR thought the work worthwhile – it was not inconsiderable after all, for new connections had to be made and the old ones blanked off. Photograph T.G. Hepburn, Rail Archive Stephenson.

Long-time Aberdeen Ferryhill WD 90097; it was there all its BR life until withdrawal in August 1963 and disposal at Cowlairs Works, though this must be fairly early on. It still has the external pipe to the top feed and the loop in the hand rail and has yet to acquire a proper smokebox number plate. Photograph Paul Chancellor Collection.

90100 12/51 3100 4/47 63100 11/48
78550: WD 3/45; Colwick 3/46; Neville Hill 8/48; St
Rollox 4/9/48; York 9/49; Dairycoates 6/10/56;
Wakefield 7/9/57; Ardsley 14/7/62
WITHDRAWN 1/64; Darlington Works 2/64

90101 3/51
77000: Eastfield 13/2/43; Tay Bridge 4/12/43; WD 12/44;
Canton 9/8/47; Old Oak 12/6/48; Newton Heath
16/12/50; Wakefield 24/11/51; Aintree 17/7/54
WITHDRAWN 5/64; Slag Reduction Co. Rotherham 9/64

90102 10/51
77001: Eastfield 13/2/43; Tay Bridge 4/12/43; WD 12/44;
Newton Abbot 22/2/47; Swansea Victoria 3/6/50;
Agecroft 16/12/50; Wigan (LYR) 23/2/57; Bolton 20/4/57
WITHDRAWN 11/63; Wards, Killamarsh 1/64

90103 3/49
77003: Eastfield 13/2/43; WD 12/44; New England 2/47;
Mexborough 4/47; Neville Hill 11/47; Colwick 8/49
WITHDRAWN 11/65; Garnham, Harris and Elton,
Chesterfield 4/66

90104 9/50
77004: Eastfield 13/2/43; New England 5/43; WD 12/44;
York 3/47; Springhead 5/47; Mexborough 10/48;
March 11/51; Mexborough 7/3/53; Colwick 28/1/56
WITHDRAWN 2/66; Drapers, Hull 6/66

90105 1/52
77005: Eastfield 13/2/43; WD 12/44; Old Oak 19/4/47;
Newton Heath 16/12/50
WITHDRAWN 12/62; Horwich Works 5/63

90106 8/50
77006: Eastfield 13/2/43; New England 3/43; WD 1/45;
Newport 3/47; New England 8/49; Tilbury 22/2/58; March
11/7/59; Plaistow 3/10/59; Tilbury 14/11/59;
New England 16/12/61
WITHDRAWN 9/62; Crewe Works 12/62

90107 6/49
77007: Eastfield 13/2/43; New England 3/43; WD 1/45;
Brighton 12/47; Redhill 31/5/49; Hither Green 13/12/49;
Mirfield 16/12/50; Aintree 11/9/54
WITHDRAWN 11/63; Crewe Works 12/63

90108 4/49
77008: Eastfield 13/2/43; New England 4/43; WD 12/44;
Mexborough 10/47; Doncaster 5/51; New England
22/3/52; Doncaster 17/5/52; Kingmoor 14/6/52;
Doncaster 29/11/52; March 6/10/56;
Frodingham 20/2/60
WITHDRAWN 8/65; Arnott Young, Parkgate and
Rawmarsh 10/65

90109 10/51
77010: Eastfield 4/43; New England 5/43; WD 1/45;
Heaton 1/47; Newport 5/47; Rose Grove 29/1/49
WITHDRAWN 5/64; Central Wagon Co, Ince, Wigan 9/64

90110 1/52
77012: Eastfield 3/43; New England 3/43; WD 12/44; Oxley
2/11/46; Banbury 12/7/47; Shrewsbury 12/8/50; Bolton
24/3/51; Agecroft 10/2/62; Bolton 5/10/63;
Agecroft 2/11/63
WITHDRAWN 3/64; Looms, Spondon 12/64

90111 5/50
77013: Eastfield 3/43; WD 12/44; Neville Hill 9/47; York
5/48; Colwick 10/48; March 10/50; Frodingham 4/51
WITHDRAWN 4/64; Smiths, Ecclesfield 7/64

90112 3/51
77014: Eastfield 3/43; York 4/43; WD 12/44; Oxley
17/5/47; Banbury 12/7/47; Lostock Hall 23/4/49; Lower
Darwen 6/10/51; Accrington 14/6/52; Mirfield 19/11/55;
Wakefield 14/6/58; Sunderland 3/12/66
WITHDRAWN 1/67; Arnott Young, Dinsdale 12/67

90113 2/52
77015: Eastfield 3/43; Longmoor 3/43; Bishopbriggs
17/3/43; Old Oak 25/1/47; Shrewsbury 12/8/50; Newton
Heath 16/12/50; Sowerby Bridge 28/12/57;
Wakefield 25/1/64
WITHDRAWN 9/66; Cashmores, Great Bridge 11/66

90114 3/50
77016: Eastfield 3/43; WD 12/44; Heaton 1/3/47; Newport
5/47; St Margarets 12/48; Motherwell 3/51; Dawsholm
1/12/51; Eastfield 1/12/62; Grangemouth 23/11/63
WITHDRAWN 7/64; Motherwell Machinery and Scrap Co,
Wishaw 10/64

90115 6/51
77017: Eastfield 3/43; WD 1/44; New England 3/47;
Staveley 2/49; Colwick 16/7/55; Frodingham 8/10/60
WITHDRAWN 5/65; Garnham, Harris and Elton,
Chesterfield 8/65 or Cashmores, Great Bridge

90116 3/49
77018: Eastfield 3/43; WD 12/44; Springhead 3/47; Goole
17/5/58; Darlington 14/6/58; Wakefield 20/9/58;
West Hartlepool 3/12/66
WITHDRAWN 6/67; Drapers, Hull 10/67

90117 3/51
77019: Dunfermline 3/43 WD 1/45; Thornton Jct 2/12/56
WITHDRAWN 1/67; McWilliams, Shettleston 5/67

90118 9/49
77020: Eastfield 3/43; New England 3/43; WD 1/45;
Mexborough 12/47; Immingham 11/49; March 7/50;
Colwick 28/1/56; Canklow 20/2/60
WITHDRAWN 11/63; Doncaster Works 2/64

90119 2/49
77022: Eastfield 3/43; New England 4/43; WD 1/45;
Annesley 2/47; March 7/50; Colwick 28/1/56; March 25/
2/56; Doncaster 23/3/57; Mexborough 14/6/58;
Frodingham 11/8/62
WITHDRAWN 1/65; Wards, Beighton, Sheffield 5/65

90120 1/49
77023: Eastfield 3/43; York 4/43; WD 12/44; Mexborough
10/47; Colwick 28/1/56; Frodingham 8/10/60
WITHDRAWN 4/65; Arnott Young, Dinsdale 7/65

90121 12/50
77024: Eastfield 3/43; York 4/43; WD 12/44; Aberdeen
Ferryhill 17/7/48; Wigan (LYR) 28/11/53; Bolton 20/2/60;
Langwith Jct 3/10/64; Barrow Hill 19/6/65
WITHDRAWN 6/65; Arnott Young, Parkgate and
Rawmarsh 9/65

90122 12/49
77025: Eastfield 4/43; York 4/43; WD 12/44; Rose Grove
24/12/49; Colwick 2/12/50; Belle Vue 26/1/52; Sowerby
Bridge 10/11/56; Wakefield 25/1/64
WITHDRAWN 10/65; Steelbreaking and Dismantling Co,
Chesterfield 11/65

90107, in excellent nick, waits to proceed at Cheadle Heath on 5 September 1957. Still retains outside pipe to the top feed. At the time it was an Aintree loco so now, in south Manchester and rather clean, it might be running in after overhaul at Crewe. It was eventually scrapped there. Photograph D. Forsyth, Paul Chancellor Collection.

The WDs may have been a homogeneous lot, at least in engine picking terms, but they had their eyebrow-raising moments when you really start to think again, like the extra filler on 90076. Well, have you spotted it yet? Yes, 90111's tender has the fire iron stowing point on this, the 'wrong' side. How many firemen were completely flummoxed by this? This tender may or may not have been unique but it shows how you just can't *assume* anything... Photograph Peter Groom.

With so many of the class on the LMR a good number were overhauled at Crewe, though Horwich seems to have taken more than its 'share'. 90112 is ex-works, outside Crewe's Ten Shop; note the capstans for manoeuvring the locos around, attaching hawsers to the draw bar. Here the final touches would be made, setting up the brick arch and so on before reuniting the engine with the tender and steaming. During 90112's time at Mirfield the shed transferred to the NER, though whether maintenance then passed to Darlington or remained with Crewe is not clear. 90112 subsequently passed to Wakefield and then to the NER 'proper', at Sunderland.

Up evening freight behind 90115 climbing towards Stoke (near Little Ponton) on 19 July 1958. It has acquired the later type washout plugs (but not the prominent covers) and 'split' hand rail though it retains the outside feed water pipes. Photograph Peter Groom.

A beautiful study of 90117, from Dunfermline (62C), at Motherwell on 8 May 1955. For a WD it is really quite clean but again we have that odd situation of no smokebox number plate though the number is very neatly painted on. Alongside is Black Five 45099, a Motherwell regular for a time; witness the large 'Scottish' cabside numbers. Photograph J. Robertson, www.transporttreasury.co.uk

90123 11/51
77026: Eastfield 4/43; York 4/43; WD 12/44; Oxley 19/4/47; Banbury 12/7/47; Leamington 3/12/49; Shrewsbury 12/8/50; Newton Heath 16/12/50; Bury 31/12/51; Agecroft 5/10/57; Lees 28/12/57; Newton Heath 18/4/64; Aintree 11/7/64; Lower Darwen 8/8/64; Rose Grove 28/11/64
WITHDRAWN 3/65; Drapers, Hull 7/65

90124 8/51
77027: Eastfield 4/43; York 4/43; WD 12/44; Canton 17/4/48; Wakefield 18/6/49; Mirfield 24/3/51; Wakefield 14/6/58
WITHDRAWN 6/65; Ellis Metals, Swalwell, Derwenthaugh 10/65

90125 10/50
77028: Eastfield then York 4/43; WD 12/44; Oxley 19/4/47; Motherwell 11/2/50; Oxley 8/9/51; Ebbw Jct 6/10/51; Canton 6/11/54; Warrington Dallam 22/9/62; Aintree 26/1/63; Springs Branch 13/7/63; Lostock Hall 5/10/63; Kirkby-in-Ashfield 28/12/63; Lostock Hall 18/4/64
WITHDRAWN 7/65; Cashmores, Great Bridge, 11/65

90126 3/49
77029: Eastfield 4/43; New England 4/43; WD 1/45; Rose Grove 26/3/49; Colwick 2/12/50; Warrington 8/9/51; Belle Vue 26/1/52; Low Moor 10/11/56; Darlington 14/6/58; Mirfield 20/9/58; Wakefield 3/11/60; Mirfield 15/7/61; Ardsley 14/7/62; Wakefield 27/11/65
WITHDRAWN 1/67; Cox and Danks, Wadsley Bridge 6/67

90127 9/50
77030: Eastfield then New England 4/43; WD 1/45; Feltham 9/47; Hither Green 4/2/50; Aintree 16/6/51; Wakefield 11/8/51; Aintree 17/7/54; Farnley Jct 21/4/56; Royston 7/10/61
WITHDRAWN 10/64; Drapers, Hull 12/65

90128 6/49
77031: Eastfield then York 4/43; WD 12/44; Thornton Jct 3/47; Eastfield 13/6/59; Grangemouth 23/12/61
WITHDRAWN 11/62; Cowlair Works 2/63

90129 10/50
77032: Eastfield then York 4/43; WD 12/44; Dairycoates 8/47; Colwick 10/48; March 16/1/54; Stratford 4/4/59; Hornsey 21/5/60; New England 15/7/61; Immingham 22/9/62
WITHDRAWN 7/64; Wards, Killamarsh 1/65

90130 11/49
77034: Eastfield then York 4/43; WD 12/44; New England 3/47; Mexborough 1/12/51; Colwick 28/1/56; New England 21/5/60; Retford 20/4/63; Colwick 19/6/65
WITHDRAWN 10/65; Drapers, Hull 2/66

90131 2/49
77035: Eastfield then New England 5/43;WD 1/45; March 8/47; Immingham 3/10/53; Retford 5/10/63
WITHDRAWN 3/65; Drapers, Hull 7/65

90132 8/49
77036: Eastfield 4/43; New England 5/43; WD 1/45; Newport 3/47; Thornaby 14/6/58; Goole 7/9/63
WITHDRAWN 4/67; Drapers, Hull 8/67

90133 5/49
77037: Eastfield 4/43; New England 5/43; WD 1/45; Annesley 4/47; Colwick 11/47; Immingham 5/48; Frodingham 5/51
WITHDRAWN 10/65; Arnott Young, Dinsdale 4/66

90134 10/49
77039: Eastfield 5/43; Aberdeen Ferryhill 12/43; WD 1/45; Dunfermline 9/47; Grangemouth 18/6/49; Polmadie 23/2/52; Dawsholm 7/10/61; St. Rollox 23/12/61
WITHDRAWN 7/62; Cowlair Works 1/63

90135 6/52
77040: Eastfield 5/43; Aberdeen Ferryhill 12/43; Reading 11/11/44; WD 12/44; Oxley 2/11/46; Birkenhead 17/4/48; Lower Darwen 4/11/50; Goole 15/11/52; Darlington 14/6/58; Mirfield 14/11/59; Wakefield 21/1/61; Mirfield 15/7/61; Ardsley 21/3/64; Wakefield 19/6/65; Sunderland 3/12/66
WITHDRAWN 9/67; Hughes Bolckows, North Blyth 10/67

90136 10/50
77041: Eastfield 5/43; Aberdeen Ferryhill 12/43; Reading 11/11/44; WD 12/44; Annesley 8/47; Colwick 11/47; Mexborough 14/6/58; Canklow 29/12/62
WITHDRAWN 4/65; Cashmores, Great Bridge 7/65

90137 5/51
77042: Kingmoor 5/43; Oxley 9/44; WD 1/45; Colwick 1/47; Barnsley 5/47; Neville Hill 11/47; Woodford Halse 7/49
WITHDRAWN 12/62; Crewe Works 5/63

90138 6/51
77044: Kingmoor 5/43; Oxley 9/44; WD 16/9/44; St Margarets 3/47; Rose Grove 29/1/49
WITHDRAWN 4/64; Crewe Works 5/64

90139 11/50
77047: Kingmoor 19/6/43; Severn Tunnel Jct 24/10/44; WD 1/45; Annesley 9/47; Woodford Halse 11/47; Colwick 10/48; Woodford Halse 7/49; Colwick 3/50; Staveley 1/12/51; Colwick 29/12/51; Mexborough 14/6/58; Canklow 29/12/62
WITHDRAWN 5/65; Drapers, Hull 7/65

90140 3/50
77048: Kingmoor 19/6/43; Oxley 9/44; WD 1/45; Farnley Jct 12/48; Colwick 2?12/50; Warrington 8/9/51; Belle Vue 26/1/52; Lees 2/11/57; Patricroft 22/9/62; Widnes 26/1/63; Springs Branch 23/3/63; Agecroft 8/6/63
WITHDRAWN 10/64; Central Wagon Co, Ince, Wigan 1/65

90141 2/49
77049: Kingmoor 19/6/43; Banbury 11/44; WD 1/45; Oxley 2/11/46; Wakefield 4/11/50; Aintree 17/7/54; Lees 28/12/57; Patricroft 22/9/62; Aintree 26/1/63
WITHDRAWN 2/64; J. Routledge, Bootle, Liverpool 8/64

90142 5/51
77150: Kingmoor 19/6/43; Stourbridge 11/44; WD 1/45; Feltham 12/47; Hither Green 4/2/50; Aintree 16/6/51; Wakefield 11/8/51; Aintree 17/7/54; Belle Vue 19/2/55; Agecroft 20/5/61; Immingham 3/10/64
WITHDRAWN 12/65; Drapers, Hull 5/66

90143 3/49
77151: Kingmoor 19/6/43; Wellingborough 11/11/44; WD 10/2/45; Oxley 9/46; Birkenhead 17/4/48; Rose Grove 4/11/50
WITHDRAWN 6/64; Connels, Calder 9/64

90144 3/49
77152: Kingmoor 19/6/43; Wellingborough 11/11/44; WD 27/1/45; Mexborough 11/47; Colwick 28/1/56; March 25/2/56; Doncaster 23/3/57
WITHDRAWN 12/63; Doncaster Works 3/64

Wakefield's 90124 by the 'coal hole' at Stockport Edgeley shed, about 1960. Alongside is Black Five 45198 which for a while was a resident of Crewe South shed. Photograph D. Forsyth, Paul Chancellor Collection.

90130 in Kings Cross shed yard, 19 August 1962. AWS fitted, with a glimpse of the pipework behind the protective plate, for once. A New England example, though the second emblem just struggles to the surface of the grime. This was the last summer of steam working into London on the GN and the WDs were much thinner on the ground than they used to be; indeed these two probably would not have got past Hornsey had that shed not been dieselised a few months before. Photograph Peter Groom.

Occasionally we would stumble across a clean WD and stare in wonder for a while; the altered 'mudhole doors' in place of the conventional washout plugs are prominent when the engine is clean, as here at Annesley on 24 June 1962. 90232 is visiting from Frodingham; the adaptation (they were washout plug covers really) meant that (as we have seen frequently already) the hand rail had to be divided in two. Photograph Stephen Gradidge.

A Woodford Halse WD, 90137, in the early 1960s but in good condition. The angle allows a glimpse, for a change, of the pony truck framing. Photograph Paul Chancellor Collection.

A WD soon after overhaul at Crewe. 90140, looking very clean, is due to return to 26E Lees (Oldham) and still retains the outside pipe to the top feed; in addition it has a steam heating hose and the overhead wire warning signs, probably newly fitted. Photograph D. Forsyth, Paul Chancellor Collection.

And now we are at Lees (which often used Newton Heath locos on its diagrams) with Newton Heath's 90142 in May 1959. The big Manchester shed only had a small allocation of the class at first though by 1959 there were 25 on its books, replacing old L&Y 0-6-0s and the failing LMS 0-8-0s. Photograph J. Davenport, Initial Photographics.

Winters as they should be; even the coal in the wagons has a covering of snow. 90143 was a long term Rose Grove resident (I guess we are up that way in this picture) having come from Oxley in November 1950; even so it has a boiler with the altered washout plugs which it must have got at Crewe. Rowledge notes that a supply of these amended boilers was kept there. Photograph Paul Chancellor Collection.

90145 3/50
77155: Wellingborough 19/6/43; WD 27/1/45; Thornton Jct 8/47; March 22/3/52; Immingham 3/10/53; Canklow 5/9/59; Langwith Jct 22/4/61
WITHDRAWN 6/64; Wards, Killamarsh 10/64

90146 2/49
77157: Wellingborough 19/6/43; WD 1/45; Mexborough 11/47; Colwick 28/1/56; New England 21/5/60; Retford 20/4/63
WITHDRAWN 6/65; Wards, Killamarsh 8/65

90147 5/49
77160: Wellingborough 19/6/43; WD 10/2/45; Wakefield 11/6/49; Mirfield 18/11/50; Colwick 2/12/50; Mold Jct 17/5/52; Stafford 27/2/60; Mold Jct 21/5/60; Widnes 12/5/62; Gorton 23/3/63; Sutton Oak 1/6/63; Springs Branch 15/6/63
WITHDRAWN 5/64; Central Wagon Co, Ince, Wigan 1/65

90148 2/49
77161: Wellingborough 19/6/43; WD 10/2/45; Laira 25/1/47; Newton Abbot 12/7/52; Canton 24/4/54; Shrewsbury 13/7/57; Banbury 22/3/58; Gloucester Barnwood 30/12/61; Stourbridge 24/2/62; Springs Branch 14/7/62; Sutton Oak 27/3/65; Lower Darwen 24/6/65; Barrow Hill 24/6/65; Frodingham 4/12/65; Doncaster 26/3/66
WITHDRAWN 4/66; Drapers, Hull 9/66

90149 6/51
77162: Eastfield 19/6/43; Parkhead 10/44; WD 12/44; Eastfield 17/4/48; Motherwell 18/9/48; Eastfield 11/48; Ebbw Jct 3/11/51; Chester (WR) then Ebbw Jct 1/12/51; Gloucester Horton Road 16/5/53; Ebbw Jct 4/10/58; Canton 31/10/59; Southall 6/10/62; Mexborough 29/12/62; Canklow 22/2/64; Langwith Jct 19/6/65
WITHDRAWN 1/66; Drapers, Hull 5/66

90150 5/49
77163: Eastfield 19/6/43; Parkhead 10/44; WD 12/44; Mexborough 11/47; Colwick 28/1/56; March 25/2/56; Doncaster 7/10/61
WITHDRAWN 9/62; Doncaster Works 12/62

90151 11/50
77164: Eastfield 6/43; Parkhead 10/44; WD 12/44; New England 3/47
WITHDRAWN 5/63; Doncaster Works 7/63

90152 3/51
77165: Eastfield 6/43; Parkhead 10/44; WD 1/45; Oxley 2/11/46; Motherwell 11/2/50; Oxley 8/9/51; Southall 3/11/51; Westhouses 8/8/59; Gorton 30/6/62; Lower Darwen 28/11/64
WITHDRAWN 5/65; Arnott Young, Dinsdale 8/65

90153 10/51
77166: Eastfield 6/43; WD 12/44; Mexborough 12/47; Colwick 28/1/56; Mexborough 14/6/58; Canklow 29/12/62; Langwith Jct 19/6/65
WITHDRAWN 2/66; Drapers, Hull 5/66

90154 2/49
77167: Eastfield 6/43; WD 12/44; York 3/47; Springhead 5/47; Mexborough 10/48; Colwick 17/5/52; New England 19/12/59; Doncaster 5/10/63
WITHDRAWN 4/66; Drapers, Hull 9/66

90155 8/49
77169: Eastfield 6/43; Parkhead 12/43; WD 1/45; Retford 7/47; Stockton on Tees 11/47; Darlington 11/7/59; Wakefield 23/2/63
WITHDRAWN 1/67; Cox and Danks, Wadsley Bridge 5/67

90148, a one-time Laira engine, at Aller Junction on 1 April 1953 on a down goods with the road set for the train to cross over to the Down Relief. The loco has the WR modifications, covered top feed and 'tunnel' on running plate for the fire irons. Photograph A. Lathey, www.transporttreasury.co.uk

90152 outside Swindon Works on 6 September 1953; modified top feed, fire iron 'tunnel' though an iron and a shovel sit on a heap of spilled coal on the tender inset. 90152 went from Oxley to Motherwell in February 1950 and returned to Oxley in September 1951, moving to Southall a couple of months later. Photograph B. Hilton, www.transporttreasury.co.uk

90156 9/51
77170: Eastfield 6/43; Parkhead 12/43; WD 1/45; Newton Heath then Neville Hill 5/47; New England 8/49; Peterborough (LMR) 16/1/54; New England 25/2/56; March 2/11/57; Stratford 4/4/59; Hornsey 21/5/60; Doncaster 15/7/61
WITHDRAWN 4/66; Drapers, Hull 9/66

90157 5/49
77171: Eastfield 6/43; WD 12/44; Accrington 14/5/49; Wakefield 16/7/49; Colwick 2/12/50; Staveley 3/51; Mold Jct 17/5/52; Widnes 8/8/59; Tebay 25/3/61; Birkenhead 16/6/62; Widnes 22/9/62; Springs Branch 23/3/63
WITHDRAWN 7/64; Central Wagon Co, Ince, Wigan 4/65

90158 3/51
77173: Eastfield then Aberdeen Ferryhill 7/43; WD 1/45; March 12/47; New England 10/48; Retford 2/11/63; Doncaster 19/6/65
WITHDRAWN 12/65; W. George, Station Steel, Wath 2/66

90159 4/51
77174: Eastfield then Aberdeen Ferryhill 7/43; WD 2/45; Newport 3/47; Rose Grove 29/1/49
WITHDRAWN 11/63; Butlers, Otley 7/64

90160 12/50
77175: Eastfield then Tay Bridge 7/43; WD 12/44; Annesley 1/47; Barnsley 5/47; Neville Hill 11/47; Springhead 5/48; Dairycoates 12/50; Goole 13/2/60; Wakefield 8/8/64
WITHDRAWN 6/67; Drapers, Hull 2/68

90161 8/51
77176: Eastfield then Tay Bridge 7/43; WD 12/44; Mexborough 11/47; Abergavenny 23/2/52; Colwick 28/1/56; Immingham 26/3/60; Frodingham 8/10/60
WITHDRAWN 2/64; Doncaster Works 3/64

90162 5/49
77178: Eastfield then Thornton Jct 7/43; WD 12/44; Annesley 4/10/47; Colwick 11/47; New England 5/51; Langwith Jct 31/12/54; Canklow 11/7/59; Immingham 5/9/59; Canklow 16/1/60
WITHDRAWN 2/64; Wards, Beighton, Sheffield 5/64

90163 5/49
77179: Eastfield then Thornton Jct 7/43; WD 12/44; Accrington 14/5/49; Wakefield 16/7/49; Colwick 2/12/50; Warrington 8/9/51; Belle Vue 26/1/52; Newton Heath 25/2/56
WITHDRAWN 12/62; Crewe Works 10/63

90164 5/49
77180: Eastfield 7/43; Stratford 7/43; March 10/43; WD 12/44; Bricklayers Arms 1/46; Aintree 14/7/51; Wakefield 11/8/51; Aintree 17/7/54; Rose Grove 22/9/62; Gorton 18/4/64; Langwith Jct 3/10/64
WITHDRAWN 4/65; Cashmores, Great Bridge 7/65

90165 5/51
77181: Eastfield 7/43; Stratford 7/43; March 10/43; WD 12/44; Annesley 9/47; Staveley then Colwick 11/47; Annesley 11/48; Colwick 12/48; New England 7/49; Frodingham 22/9/62; Mexborough 26/1/63; Doncaster 5/10/63
WITHDRAWN 4/64; Smiths, Ecclesfield 1/65

90166 8/51
77182: Eastfield then Stratford 7/43; WD 12/44; Mexborough 11/47; Colwick 28/1/56; Immingham 26/3/60; Frodingham 8/10/60
WITHDRAWN 5/65; Cashmores, Great Bridge 8/65

90167 8/51
77184: Eastfield 8/43; Dairycoates then March 9/43; Springhead then WD 12/44; Old Oak 19/4/47; Ebbw Jct 17/6/50; Pontypool Road 30/12/50; Carmarthen 22/3/58; LLlanelly 18/6/60; Canton 10/9/60
WITHDRAWN 5/62; Crewe Works 5/62

90168 9/50
77185: Eastfield 8/43; Dairycoates 9/43; WD 12/44; Thornton Jct 3/47
WITHDRAWN 8/66; McWilliams, Shettleston 11/66

90169 2/50
77186: Eastfield 8/43; Dairycoates 9/43; Springhead 4/44; WD 12/44; March 7/47; New England 10/48; Colwick 30/6/62; Retford 5/10/63; Doncaster 19/6/65
WITHDRAWN 8/65; Garnham, Harris and Elton, Chesterfield 11/65

90170 4/51
77187: Eastfield then Stratford 8/43; March 9/43; WD 1/45; Thornton Jct 3/47; Kingmoor 22/5/54; Sutton Oak 10/9/60; Agecroft 8/6/63
WITHDRAWN 8/63; Smiths, Ecclesfield 2/65

90171 4/49
77192: Eastfield 8/43; Dairycoates 9/43; WD 12/44; Lostock Hall 23/4/49; Accrington 19/11/49; Rose Grove 24/12/49
WITHDRAWN 7/65; Wards, Killamarsh 10/65

90172 11/50
77195: Longmoor 9/43; York 4/47; Stockton on Tees 8/47; Darlington 11/7/59; Dairycoates 7/9/63; Goole 30/11/63
WITHDRAWN 6/67; Drapers, Hull 12/67

90173 7/52
77196: Eastfield 8/43; Dairycoates 9/43; WD 12/44; Laira 22/3/47; Swansea Victoria 3/6/50; Newton Heath 13/1/51; Birkenhead 17/10/53; Mold Jct 4/12/54; Birkenhead 11/2/56; Springs Branch 27/2/60; Lancaster 3/11/62; Springs Branch 13/7/63
WITHDRAWN 7/64; Central Wagon Co, Ince, Wigan 1/65

90174 3/50
77198: Eastfield 8/43; March 9/43; WD 1/45; Eastfield 9/47; Ebbw Jct 3/11/51; Southall 14/6/52
WITHDRAWN 10/62 Crewe Works 6/63

90175 3/49
77199: Eastfield then Tyne Dock 9/43; New England 9/44; WD 11/44; March 4/47; Immingham 31/10/53
WITHDRAWN 4/65; Drapers, Hull 8/65

90176 9/51
77200: Eastfield 8/43; March 9/43; WD 1/45; St Philips Marsh 30/11/46; Shrewsbury 5/11/55; St Philips Marsh 28/12/57; Wakefield 4/4/59; Westhouses 8/8/59; Gorton 30/6/62
WITHDRAWN 2/63; Crewe Works 6/63

90177 9/50
77201: Eastfield 8/43; March 9/43; WD 1/45; Thornton Jct 1/3/47; Dunfermline 6/11/54
WITHDRAWN 6/63; Cowlairs Works 7/63

90178 3/49
77202: Eastfield 8/43; March 9/43; WD 1/45; Oxley 19/4/47; Lower Darwen 14/5/49; Colwick 2/12/50; Mold Jct 17/5/52; Widnes 8/8/59; Carnforth 20/2/60; Sutton Oak 8/10/60; Frodingham 22/5/65
WITHDRAWN 2/66; Drapers, Hull 7/66

WDs were not often to be found amid the jumble of Willesden shed (I certainly never saw any on 1A during my frequent visits) but 90153 was there on 16 May 1964. It was a visitor for the shed never had an allocation and the bush telegraph would have thrummed to the knowledge that a Canklow engine was in town. Photograph Stephen Gradidge.

AWS fitted 90172 at Goole shed in March 1965. I'm at a loss to explain the projections on the cab roof though it was this one, as 7195, that had been done up as an armoured loco in September 1943, going to the Melbourne Military Railway and then Longmoor. The plating (there was an extra roof sheet) was taken off before it went to Europe. Photograph J. Davenport, Initial Photographics.

90179 2/52
77203: Eastfield 8/43; Tyne Dock 9/43; WD 1/45; Worcester 19/4/47; Gloucester Horton Road 12/7/47; Worcester 24/3/51; Severn Tunnel Jct 19/4/52; Pontypool Road 21/3/53; Canton 11/9/54; Pontypool Road 9/10/54; Ebbw Jct 1/1/55; Worcester 13/7/57; Carmarthen 22/3/58; Llanelly 18/6/60; Gorton 16/6/62
WITHDRAWN 4/64; Slag Reduction Co, Ickles, Sheffield 10/64

90180 3/51
77204: Eastfield 8/43; WD 1/45; New England 1/3/47; Immingham 22/9/62
WITHDRAWN 3/65; Drapers, Hull 6/65

90181 10/50
77205: Eastfield then Thornton Jct 9/43; Bricklayers Arms 20/3/46; Huddersfield 17/6/50; Sowerby Bridge 16/2/52; Rose Grove 8/8/53
WITHDRAWN 5/65; Cashmores, Great Bridge 8/65

90182 4/50
77206: Eastfield 9/43; WD 12/44; Thornton Jct 3/47
WITHDRAWN 12/63; Wards, Inverkeithing 6/64

90183 12/51
77207: Eastfield then Thornton Jct 9/43; To WD 1/45; St Margarets 1/3/47; Rose Grove 29/1/49; Patricroft 30/1/60; Newton Heath 26/1/63; Springs Branch 28/12/63; Frodingham 22/5/65
WITHDRAWN 8/65; Drapers, Hull 11/65

90184 5/49
77208: Eastfield 9/43; WD 12/44; Retford 26/7/47; Stockton on Tees 29/11/47; Darlington 11/7/59; Mirfield 14/11/59
WITHDRAWN 10/64; Arnott Young, Dinsdale 10/65

90185 4/51
77209: Eastfield 9/43; WD 12/44; Annesley 4/10/47; Colwick 29/11/47; Wakefield 2/50; Colwick 3/50; Woodford Halse 4/50; Colwick 10/50; New England 21/5/60; Immingham 22/9/62
WITHDRAWN 3/65; Drapers, Hull 6/65

90186 2/49
77210: Eastfield then Tyne Dock 9/43; WD 1/45; Newton Abbot 19/4/47; Swansea Victoria 3/6/50; Bolton 16/12/50; Goole 15/11/52
WITHDRAWN 8/63; Darlington Works 9/63

90187 9/49
77212: Eastfield then Tyne Dock 9/43; Banbury 24/10/44; WD 1/45; Wakefield 8/10/49; Colwick 4/11/50; Woodford Halse 8/51; Colwick 2/12/51; Mold Jct 17/5/52; Carnforth 25/3/61; Kikrby-in-Ashfield 28/12/63; Carnforth 18/4/64; Sutton Oak 16/5/64; Lower Darwen 13/6/64; Colwick 19/6/65; Doncaster 4/12/65
WITHDRAWN 2/66; Drapers, Hull 7/66

90188 2/51
77214: Eastfield then Thornton Jct 9/43; WD 1/45; Newton Abbot 19/4/47; Swansea Victoria 3/6/50; Canton 24/2/51; Ebbw Jct; 16/6/51; Canton 11/8/51; Banbury 5/11/60; Ebbw Jct 3/12/60; Mexborough 29/12/62; Barrow Hill 25/1/64
WITHDRAWN 4/65; Cashmores, Great Bridge 7/65

90189 3/49
77215: Eastfield then Thornton Jct 9/43; WD 2/45; Mexborough 25/10/47; Colwick 28/1/56; Frodingham 20/2/60; Barrow Hill 25/1/64; Langwith Jct 9/10/65
WITHDRAWN 11/65; Drapers, Hull 3/66

90190 3/49
77218: Eastfield 9/43; Thornton Jct 11/43; WD 2/45; Springhead 29/3/47; Mexborough 10/48; Doncaster; 6/10/62; Mexborough 26/1/63; Canklow 21/3/64; Langwith Jct 8/8/64; Barrow Hill 2/1/65; Colwick 9/10/65; Immingham 4/12/65
WITHDRAWN 2/66; Drapers, Hull 6/66

90191 10/50
77221: Eastfield 9/43; Thornton Jct 11/43; WD 1/45; New England 1/3/47; March 2/11/57
WITHDRAWN 1/60; Stratford Works 2/60

90192 1/51
77222: Eastfield 10/43; Tyne Dock 10/43; WD 2/45; Eastfield 23/8/47; Motherwell 18/9/48; Eastfield 11/48; Banbury 1/12/51; Canton 12/7/52; Pontypool Road 9/10/54; Birkenhead 25/2/61; Widnes 22/9/62; Polmadie 23/3/63; Springs Branch 20/4/63
WITHDRAWN 4/63; Crewe Works 10/63

90193 2/51
77225: Eastfield 10/43; Newport 11/4/44; WD 2/45; Eastfield 21/2/48; Dairycoates 7/2/48; Dawsholm 14/7/51; Thorton Jct 1/8/62
WITHDRAWN 8/63; Inverurie Works 9/63

90194 9/51
77226: Eastfield then Tay Bridge 10/43; WD 1/45; Bricklayers Arms 20/3/46; Accrington 6/10/51; Bury 31/12/51; Lees 24/12/60
WITHDRAWN 3/64; Crewe Works 5/64

90195 6/49
77227: Eastfield then Dunfermline 10/43; WD 1/45; Mexborough; 25/10/47; Doncaster 11/8/62
WITHDRAWN 10/65; Drapers, Hull 1/66

90196 10/49
77228: Eastfield then Dunfermline 10/43; WD 1/45; Mexborough 27/12/47; Plaistow 21/5/55; Tilbury 14/11/59
WITHDRAWN 9/62; Stratford Works 11/62

90197 6/49
77229: Eastfield then Dunfermline 10/43; Worcester 23/11/44; WD 2/45; Wakefield 11/6/49; Colwick 2/12/50; Warrington 8/9/51; Belle Vue 26/1/52; Newton Heath 6/10/56
WITHDRAWN 5/64; Slag Reduction Co, Ickles, Rotherham 12/64

90198 8/50
77230: Eastfield then St Margarets 10/43; WD 2/45; Tay Bridge 14/5/47; St Rollox 18/9/48; Dawsholm 10/8/57; Polmadie 9/8/58; Aberdeen Ferryhill 27/1/62; Ardrossan 7/4/62; Ayr 21/4/62
WITHDRAWN 12/62; Cowlair Works 4/63

90199 2/50
77231; Eastfield 10/43; Old Oak 23/11/44; WD 1/45; Dunfermline 4/10/47; Thornton Jct 7/8/54; Grangemouth 8/10/55; Polmadie 9/8/58; Eastfield 1/12/62; Dunfermline 4/12/65
WITHDRAWN 11/66; Arnott Young, Old Kilpatrick 5/67

A WR-adapted WD (note the top feed and lamp irons) and an old friend, 90174, still at its Southall home on 28 April 1963, despite withdrawal six months before. WR ATC conduit on running plate this side. That curious Southall habit of the time, painting the smokebox door straps, extended to WDs evidently; plate removed for safe-keeping (or pinched) like the nameplate of the Hall behind. 90174's other claim to fame was that it was the only WD I photographed, at Swindon the previous April. In a few weeks it was sent to Crewe for breaking up; it was practice at the time for parts to be used again for WDs still undergoing overhaul there. Photograph Stephen Gradidge.

A former Western WD (note the covered top feed) comprehensively begrimed 90179 is now working out of its final shed, Gorton. The location is unknown to me but doubtless obvious to any reader with local knowledge; a train of empties 'somewhere in the North West'. The overhead wires in the background should help; but DC or AC? The locals' washing looks in mortal danger. Photograph D. Forsyth, Paul Chancellor Collection.

90194 ex-works and naturally in splendid order, presumably at Crewe; another WD, ex-WR, behind. Photograph Paul Chancellor Collection.

90200 6/49
77232: Eastfield 10/43; WD 12/44; Neville Hill 29/11/47; York 9/49; Darlington 16/6/56; York 7/2/59; Wakefield then to Low Moor 14/11/59; Sowerby Bridge 15/7/61; Wakefield 25/1/64; Sunderland 13/8/66
WITHDRAWN 7/67; Drapers, Hull 10/67

90201 3/49
77234: Eastfield 10/43; Springhead 4/44; WD 2/45; Stourbridge 17/5/47; Oxley 14/6/47; Canton 26/3/55; Didcot 25/3/61; Ebbw Jct 15/7/61; Gorton 16/6/62
WITHDRAWN 7/64; Carrex Metals Ltd, Rochdale 2/65

90202 11/50
77235: Eastfield 10/43; Heaton 9/44; WD 12/44; Colwick 25/1/47; Annesley 1/3/47; Woodford Halse 29/11/47; Colwick 12/48; Canklow 27/2/60
WITHDRAWN 4/65; Cashmores, Great Bridge 7/65

90203 4/51
77237: Eastfield 10/43; WD 1/45; Aberdeen Ferryhill 12/6/48; March 22/3/52; Immingham 31/10/53; March 6/10/56; Doncaster 23/3/57; Mexborough 14/6/58; Canklow 1/6/63; Doncaster 19/6/65
WITHDRAWN 10/65; Arnott Young, Dinsdale 4/66

90204 1/50
77239: Eastfield 10/43; WD 1/45; Farnley Jct 28/1/50; Colwick 2/12/50; Warrington 8/9/51; Belle Vue 26/1/52; Aintree 4/12/54; Lower Darwen 24/6/65
WITHDRAWN 6/65; Wards, Killamarsh 10/65

90205 2/52
77241: Eastfield then WD 11/43; Newton Abbot 19/4/47; Swansea Victoria 3/6/50; Bolton 16/12/50; Kirkby-in-Ashfield 23/11/63; Bury 25/1/64
WITHDRAWN 3/64; Looms, Spondon 7/65

90206 3/49
77242: Eastfield 11/43; WD 1/45; Rose Grove 26/3/49; Accrington 24/12/49; Bolton 14/7/51
WITHDRAWN 5/63; Horwich Works 9/63

90207 6/51
77247: Eastfield 11/43; St Margarets 12/43; WD 1/45; St Philips Marsh 19/4/47; Southall 14/7/51; Carmarthen 22/3/58; Llanelly 18/6/60; Gorton 16/6/62; Rose Grove 27/2/65
WITHDRAWN 5/65; Arnott Young, Dinsdale 8/65

90208 3/50
77248: Eastfield 11/43; St Margarets 12/43; WD 1/45; Dairycoates; 23/8/47; Neville Hill 5/49; New England 8/49; Colwick 24/4/54; Woodford Halse 11/2/56; March 6/10/56; Doncaster 7/10/61
WITHDRAWN 3/64 Doncaster Works 3/64

90209 2/49
77249: Eastfield 11/43; St Margarets 12/43; WD 1/45; Mexborough 25/10/47; Langwith Jct 29/12/62
WITHDRAWN 7/64; Wards, Killamarsh 2/65

90210 3/49
77252: Eastfield 11/43; St Margarets 12/43; WD 1/45; New England 1/3/47; Mexborough 26/4/47; Tyne Dock 29/11/47; Dairycoates 3/51; York 19/11/55; Darlington 16/6/56; Sowerby Bridge 20/9/58; Wakefield 25/1/64; Sunderland 13/8/66; West Hartlepool 25/3/67
WITHDRAWN 7/67; Drapers, Hull 12/67

90211 7/49
77253: Eastfield 11/43; Canal 12/43; WD 1/45; Mexborough 1/48; Canklow 1/6/63; Doncaster 19/6/65
WITHDRAWN 7/65; Wards, Beighton, Sheffield 10/65

90212 2/49
77255: Eastfield 11/43; Canal 12/43; WD 1/45; St Philips Marsh 19/4/47; Laira 9/8/47; Wakefield 18/6/49; Colwick 2/12/50; Mold Jct 17/5/52; Birkenhead 10/11/56; Carnforth 16/1/60; Sutton Oak 10/9/60; Frodingham 22/5/65
WITHDRAWN 8/65; Garnham, Harris and Elton, Chesterfield 10/65

90213 10/49
77256: Eastfield 11/43; Canal 12/43; March 2/12/44; WD 2/45; Bricklayers Arms 20/3/46; Hither Green 13/12/49; Goole 11/8/51; Dairycoates 8/8/64
WITHDRAWN 2/66; Drapers, Hull 6/66

90214 1/51
77257: Eastfield 11/43; Tyne Dock 29/1/44; Newport 11/11/44; WD 2/45; Oxley 17/5/47; Chester (WR) 9/8/47; Springs Branch 27/2/60; Westhouses 16/7/60; Gorton 30/6/62
WITHDRAWN 3/64; Hesslewoods, Attercliffe, Sheffield 12/64

90215 10/51
77258: Eastfield 11/43; Tyne Dock 29/1/44; Tyseley 24/10/44; WD 2/45; Mexborough 25/10/47; Grangemouth 5/49; Colwick 6/50; New England 21/5/60; Immingham 22/9/62
WITHDRAWN 4/65; Drapers, Hull 8/65

90216 2/50
77259: Eastfield 12/43; Newport 29/1/44; Neath 24/10/44; WD 2/45; Bricklayers Arms 20/3/46; Farnley Jct 11/8/51; Agecroft 16/2/52; Aintree 22/3/52
WITHDRAWN 8/64; Central Wagon Co, Ince, Wigan 8/65

90217 9/49
77260: Eastfield 12/43; Tyne Dock 1/44; Heaton 9/44; WD 12/44; Annesley 1/3/47; Barnsley 26/4/47; Neville Hill 29/11/47; Springhead 5/48; Dairycoates 2/50; Woodford Halse 3/50; Springhead 6/50; Dairycoates 15/11/58; York 18/11/61
WITHDRAWN 6/65; Ellis Metals Ltd, Swalwell, Derwenthaugh 10/65

90218 5/51
77261: Eastfield then Colwick 12/43; Bath Road 24/10/44; WD 11/44; Gorton 29/3/47; Annesley 26/4/47; Woodford Halse 29/11/47; Colwick 12/48; Toton 23/11/63; Woodford Halse 18/4/64
WITHDRAWN 5/64; Cashmores, Great Bridge 10/64

90219 5/50
77302; Eastfield then York 4/43; WD 12/44; Thornton Jct, 4/10/47; Grangemouth 18/6/49; Newton Heath 8/9/51; Bury 7/3/53; Aintree 3/11/60; Rose Grove 22/9/62
WITHDRAWN 5/64; Central Wagon Co, Ince, Wigan 1/65

90220 12/50
77303: Eastfield then York 4/43; WD 12/44; New England 1/3/47; Mexborough 26/4/47; Doncaster 10/51; New England 22/3/52; Doncaster 17/5/52; Mexborough 22/6/54; Barrow Hill 19/6/65; Canklow 1/6/63; Langwith Jct 9/10/65
WITHDRAWN 11/65; Drapers, Hull 3/66

90221 11/50
77305: Eastfield 4/43; WD 1/45; March 26/7/47; Immingham 31/10/53
WITHDRAWN 1/65; Cox and Danks, Wadsley Bridge 4/65

Ais Gill summit, with Wild Boar Fell in the background, in August (a good time of the year to visit here) 1964, with 90204 on a stone train. Sadly the signals have all gone now but the lonely wire running alongside the track must have operated that signal in the distance. It must have been some pull on the lever in the signalbox. 'Top' lamp iron now on smokebox door, middle iron moved to side. Photograph J.G. Walmsley, www.transporttreasury.co.uk

The same WD, then an Aintree engine, at Cheadle Heath about 1960; a good view of the ventilation 'air holes' along the cab roof line. Photograph D. Forsyth, Paul Chancellor Collection.

Bolton's snowplough-fitted 90206 in the North West, coming south past Long Preston (north of Hellifield). The train is most likely the Heysham-Haverton Hill which would have travelled via Bolton Abbey from Skipton. The load was something noxious like ammonia; hence the barrier wagons either end. Photograph A. Robey, www.transporttreasury.co.uk

90206 at its home shed, Bolton; the code is not much help dating the period, for poor old 90206 was withdrawn before Bolton went into the '9' District, in September 1963. Condition is what you might call 'BR original' apart from the second tender emblem; note the welded patch below it. Photograph Paul Chancellor Collection.

An unusual view of a renumbered WD on the SR with 90213 of Hither Green, down on the coast at St Leonards awaiting its return duty; tender generously overflowing as usual. Number on tender rear in WD (and SR!) fashion; the tender still has a toolbox or some such fitting, presumably a leftover from its days abroad. 90213 moved to Goole in August 1951.

A day in the life of a WD. New England's 90215 at Abbots Ripton on a very mixed goods, 15 July 1961. Photograph Paul Chancellor Collection.

Woodford Halse, host to Colwick's 90218 on 23 June 1963. 'Dog leg' ejector pipe and modified washout plugs but fancy covers left in a shed yard somewhere. In this state, a WD could present a curious overall livery of grey, rust-brown and streaky off-white. Photograph Stephen Gradidge.

90222 8/49
77306: Eastfield then York 4/43; WD 12/44; Eastfield 14/2/48; Newton Heath 8/9/51; Patricroft 20/2/60; Agecroft 26/1/63; Aintree 31/10/64
WITHDRAWN 8/65; Cashmores, Newport 6/66

90223 3/51
77307: Eastfield 4/43; WD 1/45; Neville Hill 14/6/47; Colwick 10/48; Lincoln 29/12/51; Immingham 18/4/53; New England 7/2/59; Lincoln 22/9/62; Retford 5/10/63; Frodingham 19/6/65
WITHDRAWN 8/65; Garnham, Harris and Elton, Chesterfield 10/65

90224 11/50
77309: Eastfield 5/43; WD 1/45; March 23/8/47; Immingham 3/10/53; Retford 15/7/61; Doncaster 16/12/61; Langwith Jct 23/3/63
WITHDRAWN 3/64; Wards, Killamarsh 7/64

90225 9/49
77310: Polmadie 5/43; Wellingborough 11/4/44; WD 12/44; Neath 17/5/47; Llanelly 6/9/47; Westbury 27/1/51; Ebbw Jct 16/6/51; Llanelly 18/6/60; Ebbw Jct 10/9/60; Mexborough 29/12/62; Doncaster 5/10/63; Barrow Hill 2/1/65
WITHDRAWN 4/65; Cashmores, Great Bridge 7/65

90226 7/49
77311: Kingmoor 5/43; Wellingborough 11/4/44; WD 2/45; Bricklayers Arms 20/3/46; Newton Heath 19/5/51; Sowerby Bridge 6/10/51; Newton Heath 3/11/51; Bury 3/10/53; Lees 14/11/59; Bury 28/11/59
WITHDRAWN 12/63; Crewe Works 2/64

90227 9/50
77312: Kingmoor 5/43; Wellingborough 11/4/44; WD 1/45; St Margarets 4/10/47; Rose Grove 12/3/49; Birkenhead 17/10/53; Mold Jct 13/2/54; Widnes 8/8/59; Mold Jct 5/9/59; Birkenhead 12/5/62; Warrington Dallam 22/9/62; Bury 23/3/63; Bolton 18/5/63; Langwith Jct 3/10/64; Staveley Central 2/1/65; Barrow Hill 19/6/65
WITHDRAWN 9/65; Cashmores, Great Bridge 2/66

90228 9/49
77313: Kingmoor 5/43; Wellingborough 11/4/44; WD 2/45; Thornton Jct 23/8/47; Kingmoor 16/7/49; Goole 15/7/50
WITHDRAWN 9/63; Darlington Works 9/63

90229 9/51
77314: Kingmoor 6/43; Wellingborough 11/4/44; WD 2/45; Mexborough 26/4/47; Polmadie 23/3/57; Thornton Jct 15/6/62
WITHDRAWN 9/66; McWilliams, Shettleston 12/66

90230 6/49
77315: Kingmoor 6/43; Wellingborough 9/12/44; WD 2/45; Newport 29/3/47; Springhead 5/48; Neville Hill 2/11/57; York 14/6/58; Wakefield 14/11/59; West Hartlepool 27/11/65
WITHDRAWN 5/67; Drapers, Hull 10/67

90231 4/51
77317: Kingmoor 6/43; Wellingborough 11/4/44; WD 2/45; York 4/10/47; Rose Grove 29/1/49
WITHDRAWN 9/63; Horwich Works 10/63

90232 11/51
77319: Wellingborough 6/43; WD 1/45; Mexborough 25/10/47; Frodingham 18/4/53
WITHDRAWN 1/66; Drapers, Hull 4/66

90233 3/49
77320: Wellingborough 6/43; WD 2/45; Neville Hill 23/8/47; Dairycoates 4/51; Springhead 10/51; Dairycoates 13/12/58; Darlington 11/7/59; Mirfield 3/10/59; Normanton 14/11/59; Sowerby Bridge 18/6/60; Wakefield 25/1/64; Mirfield 26/2/66; Wakefield 28/1/67
WITHDRAWN 5/67; Drapers, Hull 12/67

90234 4/50
77321: Wellingborough 6/43; WD 1/45; Bricklayers Arms 20/3/46; Aintree 16/6/51; Wakefield 11/8/51; Aintree 19/5/56; Polmadie 20/4/57; Grangemouth 11/8/62
WITHDRAWN 11/63; McWilliams, Shettleston 5/64

90235 3/49
77323: Wellingborough 7/43; WD 1/45; Colwick 1/3/47; Barnsley 26/4/47; Neville Hill 29/11/47; York 9/49; Dairycoates 10/51; Mold Jct 16/2/52; Colwick 17/5/52; Doncaster 8/10/60
WITHDRAWN 10/65; Drapers, Hull 1/66

90236 10/49
77324: Eastfield 6/43; St Margarets 9/43; Thornton Jct 10/43; WD 1/45; Thornton Jct 23/8/47; Grangemouth 18/6/49; Wakefield 8/9/51; Newton Heath 19/5/56; Sowerby Bridge 14/7/56; York 14/6/58; Wakefield then to Low Moor 14/11/59; Mirfield 23/9/61; Ardsley 14/7/62; Wakefield 27/11/65; Normanton 17/6/67
WITHDRAWN 9/67; Drapers, Hull 2/68

90237 4/49
77325: Eastfield 6/43; St Margarets 9/43; Thornton Jct 10/43; WD 1/45; St Philips Marsh 17/5/47; Laira 9/8/47; Wakefield 8/10/49; Goole 6/10/51; Wakefield 24/11/51; Birkenhead 17/10/53; Mold Jct 13/2/54; Woodford Halse 22/3/58; Toton 23/11/63; Woodford Halse 25/1/64
WITHDRAWN 1/64; Cashmores, Great Bridge 7/64

90238 9/51
77326: Eastfield 6/43; St Margarets 9/43; Thornton Jct 9/43; WD 1/45; Gorton 28/9/46; St Philips Marsh 25/1/47; Canton 6/10/51; Westhouses 8/8/59; Gorton 30/6/62
WITHDRAWN 3/63; Crewe Works 6/63

90239 5/51
77327: Eastfield 6/43; St Margarets 9/43; Dunfermline 10/43; WD 1/45; Heaton 26/4/47; Annesley 23/8/47; New England 5/11/49; Frodingham 22/9/62
WITHDRAWN 11/63; Doncaster Works 1/64

90240 5/51
77328: Eastfield 6/43; Dunfermline 10/43; WD 1/45; Retford 14/6/47; Stockton on Tees 29/11/47; Newport 2/11/57; Thornaby 14/6/58; Ardsley 30/6/62; Dairycoates 27/11/65
WITHDRAWN 1/67; Drapers, Hull 6/67

90241 11/50
77329: Eastfield 6/43; St Margarets then Dunfermline 9/43; Tay Bridge 12/43; WD 1/45; York 25/10/47; Rose Grove 29/1/49; Colwick 19/6/65; Frodingham 4/12/65
WITHDRAWN 1/66; Drapers, Hull 5/66

90242 5/49
77330: Eastfield 6/43; Tay Bridge 9/43; WD 1/45; Accrington 14/5/49; Wakefield 16/7/49; Colwick 2/12/50; Mold Jct 17/5/52; Widnes 8/8/59; Gorton 23/3/63; Springs Branch 1/6/63; Fleetwod 30/11/63; Aintree 28/12/63; Immingham 3/10/64
WITHDRAWN 9/65; Drapers, Hull 1/66

A marvellous study of Mirfield's 90233 in the country near Todmorden on 4 June 1966; note repositioned smokebox door and middle buffer beam lamp irons. This was its second spell at Mirfield though it was only there for a short while (a shame, given the care painting the name on the buffer beam) from February 1966 to January 1967 when it moved on to Wakefield, where so many WDs ended up. It was one of Mr Draper's infamous '205'. Photograph Brian Stephenson.

90243 9/49
77332: Eastfield 7/43; Tay Bridge 9/43; WD 1/45; Wakefield 8/10/49; Huddersfield 16/6/56; Royston 11/7/59; Normanton 3/10/64
WITHDRAWN 6/67; Arnott Young, Parkgate and Rawmarsh 11/67

90244 7/51
77334: Eastfield 7/43; St Margarets 12/43; WD 1/45; Woodford Halse 26/4/47; Annesley 23/8/47; Woodford Halse 29/11/47; Colwick 12/48; New England 11/49; Colwick 11/2/56; Plaistow 19/4/58; March 11/7/59; Plaistow 3/10/59; Tilbury 14/11/59
WITHDRAWN 7/62; Stratford Works 11/62

90245 1/50
77335: Eastfield 7/43; St Margarets 12/43; WD 1/45; Farnley Jct 28/1/50; Newton Heath 19/5/51; Aintree 19/12/59
WITHDRAWN 5/64; Central Wagon Co, Ince, Wigan 8/65

90246 2/51
77338: Eastfield then Stratford 7/43; March 9/43; WD 2/45; York 29/3/47; Springhead 26/4/47; Colwick 10/48; Mexborough 2/50; New England 10/51; Retford 2/11/63
WITHDRAWN 4/65; Arnott Young, Dinsdale 7/65

90247 12/49
77340: Eastfield 8/43; Dairycoates 9/43; WD 1/45; Brighton 12/47; Aintree 14/7/51; Wakefield 11/8/51; Normanton 5/10/57
WITHDRAWN 10/62; Gorton Works 3/63

90248 12/49
77342: Eastfield then Stratford 8/43; March 9/43; WD 2/45; Newport 29/3/47; St Margarets 12/48; Newton Heath 8/9/51; Patricroft 22/9/62; Newton Heath 26/1/63; Bolton 21/3/64; Aintree 3/10/64; Frodingham 24/6/65
WITHDRAWN 11/65; W George, Station Steel, Wath 3/66

90249 6/49
77348: Eastfield 8/43; March 9/43; WD 2/45; Wakefield 11/6/49; Huddersfield 16/6/56; Normanton 14/11/59
WITHDRAWN 12/63; Darlington Works 2/64

90250 2/49
77350: Eastfield 8/43; March 9/43; WD 1/45; Mexborough 25/10/47
WITHDRAWN 3/63; Doncaster Works 5/63

90251 7/49
77351: Eastfield 8/43; Tyne Dock 9/43; New England 9/44; WD 12/44; March 14/5/47; New England 10/48; Grantham 2/49; Colwick 2/50; Oxley 3/11/51; St Philips Marsh 19/4/52; Oxford 16/6/56; Westhouses 8/8/59; Woodford Halse 3/10/59; Westhouses 19/12/59; Gorton 30/6/62
WITHDRAWN 5/63; Crewe Works 10/63

90252 2/49
77352: Eastfield 9/43; Tyne Dock 9/43; WD 2/45; Mexborough 25/10/57; Doncaster 5/10/63
WITHDRAWN 9/65; Drapers, Hull 12/65;

90253 3/50
77353: Eastfield then Thornton Jct 9/43; Springhead 29/3/47; March 7/50; New England 8/50
WITHDRAWN 12/62; Doncaster Works 5/63

90254 10/50
77355: Eastfield then Thornton Jct 9/43; WD 1/45; Bricklayers Arms 20/3/46; Agecroft 16/6/51; Farnley Jct 21/4/56; Normanton 14/11/59; Royston 11/8/62; Farnley Jct 13/7/63; Royston 28/12/63; Normanton 8/8/64; Wakefield 9/10/65; York 4/12/65; West Hartlepool 10/9/66
WITHDRAWN 1/67; Drapers, Hull 9/67

90255 3/49
77356: Eastfield 9/43; St Margarets 12/43; WD 1/45; Mexborough 26/4/47; March 6/10/56; Doncaster 23/3/57
WITHDRAWN 12/65; W. George, Station Steel, Wath 3/66

90256 5/49
77358: Eastfield 9/43; Tyne Dock 9/43; Heaton 9/44; WD 12/44; Gorton 29/3/47; New England 26/4/47; Grantham 2/49; New England 6/49; Plaistow 21/5/55; Tilbury 14/11/59
WITHDRAWN 8/62; Stratford Works 11/62

90257 7/50
77359: Eastfield 9/43; Tyne Dock 9/43; Heaton 9/44; WD 12/44; Feltham 30/11/46; Mirfield 24/3/51; Birkenhead 17/10/53; Mold Jct 13/2/54; Widnes 8/8/59; Birkenhead 14/11/59; Springs Branch 27/2/60
WITHDRAWN 8/64; Central Wagon Co, Ince, Wigan 1/65

90258 12/50
77362: Eastfield 9/43; Dunfermline 10/43; WD 12/44; St Margarets 29/3/47; Rose Grove 29/1/49; Lostock Hall 26/1/52; Langwith Jct 3/10/64; Barrow Hill 2/1/65; Staveley Central 19/6/65; Barrow Hill 31/7/65; Langwith Jct 9/10/65
WITHDRAWN 1/66; Cashmores, Newport 6/66

90259 3/49
77364: Eastfield 9/43; Dunfermline 10/43; WD 2/45; March 26/4/47; New England 12/48; Langwith Jct 31/12/54; Colwick 21/5/60
WITHDRAWN 10/65; Drapers, Hull 1/66

90260 2/51
77365: Eastfield 9/43; Dunfermline 11/43; WD 2/45; Aberdeen Ferryhill 12/6/48; Wakefield 8/9/51; Goole 10/9/55
WITHDRAWN 9/63; Darlington Works 9/63

90261 10/51
77368: Eastfield then Tay Bridge 10/43; WD 2/45; Reading 1/11/47; Ebbw Jct 17/6/50; Shrewsbury 31/10/53; Leamington 14/7/56; Banbury 5/9/59; Stourbridge 24/2/62; Springs Branch 14/7/62; Agecroft 1/6/63; Rose Grove 31/10/64; Lower Darwen 28/11/64
WITHDRAWN 7/65; Cashmores, Great Bridge 12/65

90262 12/49
77371: Eastfield 10/43; Heaton 9/44; WD 12/44; Thornton Jct 26/4/47; Goole 15/7/50; Dairycoates 30/11/63
WITHDRAWN 6/67; Drapers, Hull 1/68

90263 8/51
77372: Eastfield then Parkhead 10/43; March 2/12/44; WD 2/45; Annesley 1/3/47; Neville Hill 29/11/47; Colwick 10/48; Annesley 11/48; Colwick 2/49; Woodford Halse 7/49; Staveley 29/11/52; Woodford Halse 8/1/53; Colwick 18/4/53; Immingham 13/12/58; Colwick 8/8/59
WITHDRAWN 1/64; Doncaster Works 5/64

90264 9/50
77374: Eastfield then Parkhead 10/43; WD 2/45; Eastfield 17/4/48; Dawsholm 10/48; Rose Grove 12/3/49; Lostock Hall 25/1/64
WITHDRAWN 8/64; Cashmores, Great Bridge 2/65

Just another WD 2-8-0 going about its everyday business, 90246 in Hadley Woods on 4 July 1953 and in good nick by the look of it, with a decent tenderful of coal and fire irons neatly stacked away. The photograph is from the first overbridge, south of the tunnels, a lovely spot in the midst of the woods; the brake van can just be seen leaving the double line section opposite Greenwood box, as the train takes the slow line towards New Barnet. The train is one of many Class H coal trains that ran each day from New England to Ferme Park, worked almost exclusively by New England WDs. The crews came from Hornsey and Hitchin as well as New England and the trains were remanned en route depending on how well the services were running. Much of the coal came from the East Midlands, tripped to Peterborough from Colwick; then the trains were remarshalled and sent south either on the GN or on the Joint line via March. This is an archetypal picture of the service of the time, as it was in the mid-1950s before the 9Fs began to take such a part in the workings. The condition of 90246 is above the average for the period, suggesting it is ex-works; from Doncaster to judge from the size of the numbers. It is interesting to note how prevalent wooden bodied wagons still were in coal trains, this far into the 1950s. See too, *Eastern Region Memories*. Photograph B.K.B. Green, Initial Photographics.

By now 90246 has fallen on hard times. Wherever they were, they were neglected of course, apart from one or two corners of Scotland perhaps. Needless to say, 90246 is one New England's finest; here she is in the yard there on 10 April 1960 with one of the new NBL Type 2s dumped in the background. It's odd to think that NBL built both these locos... Photograph R.J. Buckley, Initial Photographics.

A rather splendid WD, 90260 at Goole shed in the summer of 1959; 'RA6' in lower corner of cab, ER washout plug arrangement and so on. Smokebox sides free of all bolt/rivet heads. Photograph J. Davenport, Initial Photographics.

90265 7/50
77375: Eastfield then St Margarets 10/43; WD 2/45; Eastfield 23/8/47; Wakefield 8/9/51; Huddersfield 16/6/56; Springhead 22/2/58; Goole 17/5/58; Dairycoates 30/11/63
WITHDRAWN 6/67; Drapers, Hull 12/67

90266 3/49
77378: Eastfield 10/43; Heaton 9/44; WD 12/44; Old Oak 19/4/47; Reading 14/5/47; Laira 30/10/48; Reading 27/11/48; Lower Darwen 14/5/49; Accrington 19/11/55; Lostock Hall 20/4/57; Rose Grove 11/8/62; Gorton 16/5/64; Langwith Jct 3/10/64; Staveley Central 2/1/65; Barrow Hill 19/6/65
WITHDRAWN 7/65; Arnott Young, Parkgate and Rawmarsh 9/65

90267 4/50
77379: Eastfield 10/43; Heaton 9/44; WD 12/44; Feltham 12/7/47; Hither Green 17/6/50; Accrington 24/11/51; Farnley Jct 31/12/51; Aintree 16/2/52; Rose Grove 4/10/52; Bolton 18/4/53; Aintree 3/10/64
WITHDRAWN 3/65; Wards, Beighton, Sheffield 6/65

90268 12/51
77380: Eastfield 10/43; Heaton 9/44; WD 12/44; Canton 17/5/47; Pontypool Road 10/7/48; Pill 30/12/50; Southall 24/3/51; Banbury 11/7/59; Stourbridge 24/2/62; Springs Branch 14/7/62; Agecroft 1/6/63; Gorton 31/10/64; Lower Darwen 28/11/64
WITHDRAWN 4/65; Hayes, Bridgend 8/65

90269 1/51
77381: Eastfield 10/43; Springhead 4/44; WD 1/45; Annesley 23/8/47; Staveley Central 29/11/47; Colwick 22/6/54; New England 7/2/59
WITHDRAWN 5/63; Doncaster Works 7/63

90270 8/49
77386: Eastfield 11/43; Ebbw Jct 23/11/44; WD 12/44; Mexborough 27/12/47; Doncaster 5/51; Mexborough 21/5/55; New England 18/11/61
WITHDRAWN 12/62; Doncaster Works 7/63

90271 1/53
77388: Eastfield 11/43; Canal 12/43; WD 1/45; Newton Abbot 19/4/47; Exeter 12/7/47; Canton 1/11/47; Bolton 13/1/51; Lees 28/12/57; Newton Heath 12/7/58; Aintree 11/7/64; Rose Grove 8/8/64; Langwith Jct 3/10/64
WITHDRAWN 7/65; Wards, Beighton, Sheffield 11/65

90272 3/49
77390: Eastfield 11/43; Haymarket 12/43; WD 2/45; Annesley 1/3/47; Tyne Dock 29/11/47; Dairycoates 2/49; York 10/49; Dairycoates 11/49; Tyne Dock 2/50; Dairycoates 3/51; Langwith Jct 13/8/55; Dairycoates 6/10/56; Goole 20/5/67
WITHDRAWN 6/67; Drapers, Hull 12/67

90273 1/51
77392: Eastfield 11/43; Haymarket 12/43; WD 1/45; Heaton 1/3/47; Newport 26/4/47; Thornaby 14/6/58; Goole 7/9/63
WITHDRAWN 10/65; Drapers, Hull 2/66

90274 9/50
77393: Eastfield 11/43; Haymarket 12/43; WD 2/45; Reading 27/12/47; Rose Grove 12/3/49; Gorton 16/5/64; Aintree 14/11/64; Frodingham 24/6/65
WITHDRAWN 1/66; Drapers, Hull 4/66

90275 8/49
77394: Eastfield 11/43; Canal 12/43; WD 2/45; Mexborough 25/10/47; Immingham 11/49; March 7/50; Immingham 31/10/53; Langwith 22/6/54
WITHDRAWN 7/65; Cashmores, Great Bridge 11/65

90276 12/50
77395: Eastfield 11/43; Canal 12/43; WD 1/45; Annesley 23/8/47; Staveley Central 29/11/47; Colwick 22/6/54; Staveley Central 28/1/56; Langwith Jct then back to Staveley Central 27/2/60; Canklow 26/3/60
WITHDRAWN 2/65; Steelbreaking and Dismantling Co, Chesterfield 8/65

90277 7/50
77398: Eastfield 11/43; Tyne Dock 11/44; Heaton 9/44; WD 12/44; Sowerby Bridge 12/8/50; Wakefield 4/11/50; Huddersfield 16/6/56; Wigan (L&Y) 8/9/56; Lostock Hall 6/10/56; Doncaster 3/10/64
WITHDRAWN 10/65; Drapers, Hull 3/66

90278 5/50
77399: Eastfield 11/43; Newport 1/44; Bath Road 23/11/44; WD 12/44; Aberdeen Ferryhill 12/6/48; CME Rugby 11/48; Dunfermline 19/11/49; Accrington 8/9/51; Farnley Jct 31/12/51; Aintree 16/2/52
WITHDRAWN 12/62; Horwich Works 5/63

90279 2/49
77401: Eastfield 12/43; Newport 29/1/44; Neath 23/11/44; WD 12/44; March 14/6/47 ; New England 10/48; March 2/11/57; Doncaster 7/10/61
WITHDRAWN 6/65; Arnott Young, Parkgate and Rawmarsh 10/65

90280 5/49
77402: Eastfield 12/43; Colwick 29/12/43; WD 11/44; Gorton 29/3/47; Annesley 26/4/47; Mexborough 29/11/47; March 5/51; Immingham 3/10/53; Retford 5/10/63; Frodingham 19/6/65
WITHDRAWN 9/65; Drapers, Hull 12/65

90281 3/49
77404: Eastfield 12/43; Newport 29/1/44; Worcester 23/11/44; WD 12/44; Thornton Jct 29/3/47; Goole 15/7/50; Mirfield 11/7/59; Sowerby Bridge 18/6/60; Wakefield 25/1/64
WITHDRAWN 6/67; Cox and Danks, Wadsley Bridge 11/67

90282 4/49
77406: Eastfield 12/43; Colwick 29/12/43; WD 1/45; Thornton Jct 26/7/47; Aintree 8/9/51; Colwick 3/10/64
WITHDRAWN 1/65; Cashmores, Great Bridge 3/65

90283 12/50
77407: Eastfield 12/43; Colwick 29/12/43; WD 11/44; Neath 17/5/47; Llanelly 6/9/47; Rose Grove 12/3/49; Newton Heath 28/11/53; Aintree 14/7/56; Springs Branch 8/8/64; Frodingham 3/10/64
WITHDRAWN 10/65; Drapers, Hull 1/66

90284 1/52
77408: Eastfield 12/43; Colwick 29/1/44; WD 12/44; Oxley 17/5/47; Banbury 12/7/47; Worcester 3/12/49; Southall 11/8/51; Oxley 19/4/52; St Philips Marsh 3/10/53; Southall 31/12/54; St Philips Marsh 26/2/55; Oxford 16/6/56; Westhouses 8/8/59; Gorton 30/6/62; Aintree 14/11/64
WITHDRAWN 3/65; Wards, Beighton, Sheffield 5/65

90285 11/49
77411: Eastfield 12/43; Colwick 29/1/44; WD 12/44; New England 25/1/47; Mexborough 26/4/47; Immingham 29/12/51; Retford 5/10/63
WITHDRAWN 6/65; Cox and Danks, Wadsley Bridge 9/65

90286 2/51
77413: Eastfield 12/43; Newport 25/3/44; Neath 23/11/44; WD 12/44; Annesley 29/3/47; Mexborough 29/11/47; Doncaster 24/12/60
WITHDRAWN 7/62; Gorton Works 9/62

There were probably no locos like the WDs when it came to the wide variety of works that repaired them. This is the late lamented A shop at Swindon with 90261 at the end of its overhaul, vacuum pipe and screw coupling to be added, covered top feed and GW lamp irons evident. Shed code indicates it belongs to Shrewsbury where it stayed for another four years. Photograph A.R. Carpenter, www.transporttreasury.co.uk

The turntable at Gowhole, a curious sight to come across in the middle of the countryside. It was remote – note the enthusiasts' cars in the lane beyond – and was there because this was a longstanding boundary/changeover point between the old Central Division and the Midland lines. Compare with 92016 at the same location in *The Book of the 9F 2-10-0s*. 90267 of Bolton is on the turntable on 14 June 1961; the ladder was to enable a man to get down into the pit and back out again. Photograph Dr A.H. Roscoe, www.transporttreasury.co.uk

A Westernised WD, 90268 at Langley, on the WR main line on 6 September 1952. Swindon alterations included the 'tunnel' on the running plate for the fire irons and the covered top feed, though inevitably the fire irons are in the original place on the tender 'inset'. And this is on the WR where the complaints originated! The 'tunnels', in fact, seem to have been barely used at all. The cure was worse than the disease, apparently. 90268 was a Southall loco at the time, ending its days at Lower Darwen in Lancashire. It undertook another lengthy journey for disposal, going to Hayes at Bridgend, not far from one of its old homes, Cardiff Canton. Photograph Stephen Gradidge.

Impossible to resist this one of 90271 at Oldham (Lees) shed. Jim Davenport labelled it 'clearing snow' but didn't give a date. For once, a WD with the window up, and can you blame them? Photograph J. Davenport, Initial Photographics.

A curiosity, though the location eludes me. 90273 is being stripped, I'd guess, before entry to the shops and it's relatively late on, to judge from the AWS fittings. The oddity is that the smokebox (minus chimney) is chalked 90434... It can't have *come* from that engine, outside in the yard, so is it *destined* for 90434? It can't be that 90273 is being cannibalised, surely? It wasn't withdrawn until late 1965 with 90434 following 18 months later and with so many WDs in the Region 'going west' I can't see that the authorities would have bothered. This scene must be quite a bit earlier, to judge from that elderly 0-6-0 behind; maybe 90434 was in an advanced state in the works and needed a decent smokebox, quick. Both are NER engines of course so the works *should* be Darlington; but it certainly doesn't *look* like it... Photograph Paul Chancellor Collection.

A Canklow WD at Crewe North; as it's certainly not in standard Canklow condition, it is fresh out of the nearby works and working off Crewe South for a while before returning to Yorkshire. Diagonal works plate on expansion link bracket. Photograph D. Forsyth, Paul Chancellor Collection.

90278 in what we might term 'BR original' condition, more or less, at Cheadle Heath around 1960. No washout plug modification, electrification flashes, 'flush' filler cap to rearwards gravity sanding and so on. The window (not an 'original' feature as such) is up for once. Photograph D. Forsyth, Paul Chancellor Collection.

90287 3/51
77414: Eastfield 12/43; Newport 29/1/44; Ebbw Jct 23/11/44; WD 12/44; March 26/4/47; New England 10/48; Colwick 3/11/51; Langwith Jct 22/6/54; Colwick 21/5/60
WITHDRAWN 12/62; Arnott Young, Bilston 4/63

90288 2/51
77415: Eastfield 12/43; Tyne Dock 29/1/44; Ebbw Jct 23/11/44; WD 2/45; March 27/12/47; New England 10/48; Colwick 8/8/53; Immingham 26/2/60; Colwick 16/7/60; Frodingham 8/10/60
WITHDRAWN 9/62; Crewe Works 12/62

90289 5/49
77416: Eastfield 12/43; Tyne Dock 29/1/44; Shrewsbury 23/11/44; WD 2/45; St Margarets 25/10/47; Kingmoor 18/9/48; St Margarets 11/48; Rose Grove 29/1/49; Newton Heath 8/9/51; Lancaster 12/7/58; Wakefield 4/10/58; Aintree 11/7/64; Rose Grove 8/8/64
WITHDRAWN 11/64; Smiths, Ecclesfield 5/65

90290 3/51
77418: Eastfield 29/1/44; Worcester 23/11/44; WD 12/44; Gorton 1/3/47; Annesley then Barnsley 26/4/47; Annesley 14/5/47; Mexborough 29/11/47; March 10/51; Doncaster 26/1/52; New England 22/3/52; Doncaster 17/5/52; Mexborough 22/6/54; Langwith Jct 21/5/60; Canklow 16/7/60
WITHDRAWN 5/65; Drapers, Hull 7/65

90291 5/49
77419: Eastfield 29/1/44; Stourbridge 23/11/44; WD 12/44; St Margarets 26/4/47; Kingmoor 18/9/48; St Margarets 11/48; Dunfermline 19/8/49; St Margarets 24/12/49; Newton Heath 8/9/51; Rose Grove 11/7/64
WITHDRAWN 2/65; Cashmores, Great Bridge 5/65

90292 4/49
77421: Eastfield 29/1/44; Shrewsbury 24/10/44; WD 2/45; St Philips Marsh 17/5/47; Laira 9/8/47; Wakefield 8/10/49; Agecroft 16/6/56; Sutton Oak 1/6/63; Langwith Jct 3/10/64
WITHDRAWN 10/65; Drapers, Hull 1/66

90293 9/51
77424: Eastfield 29/1/44; Stewarts Lane 26/2/44; Bricklayers Arms 25/3/44; WD 12/44; Thornton Jct 1/3/47; Kingmoor 16/7/49; Dunfermline 19/8/49; March 22/3/52; Immingham 31/10/53; Doncaster 7/10/61
WITHDRAWN 9/65; Wards, Beighton, Sheffield 10/65

90294 12/49
77425: Eastfield 29/1/44; Stewarts Lane 26/2/44; Bricklayers Arms 25/3/44; WD 12/44; March 23/8/47; Immingham 31/10/53
WITHDRAWN 7/65; Drapers, Hull 10/65

90295 2/52
77426: Eastfield 29/1/44; Stewarts Lane 26/2/44; Bricklayers Arms 25/3/44; WD 12/44; St Margarets 29/3/47; Lostock Hall 23/4/49; Rose Grove 10/2/62; Barrow Hill 19/6/65; Colwick 9/10/65
WITHDRAWN 1/66; Drapers, Hull 5/66

90296 8/49
77428: Eastfield 29/1/44; Stewarts Lane 26/2/44; Bricklayers Arms 25/3/44; Mexborough 25/10/47; March 5/51; Colwick 3/10/53; Doncaster 8/10/60
WITHDRAWN 8/65; Wards, Beighton, Sheffield 11/65

90297 3/49
77429: Eastfield 29/1/44; Bricklayers Arms 25/3/44; WD 12/44; Neath 17/5/47; Llanelly 14/6/47; Bolton 16/12/50; Aintree 27/2/60; Lower Darwen 17/6/61; Rose Grove 20/4/63; Lostock Hall 25/1/64
WITHDRAWN 8/64; Cashmores, Great Bridge 2/65

90298 6/49
77431: Eastfield 26/2/44; New Cross 25/3/44; WD 12/44; Eastfield 23/8/47; March 22/3/52; Immingham 31/10/53; March 6/10/56; Stratford 23/2/57; March 15/11/58; Stratford 17/1/59; Tilbury 16/1/60
WITHDRAWN 7/62; Stratford Works 9/62

90299 8/49
77432: Eastfield 26/2/44; New Cross 25/3/44; WD 12/44; March 27/12/47; New England 10/48; Staveley 2/49; Woodford Halse 31/12/54; Toton 21/3/64; Woodford Halse 18/4/64
WITHDRAWN 5/64; Cashmores, Great Bridge 10/64

Mexborough's 90290 is a visitor at Doncaster shed about 1951, the year it was renumbered into the BR series. Photograph J. Davenport, Initial Photographics.

Compare and contrast. Two apparently identical WDs, 90291 (top) at Wakefield on 14 September 1956 and 90294 (below) at March shed, 26 August 1958. The main technical difference of course, lies in the adjustments consequent on the modification of the washout plugs. Neither of them have the cinder guard to the cab widow. But look how the pipe to the blower is foreshortened on 90294, with a nut rather than a wheel valve, while 90291 has the lubricator oil pipes *this* side, not the right-hand side. Thre's a lot more like this... The more you look... Photographs Peter Groom.

What nice clean lines you have. 90299, almost pretty, at Woodford Halse shed in May 1953. Cinder guard to window, unlike the previous two. Photograph J. Davenport, Initial Photographics.

90300 5/49
77433: Eastfield 26/2/44; New Cross 25/3/44; WD 12/44; Thornton Jct 29/3/47; Goole 9/9/50; Mirfield 11/7/59; Wakefield 25/1/64
WITHDRAWN 6/67; Cox and Danks, Wadsley Bridge 10/67

90301 5/49 77434: Eastfield 26/2/44; New Cross 25/3/44; WD 12/44; New England 19/4/47; Annesley 23/8/47; Mexborough 29/11/47; Doncaster 5/51; Mexborough 14/6/58; Langwith Jct 21/5/60; Staveley Central 2/1/65; Langwith Jct 19/6/65
WITHDRAWN 9/65; Drapers, Hull 1/66

90302 12/50
77436: Eastfield 26/2/44; Eastleigh 25/3/44; WD 11/44; March 25/10/47; Immingham 31/10/53; Langwith Jct 13/8/55
WITHDRAWN 8/64; Wards, Killamarsh 11/64

90303 7/49
77439: Eastfield 26/2/44; Eastleigh 25/2/44; WD 11/44; Immingham 1/3/47; Neville Hill 29/11/47; Colwick 8/49
WITHDRAWN 12/62; Arnott Young, Bilston 4/63

90304 9/49
77440: Eastfield 26/2/44; Eastleigh 25/3/44; WD 12/44; March 23/8/47; Colchester 5/48; March 10/51; Mexborough 14/2/53; New England 18/11/61; Colwick 30/6/62
WITHDRAWN 9/64; Wards, Killamarsh 1/65

90305 2/51
77441: Eastfield 26/2/44; Eastleigh 25/3/44; WD 12/44; Springhead 1/3/47; Newport 26/4/47; New England 8/49; Doncaster 26/1/52; March 6/10/56; Doncaster 7/10/61
WITHDRAWN 3/66; W George, Station Steel, Wath 8/66

90306 8/49
77442: Eastfield 26/2/44; Eastleigh 25/3/44; WD 12/44; Dunfermline 23/8/47; St Margarets 18/11/50; Accrington 8/9/51; Farnley Jct 31/12/51; Agecroft 16/2/52; Lees 28/12/57; Agecroft 7/10/61; Aintree 31/10/64; Rose Grove 22/5/65; Barrow Hill 19/6/65
WITHDRAWN 6/65; Wards, Beighton, Sheffield 11/65

90307 4/49
77443: Eastfield 26/2/44; Eastleigh 25/3/44; WD 12/44; Pontypool Road 12/7/47; Swansea Victoria 3/6/50; Agecroft 16/12/50
WITHDRAWN 12/62; Crewe Works 6/63

90308 1/51
77444: Eastfield 26/2/44; Eastleigh 25/3/44; WD 12/44; Feltham 23/8/47; Farnley Jct 31/12/54; Huddersfield 15/7/50; Sowerby Bridge 16/2/52; Bury 8/8/53; Huddersfield 21/1/61
WITHDRAWN 10/62; Crewe Works 5/63

90309 11/51
77445: Eastfield 26/2/44; Eastleigh 25/3/44; WD 12/44; Immingham 29/3/47; Tyne Dock 29/11/47; Dairycoates 2/49; York 10/49; Dairycoates 11/49; Tyne Dock 2/50; Normanton 7/9/57; Darlington 15/7/61; Polmadie 23/3/63; Darlington 15/6/63; West Hartlepool 26/3/66
WITHDRAWN 7/67; Drapers, Hull 10/67

90310 5/49
77447: WD 2/44; Wakefield 14/5/49; Sowerby Bridge 16/6/56; Low Moor 29/12/62; Mirfield 3/10/64
WITHDRAWN 12/66; Drapers, Hull 3/67

90311 10/49
77449: WD 3/44;Neville Hill 4/10/47; Mexborough 25/10/47; Canklow 29/1/62
WITHDRAWN 8/64; Wards, Killamarsh 11/64

A Mexborough WD at York, 90304 amid the Pacifics and V2s on 23 May 1955. Again that foreshortened pipe to the blower; diagonal works plate. Photograph J. Robertson, www.transporttreasury.co.uk

A perfectly beautiful portrait of a WD early on in BR days. It's a Scottish one (before the clack replacement programme was even thought of) at Eastfield and its condition points to a spell in Cowlairs a few days before; fine square jawed laddie stares forth from that distinctive 'picture' side opening – we can hardly call it a 'window'. Numbering larger than you'd expect, painted smokebox number, no shed plate but '7F' and R.A.6 painted on the cabside, before BR hastily uprated everything. Photograph J. Patterson, www.transporttreasury.co.uk

Within a year or two 90306 was in the North of England where it worked out its days until 1965. Here it is, again not too long out of works, at its then home shed Lees, in June 1958. Optimism did not flow in rivers at Oldham, hence the snow plough still on 90388 alongside. Photograph J. Davenport, Initial Photographics.

90307 in somewhat dramatic pose at Crewe, 13 January 1958. Westernised long before, it nonetheless spent almost its entire BR life working from Manchester. Photograph R. Smith, www.transporttreasury.co.uk

90312 1/52
70801: WD 3/44; St Philips Marsh 30/11/46; Swindon 25/3/50; Banbury 21/4/51; Oxford 1/11/52; Ebbw Jct 8/9/56; Canton 6/10/56; Southall 26/3/60; Didcot 25/3/61; Ebbw Jct 20/5/61; Llanelly 7/10/61; Gorton 16/6/62
WITHDRAWN 12/63; Crewe Works 3/64

90313 8/49
70802: WD 3/44; Eastfield 23/8/47; Dawsholm 14/7/51; Banbury 1/12/51; Southall 24/4/54; Banbury 19/4/58; Mexborough 29/12/62; Canklow 5/10/63
WITHDRAWN 4/64; Smiths, Ecclesfield 7/64

90314 5/51
70807: WD 3/44; York 4/10/47; Rose Grove 29/1/49
WITHDRAWN 4/65; Cashmores, Great Bridge 8/65

90315 10/52
70808: WD 3/44; Croes Newydd 17/5/47; Llanelly 15/7/50; Pontypool Road 9/10/54; Gloucester Barnwood 23/4/60; Banbury 18/6/60; Warrington Dallam 8/9/62; Lancaster (Green Ayre) 26/1/63; Agecroft 7/9/63; Bolton 5/10/63; Agecroft 8/8/64; Frodingham 3/10/64
WITHDRAWN 11/65; Garnham, Harris and Elton, Chesterfield 5/66

90316 1/50
70809: WD 3/44; Farnley Jct 14/1/50; Sowerby Bridge 4/10/52; Bolton 18/4/53; Belle Vue 8/10/55; Lancaster (Green Ayre) 14/6/58; Aintree 17/1/59; Lower Darwen 17/6/61; Lancaster (Green Ayre) 26/1/63; Aintree 25/1/64; Bolton 22/2/64; Springs Branch 21/3/64; Colwick 3/10/64
WITHDRAWN 12/65; Drapers, Hull 4/66

90317 7/50
70811: WD 3/44; Ashford 14/6/47; Redhill 31/7/48; Mold Jct 3/11/51; Widnes 5/9/59; Birkenhead 14/11/59; Springs Branch 27/2/60
WITHDRAWN 3/65; Wards, Beighton, Sheffield 5/65

90318 12/49
70814: WD 3/44; Farnley Jct 31/12/49; Normanton 14/11/59; Royston 11/9/65; Normanton 28/1/67
WITHDRAWN 9/67; Drapers, Hull 2/68

90319 5/51
70817: Thornton Jct 1/3/47; Ayr 3/51; Ardrossan 25/2/61; Ayr 8/9/62; Thornton Junct. 30/11/63
WITHDRAWN 6/64; Motherwell Machinery and Scrap Co, Wishaw 1/65

90320 4/49
70825: WD 4/44; Lostock Hall 23/4/49; Polmadie 23/3/57; Dawsholm 13/7/57; Polmadie 19/4/58
WITHDRAWN 7/62; Cowlairs Works 9/62

90321 6/50
70829: Mirfield 12/8/50; Wakefield 14/6/58; Sunderland 3/12/66
WITHDRAWN 7/67; Drapers, Hull 12/67

90322 5/50
70833: WD 5/44; Farnley Jct 25/2/50; Huddersfield 31/12/51; Farnley Jct 23/2/52; Mirfield 11/7/59; Low Moor 20/2/60; Mirfield 23/9/61; Wakefield 25/1/64
WITHDRAWN 8/64; Smiths, Ecclesfield 12/64

90323 2/49
70834: WD 5/44; Retford 26/7/47; Dairycoates 29/11/47; Colwick 10/48; Ebbw Jct 1/12/51; Aberdare 1/11/52; Shrewsbury 21/3/53; Severn Tunnel Jct 13/6/53; Canton 8/10/55; Banbury 5/11/60; Ebbw Jct 3/12/60; Gorton 16/6/62
WITHDRAWN 5/64; Slag Reduction, Rotherham 10/64

90324 5/49
70836: WD 5/44; St Philips Marsh 30/11/46; Swindon 25/2/50; Swansea Victoria 2/12/50; Bolton 16/12/50; Agecroft 24/1/51
WITHDRAWN 5/64; Slag Reduction Co, Ickles, Rotherham 1/65

90325 1/50
70838: WD 5/44; Farnley Jct 14/1/50; Huddersfield 14/2/53
WITHDRAWN 9/65; Garnham, Harris and Elton, Chesterfield 11/65

90326 4/52
70839: WD 5/44; Neville Hill 30/8/47; York 5/48; Rose Grove 29/1/49; Farnley Jct 3/6/50; Mirfield 24/3/51; Wakefield 14/6/58
WITHDRAWN 11/63; Horwich Works 12/63

90327 3/52
70843: WD 6/44; Didcot 22/3/47; Shrewsbury 12/8/50; Newton Heath 16/12/50; Lancaster (Green Ayre) 12/7/58; Aintree 17/1/59; Rose Grove 29/9/62; Bolton 25/1/64; Aintree 5/9/64
WITHDRAWN 1/65; Maden and Mckee, Stanley, Liverpool 5/65

90328 3/49
70845: WD 6/44; Lostock Hall 23/4/49; Newton Heath 7/2/59; Patricroft 22/9/62; Newton Heath 26/1/63
WITHDRAWN 5/64; Slag Reduction Co, Ickles, Rotherham 9/64

90329 9/49
70849: WD 6/44; Wakefield 8/49; Sowerby Bridge 16/6/56; Wakefield 5/10/63
WITHDRAWN 10/65; Steelbreaking and Dismantling Co, Chesterfield 12/65

90330 6/49
70850: WD 6/44; Mexborough 25/20/47; Grangemouth 5/49; Colwick 6/50; Staverton Central 10/50; Colwick 6/51; Mexborough 7/3/53; Canklow 5/10/63; Doncaster 19/6/65
WITHDRAWN 12/65; W. George, Wath 3/66

90331 4/49
70851: WD 6/44; Lostock Hall 23/4/49; Lees 23/9/61; Patricroft 22/9/62; Newton Heath 23/2/63
WITHDRAWN 11/63; Crewe Works 2/64

90332 12/49
70853: WD 6/44; Hither Green 14/6/47; Huddersfield 3/6/50; Normanton 28/1/67
WITHDRAWN 1/67; Wards, Killamarsh 3/67

90333 4/49
70857: WD 7/44; Lostock Hall then Accrington 14/5/49; Wakefield 13/8/49; Low Moor 5/11/58; Mirfield 23/9/61; Wakefield 21/3/64
WITHDRAWN 10/65; Drapers, Hull 2/66

90334 8/49
70859: WD 7/44; Wakefield 13/8/49; Normanton 15/6/57; Farnley Jct 17/1/59
WITHDRAWN 11/63; Darlington Works 12/63

90335 3/49 70860: WD 7/44; Lostock Hall 23/4/49; Accrington 14/5/49; Fleetwood 10/2/62
WITHDRAWN 11/63; Horwich Works 12/63

90314 and companion, probably in the mid-1950s for though 90314 was at Rose Grove for a number of years the Black Five 45395 alongside left Walsall (3C) in June 1958 never to return. The pair are outside Crewe 10 Shop before the traverser was installed. The WD, like all plain black engines, did not go to the Paint Shop but the eagle-eyed will notice that the 4-6-0 *is* lined so it must have been through the Shop. It has presumably had to come back into 10 Shop after steam testing. Screw couplings yet to be put on, on both engines. Photograph I. Mackenzie, www.transporttreasury.co.uk

Black and white. 90314 in the snow. Photograph Paul Chancellor Collection.

90315, of Banbury, passing Severn Tunnel Junction with a train of empty hoppers on 5 June 1961. Already the signals have been returned to danger by the 'bobby' who can be seen in the signalbox observing the passing train. Photograph B.W.L. Brooksbank, Initial Photographics.

Cheadle Heath again and as 90316 awaits the road, a crewman take a rest on a proper seat. Photograph D. Forsyth, Paul Chancellor Collection.

A fine, newly overhauled and painted 90317, freshly bedecked with electrification flashes, at Stockport Edgeley. A view from the path leading down to the shed, about 1960. Largely unnoticed, Edgeley was nonetheless something of a cosmopolitan place, responsible (Lees was a bit like this) for more crew and engine changing than actual locomotives. The work was all freight of course and even North East engines were common; Dairycoates K3s could be found almost on a daily basis but as withdrawals progressed they gave way to WDs, though 90317 was a home-grown LMR engine. Photograph D. Forsyth, Paul Chancellor Collection.

This is Stockport Edgeley again, with the main line going past, though it is some years prior to the previous view, before the overhead line was put up. Excellent side-on of your average WD. Photograph D. Forsyth, Paul Chancellor Collection.

WDs at Polmadie, 21 May 1961; 90320 at front, 90387 behind, followed by another WD and one of the 2-10-0s. We are back with those Scottish clacks; this is not the best of views for the purpose but the nearest WD, 90320, can be seen to have the familiar top layout of boiler clacks while the two behind have them arranged separately, in familiar BR Standard fashion. Photograph Paul Chancellor Collection.

A beautiful 90323 ex-works (note number chalked on pony wheel) at Swindon on 24 April 1955 with the fire iron 'tunnel' and covered top feed but no smokebox number plate; WR 'E' route restriction disc below the number, no '8F' above. In front is a newly built BR 2-6-2T, 82037 or 82038 perhaps. Photograph A.R. Carpenter, www.transporttreasury.co.uk

90323 out on the road with a goods train a couple of weeks after its overhaul, passing Swindon station on 8 May 1955. It is based at Severn Tunnel Junction and already the gloss of repainting is starting to fade. The smokebox number plate has been fitted but on the top smokebox hinge strap whereas normally it was below, giving the engine an odd look. Photograph B.K.B. Green, Initial Photographics.

Crewe South and 90327 has a bit of time to work out before returning home to Aintree shed. The 27B plate indicates the period to be January 1959-September 1962. Photograph D. Forsyth, Paul Chancellor Collection.

With the WDs, some you saw every day, others never in a lifetime of looking, so we offer no excuse for two pictures of dear old 90327, this time at that familiar viewing point, the path to Stockport Edgeley shed (see, particularly, *The Book of the Stanier 2-6-0s* in this series) this time on 24 August 1961. The box is Edgeley Junction No.2 and the curious wire mesh over the windows was put up to discourage signalmen from leaning out and electrocuting themselves. The fire iron 'tunnel' on the running plate nearest to us shows that 90327 is a former WR engine but crews did as they always had and (as they did near enough everywhere else, including the WR) stowed the irons on the tender in traditional fashion. Every now and then a fireman probably wondered just what this strange compartment in front of the cab was for, exactly, full of coal dust and dirty water. As noted, we are on the famous 'cinder path' again, beloved of this fine photographer; the shed itself is out of sight to the right. Photograph D. Forsyth, Paul Chancellor Collection.

90329, ex-works at Crewe on 10 September 1950. We've included a high proportion of such pictures but wouldn't want to misrepresent the WDs; the grime and muck soon wore out over the smooth ex-works surfaces seen here. It didn't help that all-black engines such as the WDs didn't go in the Paint Shop and in any case only got a 'part paint' in some instances, as here! The piping along both sides of the WD boiler was a bit like the snowflake; no one example was the same as any other! Photograph B.K.B. Green, Initial Photographics.

90329 now of Sowerby Bridge passing through Rochdale station in April 1960 on a typical goods of the time. It moved to Wakefield in September 1963. Photograph J. Davenport, Initial Photographics.

An elegant, barely even priming yet, 90337, another WD in more or less 'BR original' condition. Compare with the wreck on page 108. Photograph Paul Chancellor Collection.

90336 1/50
70864: WD 7/44; Farnley Jct 14/1/50; Royston 11/7/59;
Wakefield 2/11/63
WITHDRAWN 1/66; Drapers, Hull 4/66

90337 6/49
70865: WD 8/44; Wakefield 18/6/49; Normanton
15/6/57; Royston 11/9/65; Normanton 8/10/66
WITHDRAWN 1/67; Cox and Danks, Wadsley Bridge
8/67

90338 11/49
70866: WD 8/44; Newton Heath 5/11/49
WITHDRAWN 11/63; Crewe Works 11/63

90339 9/49
70867: WD 8/44; Wakefield 8/49;
West Hartlepool 10/9/66
WITHDRAWN 7/67; Drapers, Hull 10/67

90340 11/49
70871: WD 8/44; New England 1/3/47; Mexborough
3/50; March 6/10/56; Doncaster 7/10/61;
Barrow Hill 25/1/64
WITHDRAWN 7/65; Cox and Danks,
Wadsley Bridge 11/65

90341 9/49
70874: WD 8/44; Wakefield 8/49
WITHDRAWN 7/65; Drapers, Hull 11/65

90342 5/49
70875: WD 8/44; Wakefield 11/6/49
WITHDRAWN 11/65; Drapers, Hull 3/66

90343 11/52
70876: WD 8/44; St Philips Marsh 25/1/47; Westbury
25/2/50; Swansea Victoria 2/12/50; Agecroft 16/12/50;
Bolton 13/1/51; Aintree 23/4/55
WITHDRAWN 12/63; Crewe Works 1/64

90344 2/49
70877: WD 8/44; Retford 26/7/47; Stockton on Tees
29/11/47; West Hartlepool 8/10/55
WITHDRAWN 11/64; Darlington Works 12/64

90345 2/51
70878: WD 8/44; Brighton 12/47; Bricklayers Arms
8/1/49; Brighton 30/6/49; Huddersfield 3/6/50; Bury
31/10/53; Royston 5/10/63; Normanton 8/8/64;
Wakefield 9/10/65
WITHDRAWN 6/67; Cox and Danks Wadsley Bridge
11/67

90346 9/50
77263: WD 6/44; Heaton 1/3/47; Newport 26/4/47;
Immingham 8/51; Staveley 29/12/51; Colwick 17/5/52;
Woodford Halse 10/11/56; Barrow Hill 19/6/65; Toton
23/11/63; Nottingham 28/12/63; Woodford Halse
18/4/64; Birkenhead 13/6/64; Rose Grove 22/5/65;
Colwick 9/10/65
WITHDRAWN 10/65; Drapers, Hull 2/66

90347 2/50
77270: WD 7/44; Brighton 12/47; New England 8/49;
Huddersfield 3/6/50; Wakefield 9/10/65; York 4/12/65;
West Hartlepool 10/9/66
WITHDRAWN 5/67; Drapers, Hull 9/67

90348 1/51
77271; WD 8/44; Newport 26/4/47; Rose Grove
29/1/49; Accrington 19/4/52; Mirfield 19/11/55; Wakefield
14/6/58; Sunderland 8/10/66
WITHDRAWN 9/67; Hughes Bolckows Ltd,
North Blyth 10/67

90349 3/51
77274: WD 8/44; New England 1/3/47; Retford 2/11/63
WITHDRAWN 6/65; Cox and Danks, Wadsley Bridge
2/66

90350 12/50
77278: WD 8/44; Thornton Jct 1/3/47
WITHDRAWN 8/66; McWilliams, Shettleston 11/66

90351 6/50
77280: WD 8/44; Farnley Jct 28/1/50; Mirfield 11/7/59;
Low Moor 20/2/60; Mirfield 3/10/64;
Wakefield 28/1/67; Normanton 17/6/67
WITHDRAWN 9/67; Arnott Young, Parkgate and
Rawmarsh 12/67

90352 12/51
77283: WD 8/44; Mexborough 26/2/47; New England
1/3/47; Tyne Dock 29/11/47; Dairycoates 9/51;
Springhead 18/4/53; Dairycoates 13/12/58;
Goole 22/4/67
WITHDRAWN 6/67; Drapers, Hull 12/67

90353 6/49
77285: WD 8/44; Wakefield 18/6/49
WITHDRAWN 2/65; Wards, Beighton, Sheffield 8/65

90354 8/49
77286: WD 8/44; Brighton 12/47; Sowerby Bridge
11/8/51; Agecroft 8/8/53
WITHDRAWN 10/64; Wards, Killamarsh 2/65

90355 3/52
77288: WD 8/44; Exeter 22/3/47; Canton 1/11/47; Severn
Tunnel Jct 15/7/50; Canton 8/10/55; Southall 19/5/56
WITHDRAWN 10/62; Crewe Works 11/62

90356 10/51
77289: WD 8/44; St Philips Marsh 19/4/47; Ebbw Jct
5/9/53; Shrewsbury 31/10/53; Southall 28/12/57
WITHDRAWN 10/62; Crewe Works 11/62

90357 3/49
77291: WD 9/44; Old Oak 27/12/47; Reading 15/5/48;
Lower Darwen 14/5/49; Normanton 15/6/57;
Wakefield 9/10/65; Sunderland 13/8/66
WITHDRAWN 9/66; Drapers, Hull 12/66

90358 11/49
77292: WD 9/44; Gorton 29/3/47; Annesley 26/4/47;
Woodford Halse 29/11/47; Colwick 12/48; Staverton
10/50; Colwick 4/51; Mexborough 7/3/53; Canklow
29/12/62
WITHDRAWN 11/63; Doncaster Works 2/64

90359 2/49
77294: WD 9/44; Newton Abbot 19/4/47; Laira 14/6/47;
Swansea Victoria 3/6/50; Agecroft 16/12/50;
Bury 4/10/52; Agecroft 5/10/57
WITHDRAWN 10/64; Central Wagon Co, Ince, Wigan
1/65

90360 11/50
77296: WD 9/44; Ashford 14/6/47; Redhill 31/7/48;
Newton Heath 11/8/51; Sowerby Bridge 14/7/56;
Wakefield 5/10/63; Normanton 17/6/67;
West Hartlepool 29/7/67
WITHDRAWN 9/67; Arnott Young, Dinsdale 11/67

90361 3/49
77297: WD 9/44; Oxley 19/4/47; Banbury 12/7/47;
Wakefield 18/6/49; Ardsley 18/6/60; Wakefield
11/9/65; Sunderland 3/12/66
WITHDRAWN 4/67; Drapers, Hull 8/67

It is April 1966 and with official attitudes towards steam turning to contempt and loathing, BR has brought poor old 90337 at Normanton shed to a condition that would probably have shocked those receiving the Austerities back from the war in Europe. An all too common sight at the end of steam, an engine in store, chimney covered over (why did they bother?), dome cover removed, front footsteps bent and the engine just looking decrepit, not least from the crude patch repair on the smokebox. 90336 was officially withdrawn only in January 1966. Photograph J. Davenport, Initial Photographics.

The huge and newly rebuilt shed at Wakefield, with Newton Heath's 90339 at the south end, in the 1950s. The block over on the right is the Wakefield 'barracks', for men on lodging turns. Among the usual ranks of WDs is 52576, an old L&Y 'A' class 0-6-0. As usual the only even half-clean spot on the WD is the area of the cab number. Photograph A. Robey, www.transporttreasury.co.uk

90341 glinting in the evening light at Stockport Edgeley. Photograph D. Forsyth, Paul Chancellor Collection.

90353 newly outshopped (and renumbered) at Crewe Works 19 June 1949; it awaits a shed plate. Alongside is a Stanier 8F, the basic 'pattern' for the WDs, also ex-works and bound for Toton.

Typically 'battered but unbowed', sagging look of a WD, 90357 at Wakefield shed on 29 July 1966; the wheels were cast in one piece, to a thickness to cater for reprofiling abroad. Basic hand rails, access ladder on the back, a good view of the inset for tender first running which must have also created a bit of a draught on the footplate. Screw coupling and a bracket on the top rear corners for lifting. Wakefield accumulated a huge stud of WDs (in comparative terms) towards the end; from Weybridge (we shared a 'W' but that was it) the shed seemed a thousand miles away, though we had our hands full with the last of Southern steam. Wakefield remained a shimmering, never to be realised prize. Photograph B.W.L. Brooksbank, Initial Photographics.

A gloriously filthy 90360 at West Hartlepool shed in the very last days of the class, on 17 August 1967. There is an 'O' added to the cab, oddly, and the mysterious WHO'S SORRY NOW written in the grime of the tender side. Something different, too, about those washout plug covers. It must be ready for one of its final duties for it was among the final batch withdrawn, in September 1967. It met its end at Arnott Young, Dinsdale. Photograph A.G. Forsyth, Initial Photographics.

The Great Western comes to Hull. 90361, once of Banbury, at Dairycoates shed in August 1952; again crews use the original fire iron bunker stowage rather than the 'tunnel' provided at Swindon. Photograph J. Robertson, www.transporttreasury.co.uk

90362 6/49
77299: WD 9/44; Wakefield 18/6/49; Normanton 15/6/57; Carnforth 23/3/63; Huddersfield 27/3/65; Normanton 28/1/67
WITHDRAWN 6/67; Arnott Young, Parkgate and Rawmarsh 11/67

90363 3/49
78510: WD 9/44; Ebbw Jct 23/8/47; Wakefield 8/49
WITHDRAWN 6/67; Cox and Danks, Wadsley Bridge 11/67

90364 11/49
78512: WD 9/44; Banbury 12/7/47; Rose Grove 12/3/49; Bury 24/12/49; Bolton 28/12/63; Gorton 3/10/64; Rose Grove 2/1/65; Doncaster 19/6/65; Immingham 27/11/65
WITHDRAWN 12/65; Drapers, Hull 5/66

90365 5/51
78514: WD 9/44; Annesley 4/10/47; Colwick 29/11/47; Woodford Halse 7/49; Toton 23/11/63; Wooford Halse 18/4/64; Gorton 16/5/64; Doncaster 3/10/64
WITHDRAWN 6/65; Arnott Young, Parkgate and Rawmarsh 11/65

90366 6/52
78521: WD 9/44; Old Oak 9/8/47; Newton Heath 16/12/50
WITHDRAWN 1/64; Crewe Works 2/64

90367 11/49
78522: WD 10/44; Old Oak 19/4/47; Reading 17/5/47; New England 3/48; Old Oak 27/11/48; Lostock Hall 23/4/49; Fleetwood 10/2/62; Bolton 20/4/63; Gorton 3/10/64; Rose Grove 2/1/65; Barrow Hill 19/6/65; Colwick 9/10/65; Frodingham 4/12/65
WITHDRAWN 2/66; Drapers, Hull 7/66

90368 5/49
78525: WD 10/44; Immingham 19/4/47; Annesley 23/8/47; Colwick 29/11/47; Canklow 5/9/59; Barrow Hill 25/1/64
WITHDRAWN 6/65; Arnott Young, Parkgate and Rawmarsh 9/65

90369 2/49
78526: WD 10/44; Neville Hill 25/10/47; York 5/48; Colwick 10/48; Woodford Halse 14/6/52; Colwick 9/8/52; Northampton 24/4/54; Birkenhead 20/4/57; Warrington Dallam 22/9/62; Nottingham 28/12/63; Carnforth 18/4/64; Springs Branch 16/5/64; Doncaster 3/10/64
WITHDRAWN 4/66; Drapers, Hull 9/66

90370 6/49
78560: WD 9/44; Wakefield 18/6/49; Sunderland 8/10/66
WITHDRAWN 5/67; Drapers, Hull 9/67

90371 7/49
78561: WD 9/44; St Margarets 1/3/47; Rose Grove 23/4/49; Patricroft 21/1/61; Newton Heath 26/1/63
WITHDRAWN 5/64; Slag Reduction Co, Ickles, Rotherham 1/65

90372 3/50
78563: WD 9/44; Farnley Jct 22/4/50; Agecroft 21/4/56; Doncaster 3/10/64
WITHDRAWN 12/65; W. George, Station Steel 7/66

90373 3/51
78564: WD 9/44; Newport 3/47; Thornaby 14/6/58; Darlington 18/6/60; Wakefield 23/2/63
WITHDRAWN 9/66; Drapers, Hull 11/66

90374 10/49
78568:WD 10/44; St Margarets 19/4/47; Lostock Hall 23/4/49; Lower Darwen 19/11/49; Accrington 19/11/55; Rose Grove 16/1/60; Accrington 20/2/60; Rose Grove 25/3/61
WITHDRAWN 4/64; Central Wagon Co, Ince, Wigan 9/64

90375 12/49
78569: WD 10/44; Bricklayers Arms 20/3/46; Mirfield 16/12/50; Lower Darwen 17/6/61
WITHDRAWN 7/64; Central Wagon Co, Ince, Wigan 11/64

90376 9/49
78572: WD 10/44; St Margarets 19/4/47; Kingmoor 18/9/48; St Margarets 11/48; Newton Heath 8/9/51
WITHDRAWN 12/62; Horwich Works 6/63

90377 4/51
78575: WD 10/44; York 1/3/47; Stockton on Tees 23/8/47; Dawsholm 11/7/59; Thornaby 3/10/59; Royston 29/12/62; Normanton 28/12/63; Royston 27/3/65
WITHDRAWN 2/66; Drapers, Hull 6/66

90378 4/49
78578: WD 10/44; Dairycoates 23/8/47; York 10/49; Dairycoates 11/49; Springhead 6/50; Dairycoates 10/50; Springhead 15/12/56; Dairycoates 11/1/58; Springhead 19/4/58; Dairycoates 13/12/58; Sunderland 17/6/67;
WITHDRAWN 9/67 Hughes Bolckows Ltd, North Blyth 10/67

90379 9/49
78580: WD 10/44; Wakefield 13/8/49
WITHDRAWN 3/66; Motherwell Machinery and Scrap Co, Wishaw 6/66

90380 8/49
78581: WD 11/44; Wakefield 13/8/49; Mirfield 26/2/66
WITHDRAWN 3/66; Drapers, Hull 8/66

90381 9/49
78583: WD 11/44; Wakefield 13/8/49; Aintree 11/2/56; Frodingham 24/6/65
WITHDRAWN 10/65; Drapers, Hull 2/66

90382 4/49
78585: WD 11/44; Dairycoates 4/10/47; Springhead 10/49; Dairycoates 11/49; Haverton Hill 10/50; Dairycoates 9/51; Wakefield 7/9/57; Sunderland 3/12/66
WITHDRAWN 9/67; Hughes Bolckows Ltd, North Blyth 10/67

90383 12/49
78587: WD 11/44; Neville Hill 29/11/47; New England 8/49; Mexborough 3/50; March 10/50; Mexborough 3/51; Doncaster 5/51; Immingham 23/2/57; Colwick 8/10/60; Barrow Hill 2/1/65
WITHDRAWN 4/65; Cashmores, Great Bridge 7/65

90384 11/49
78588: WD 11/44; March 23/8/47; Colwick 3/10/53; Mexborough 14/6/58; Canklow 22/2/64; Barrow Hill 19/6/65; Colwick 9/10/65; Frodingham 4/12/65
WITHDRAWN 2/66; Drapers, Hull 7/66

Banker at work. I confess to not having any idea where this is, though readers who do know will groan at such ignorance. It's included as a smashing picture and to show a WD hard at work to the end – and it *is* late on; 90370 has AWS and the rearranged lamp irons at the front. Photograph Paul Chancellor Collection.

Doncaster was always a good place to see WDs at work, with members of the class working in from all over the ER on goods trains and also for attention at the nearby Works. AWS-fitted 90378 was now at 50B Dairycoates (recoded from 53A in January 1960) and must have worked in from the coast with its train. The crew member seems more intent on the photographer than the road ahead and the spotters are as usual more interested in the locos in the background (a B1 and a Pacific) than the poor old WD. Photograph www.transporttreasury.co.uk

Sunderland shed on 17 August 1967 and it looks like the end for these two WDs. 90378 had moved here in June and 90382 in December 1966 and it is doubtful they did much work. The shed closed exactly one month later and their next and final movement was to the wonderfully named scrapyard of Hughes Bolckows Ltd. of North Blyth. Photograph A. G. Forsyth, Initial Photographics.

90379 of Wakefield shed on foreign territory with a goods through Lostock Hall station. Both building and signal gantry look rather rundown. 90379 ended up at Motherwell Machinery and Scrap Co., perhaps its first visit back to Scotland since it was built. It had spent its entire BR life at Wakefield. Photograph B.K.B. Green, Initial Photographics.

Another WD, 90381, pauses at Cheadle Heath, on 2 September 1957. The WD 2-8-0 was a model railway rarity for years; given the wheels, building one from a kit was the only option. The production of 4mm engines like this, from Bachmann and Hornby, to quite astonishing standards, has livened up many an attic railway. Photograph A.G. Forsyth, Initial Photographics.

90382 in 'extreme BR late' condition; that is, literally caked in filth. It was in the North East all its life and despite a fair collection of snaps taken up there I'm having trouble pinpointing this coal stage. It's an ancient NER structure that's for sure, re-clad in corrugated sheeting and bolstered by concrete framing. That signal shows that it's adjacent to the running lines – I'd plump for West Hartlepool. Photograph Paul Chancellor Collection.

90385 7/50
78590: WD 11/44; Sowerby Bridge 12/8/50;
Wakefield 4/11/50;
Huddersfield 8/10/55; Wakefield 31/12/55
WITHDRAWN 3/67; Drapers, Hull 6/67

90386 3/49
78592: WD 11/44; March 14/6/47; Dalry Road 11/2/50;
Motherwell 17/6/50; Hamilton 18/4/53; Motherwell
6/9/58; Aberdeen Ferryhill 1/6/63;
Dunfermline 6/7/63; Sunderland 3/12/66;
Dunfermline 18/2/67
WITHDRAWN 4/67; Motherwell and Machinery Scrap Co,
Wishaw 9/67

90387 3/51
78594: WD 11/44; St Margarets 29/3/47; Dawsholm
23/10/48; Rose Grove 12/3/49; Dawsholm 23/3/57; Polmadie
25/1/58
WITHDRAWN 9/62; Cowlairs Works 9/62

90388 11/49
78595: WD 11/44; Wakefield 13/8/49; Rose Grove
11/7/64
WITHDRAWN 7/64; Central Wagon Co,
Wigan 11/64

90389 11/49
78596: WD 11/44; Bricklayers Arms 14/6/47; Hither Green
1/4/48; Newton Heath 8/9/51; Rose Grove
11/7/64
WITHDRAWN 10/64; Smiths, Ecclesfield 3/65

90390 4/51
78597: WD 11/44; Hither Green 14/5/47; Newton Heath
19/5/51; Sowerby Bridge 8/9/51; Newton Heath
3/11/51; Patricroft 22/9/62; Newton Heath 26/1/63; Gorton
25/1/64; Sutton Oak 21/3/64;
Frodingham 22/5/65
WITHDRAWN 9/65; Drapers, Hull 12/65

90391 3/49
78598: WD 12/44; York 25/10/47; Colwick 10/48;
Staveley 28/1/56; Canklow 19/12/59
WITHDRAWN 8/62; Gorton Works 10/62

90392 2/49
78599: WD 12/44; March 23/8/47; Colwick 31/10/53;
Northampton 24/4/54; Birkenhead 20/4/57; Warrington
Dallam 22/9/62; Carnforth 23/3/63; Gorton 15/6/63
WITHDRAWN 12/64; Wards, Broughton Lane, Sheffield 3/65

90393 3/51
78600: WD 12/44; March 26/7/47; Immingham
3/10/53; Colwick 8/10/60
WITHDRAWN 8/65; Ellis Metals Ltd, Swalwell,
Derwenthaugh 1/66

90394 8/51
78601: WD 12/44; Immingham 1/3/47; Tyne Dock
29/11/47; Dairycoates 2/49; Neville Hill 5/49; Staveley
Central 8/49; Colwick 16/7/55; Immingham 26/3/60
WITHDRAWN 4/64; Smiths, Ecclesfield 12/64

90395 3/50
78602: WD 12/44; Farnley Jct 25/3/50; Royston
20/2/60; Normanton 28/12/63; Wakefield 9/10/65;
York 4/12/65; Sunderland 8/10/66
WITHDRAWN 10/66; Drapers, Hull 3/67

90396 4/49
78604: WD 12/44; Oxley 19/4/47; Banbury 12/7/47;
Wakefield 18/6/49
WITHDRAWN 6/67 Cox and Danks, Wadsley Bridge
11/67

90397 9/49
78605: WD 12/44; Wakefield 13/8/49;
Goole 31/12/54Low Moor
16/6/56; Darlington 14/6/58; Haverton Hill 18/10/58;
Thornaby 11/7/59; Mirfield 14/11/59; Low Moor
20/2/60; Mirfield 3/10/64; Wakefield 28/1/67
WITHDRAWN 5/67; Arnott Young, Parkgate and
Rawmarsh 8/67

90398 3/49
78606: WD 12/44; Lostock Hall 23/4/49; Bury 23/9/61;
Rose Grove 11/8/62; Newton Heath 18/4/64; Lower
Darwen 11/7/64; Langwith Jct 3/10/64
WITHDRAWN 7/65; Cox and Danks, Wadsley Bridge
9/65

90399 12/50
78607: WD 12/44; Ebbw Jct; 5/48; Rose Grove 12/3/49;
Accrington 19/4/52; Patricroft 16/1/60; Newton Heath
26/1/63; Aintree 11/7/64; Springs Branch 11/7/64
WITHDRAWN 3/65; Wards, Beighton, Sheffield 8/65

90386 ready to leave Glasgow Queen Street with a Stephenson Locomotive Society tour on 11 April 1966; obviously readied for the occasion it has a tenderful of coal, safety valves lifting and the blower is doing its job. Strange that in the December it was transferred from Scotland to Sunderland only to return to Dunfermline shed the following month, to be withdrawn in the April. Readers will have spotted, of course, the 'Scottish clacks'. Photograph Paul Cotterell.

Another one that's hard to resist... That's 90386 on the right. There are no details available for this print but the clacks tell us it's Scotland. The variation in the 'patching' over the feed pipes leading to the clacks is fascinating. The snifting valves are nearly as big as the chimney! This anti-vacuum valve, so prominent behind the chimney, was mounted on the superheater header, an echo of LNW practice. It was held on its seat when the regulator was open and dropped off when it was closed, thereby preventing pumping action by the cylinders and avoiding the drawing down of ash and so on into the blast pipe. Riddles presumably put it here because only one was needed instead of the two required if mounted on the valve chest – it all added to that metal, machining and 6,000 hours saved! In early days the valve was much less prominent but was soon changed, universally, with this 'pot' cover. On the 2-10-0s it remained as originally fitted and was much less noticeable. Photograph Paul Chancellor Collection.

90388 in a Jinty sandwich at Crewe. Photograph D. Forsyth, Paul Chancellor Collection.

90390 at Crewe; compare the piping to the blower with 90393 below; again, the only similarities are the differences...
Photograph D. Forsyth, Paul Chancellor Collection.

90393 looking very fine indeed, ex-works at Darlington shed in August 1953; 'RA6' on lower cabside, no '8F' above number, pipes to clacks outside boiler cladding. Note also diamond builder's plate on the radius link bracket. These seem largely to have disappeared after a while, though there were still plenty around in the early 1950s. Photograph W. Hermiston, www.transporttreasury.co.uk

How years of neglect transform a respectable locomotive into a near-ruin. 90393 now in perfectly awful condition, at Colwick shed, on 2 May 1965. It was withdrawn in August and has STORED HOT BOX chalked on the cab, so maybe it never ran again. Features to note include the crude riveted patch on the smokebox, original clack feed and hand rail now in place, so it has been fitted with an older style boiler; that steam feed pipe seen back at Darlington in 1953 now runs *outside* the clack feed pipe, just like in the old days! Modellers pay your money and take your pick... Photograph J. Davenport, Initial Photographics.

90399 turning at Crewe South. 47482 to left, a Patriot in the distance. Photograph D. Forsyth, Paul Chancellor Collection.

90400 2/49
78609: WD 12/44; Immingham 19/4/47; Annesley 23/8/47; Mexborough 29/11/47
WITHDRAWN 12/63; Darlington Works 1/64

90401 6/49
78610: WD 12/44; New England 1/3/47; Mexborough 26/6/47: Canklow 22/2/64; Staveley Central 24/4/65; Langwith Jct 19/6/65
WITHDRAWN 11/65; Drapers, Hull 3/66

90402 4/49
78612: WD 12/44; Lostock Hall then to Accrington 14/5/49; Bolton 14/7/51; Lees 28/12/57; Gorton 22/2/64
WITHDRAWN 4/64; Hesslewoods, Attercliffe, Sheffield 12/64

90403 2/51
78614: WD 12/44; Dairycoates 4/10/47; Neville Hill 5/49; Staveley 8/49; Woodford Halse 31/12/54; Gorton 6/10/62; Nottingham 28/12/63; Gorton 16/5/64
WITHDRAWN 5/64; Slag Reduction Co, Ickles, Rotherham 1/65

90404 8/49
78615: WD 1/45; Wakefield 13/8/49; Goole 28/1/56; Wakefield 11/2/56
WITHDRAWN 6/67; Drapers, Hull 2/68

90405 5/51
78616: WD 1/45; Retford 26/7/47; Stockton on Tees 29/11/47; York 15/6/57; Wakefield 14/11/59; Darlington 18/6/60; Ardsley 16/12/61; Wakefield 11/9/65; Normanton 17/6/67
WITHDRAWN 9/67; Arnott Young, Parkgate and Rawmarsh 12/67

90406 7/50
78621: WD 1/45; Sowerby Bridge 12/8/50; Wakefield 4/11/50; Low Moor 16/6/56; Darlington 14/6/58; Thornaby 3/10/59; Goole 7/9/63
WITHDRAWN 7/67; Drapers, Hull 12/67

90407 4/50
78624: WD 1/45; Farnley Jct 22/4/50; Royston 7/10/61; Wakefield 2/11/63
WITHDRAWN 5/67; Arnott Young, Parkgate and Rawmarsh 8/67

90408 6/50
78531: WD 1/45; Bricklayers Arms 14/6/47; Aintree 16/6/51; Bury 14/6/52; Kirkby-in-Ashfield 28/2/63; Bury 18/4/64
WITHDRAWN 4/64; Looms, Spondon 12/64

90409 8/51
78532: WD 1/45; Dairycoates 4/10/47; York 10/49; Dairycoates 11/49; York 19/11/55; Newport 16/6/56; Thornaby 14/6/58; Ardsley 30/6/62; Wakefield 22/5/65
WITHDRAWN 6/67; Cox and Danks, Wadsley Bridge 11/67

90410 12/51
78537: WD 2/45; Mexborough 26/4/47; Canklow 21/3/64; Barrow Hill 19/6/65; Colwick 9/10/65; Frodingham 27/11/65; Doncaster 26/3/66
WITHDRAWN 4/66; Drapers, Hull 9/66

90411 9/50
78538: WD 2/45; Neville Hill 25/10/47; York 5/48; Colwick 8/49; Annesley 1/51; Colwick 6/51; Woodford Halse 8/51; Colwick 17/5/52; March 16/1/54; Colwick 24/4/54; Langwith Jct 22/6/54; Canklow 11/7/59; Immingham 5/9/59; Canklow 16/1/60; Langwith Jct 16/7/60
WITHDRAWN 8/64; Wards, Killamarsh 11/64

90412 8/49
78541: WD 2/45; Wakefield 13/8/49; Sowerby Bridge 25/2/56; Wakefield 5/10/63
WITHDRAWN 10/64; Ellis Metals Ltd, Swalwell, Derwenthaugh 12/65

90413 12/51
78542: WD 2/45; Gloucester Horton Road 29/11/47; Shrewsbury 12/8/50; Newton Heath 16/12/50; Bury 31/12/51; Lostock Hall 23/2/57; Bury 23/9/61; Fleetwood 22/9/62; Aintree 28/12/63; Colwick 3/10/64
WITHDRAWN 2/66; Drapers, Hull 6/66

90414 4/49
78543: WD 2/45; Canton 10/47; Pontypool Road 10/7/48; Canton 2/10/48; Pontypool Road 30/10/48; Wakefield 8/10/49; Canklow 5/9/59
WITHDRAWN 12/62; Arnott Young, Bilston 4/63

90415 6/49
78544: WD 2/45; Wakefield 18/6/49
WITHDRAWN 1/67; Arnott Young, Parkgate and Rawmarsh 6/67

90416 3/49
78546: WD 2/45; Rose Grove 26/3/49; Accrington 24/12/49; Bolton 11/8/51; Aintree 4/12/54
WITHDRAWN 5/64; Central Wagon Co, Ince, Wigan 4/65

90417 9/49
78551: WD 3/45; Wakefield 8/49; Sunderland 8/10/66
WITHDRAWN 9/67; Hughes Bolckows Ltd, North Blyth 10/67

90418 9/51
78553: WD 3/45; Dairycoates 23/8/47; Colwick 10/48; Staveley 2/50; Colwick 16/7/55; Staveley 28/1/56; Langwith Jct 27/2/60; Darnell 26/3/60; Langwith Jct 22/4/61
WITHDRAWN 1/66; Drapers, Hull 5/66

90419 10/49
78554: WD 3/45; Wakefield 5/11/49; Bury 24/12/49; Bolton 28/12/63; Aintree 5/9/64; Barrow Hill 3/10/64
WITHDRAWN 4/65; Cashmores, Great Bridge 7/65

90420 10/49
78556: WD 3/45; Accrington 8/10/49; Rose Grove 24/12/49;
WITHDRAWN 8/65; Cashmores, Newport 2/66

90421 10/49
78559: WD 3/45; Mexborough 1/3/47; Doncaster 5/10/63; Barrow Hill 25/1/64; Doncaster 8/8/64
WITHDRAWN 8/65; Wards, Beighton, Sheffield 12/65

90407, forging through a near-derelict Knottingley station on a goods train, 20 September 1965. The place is a wreck, just the supporting pillars and no roof; it could not have survived much longer.

Wakefield shed in its last year of working, on 14 January 1967. We have three (all AWS-fitted) of the resident WDs, all in typical mucky condition of the time – enough to rival the weather in fact. On the left is 90397 which had only been transferred here this month; 90625 had been a Wakefield loco since October 1965 (its second period based here) while 90407 arrived in October 1965. All three were withdrawn in May 1967, 90625 becoming one of Draper's 205. Photograph Keith Lawrence.

Grime at Grimesthorpe, 20 February 1960. 90411 in a condition woeful enough to match anything found later in the 1960s; you can hardly read the cabside number and there is no sign of the BR totem on the tender side, though oddly someone has 'dolled it up' a bit at the front in the fairly recent past. Grimesthorpe was the old MR freight shed in Sheffield and part of the Eastern Region since 1958. Photograph J. Davenport, Initial Photographics.

90427 enters the shadow of the footbridge that crossed the line to give access to Wakefield shed, seen in the background, 10 December 1966. The WD was a Goole one; from 1 January 1957 at least 115 individual WDs came to be based at Wakefield shed. Photograph Keith Lawrence.

90422 3/50 3101 3/47 63101 9/48
77083: Gorton then New England 8/43; WD 12/44; March 20/4/46; Colchester 20/3/48; March 15/5/48; Frodingham 4/51
WITHDRAWN 6/65; Cox and Danks, Wadsley Bridge 11/65

90423 4/51 3102 3/47 63102 7/48
77091: Gorton 8/43; New England 9/43; Ebbw Jct 11/44; WD 2/45; Woodford Halse 3/46; Colwick 29/11/47; York 23/10/48; Darlington 12/2/49; Dairycoates 8/9/51; Mold Jct 16/2/52; Llandudno Jct 22/3/52; Mold Jct 19/4/52; Colwick 17/5/52; Northampton 24/4/54; Mold Jct 20/4/57; Widnes 8/8/59; Springs Branch 23/3/63; Colwick 3/10/64
WITHDRAWN 12/65; Drapers, Hull 4/66

90424 11/49 3103 2/47 63103 8/48
77093: Gorton 8/43; New England 9/43; WD 12/44; Heaton 1/47; Neville Hill 12/2/49; York 8/10/49; Selby 18/4/53; York 22/6/54; Newport 16/6/56; York 15/6/57
WITHDRAWN 12/63; Darlington Works 12/63

90425 11/49 3104 3/47 63104 6/48
77100: Gorton 9/43; March 10/43; WD 2/45; Heaton 10/46; March 28/12/46; Frodingham 4/51
WITHDRAWN 12/62; Central Wagon Co, Ince, Wigan 12/63

90426 11/50 3105 4/47 63105 6/48
77110: Gorton then Colwick 10/43; WD 11/44; Springhead 3/46; Heaton 28/5/47; Newport 12/2/49; Thornaby 14/6/58; Wakefield 12/5/62; Ardsley 25/1/64
WITHDRAWN 3/65; Drapers, Hull 6/65

90427 12/50 3106 3/47 63106 10/48
77112: Gorton then Colwick 10/43; WD 1/45; Tweedmouth 29/11/47; Dairycoates 4/51; Springhead 6/51; Dairycoates 13/12/58; Goole 30/11/63
WITHDRAWN 6/67; Drapers, Hull 1/68

90428 10/50 3107 3/47 63107 6/48
77113: Gorton then Colwick 10/43; Ebbw Jct 24/10/44; WD 2/45; Eastfield 3/46; Thornton Jct 4/46; March 28/12/46; Colchester 20/3/48; March 15/5/48; New England 3/12/49; Doncaster 20/4/63
WITHDRAWN 1/66; Drapers, Hull 4/66

90429 8/50 3108 4/47 63108 7/48
77131: Gorton then March 11/43; WD 2/45; Woodford Halse 4/46; Gorton 9/46; Mexborough 28/5/47; Springhead 23/10/48; Wakefield 7/9/57
WITHDRAWN 4/67; Drapers, Hull 9/67

90430 6/51 3109 4/47 63109 10/48
77133: Gorton then Newport 11/43; New England 9/44; WD 11/44; Heaton 2/47; Tyne Dock 12/2/49; Dairycoates 8/9/51; Goole 17/5/58; Stockton 14/6/58; Darlington 11/7/59; Wakefield 23/2/63; Normanton 17/6/67
WITHDRAWN 9/67; Drapers, Hull 4/68

90431 6/49 3110 2/47 63110 6/48
77136: Gorton then Newport 11/43; Pontypool Road 11/44; WD 2/45; March 12/45; Colchester 20/3/48; March 15/5/48; Colchester 7/8/48; Immingham 3/10/53; Langwith Jct 13/8/55
WITHDRAWN 12/62; Arnott Young, Bilston 4/63

90432 2/49 3111 3/47
77146: Gorton then Newport 12/43; Shrewsbury 11/44; WD 2/45; York 11/45; Heaton 9/46; York 12/2/49; Dairycoates 10/51; Mold Jct 16/2/52; Colwick 17/5/52
WITHDRAWN 10/65; Drapers, Hull 1/66

90433 10/50 3112 2/47
77473: Gorton 29/1/44; Bricklayers Arms 26/2/44; WD 11/44; York 26/1/46; Heaton 28/9/46; March 28/12/46; Colwick 3/10/53; Woodford Halse 11/2/56; Toton 23/11/63; Woodford Halse 18/4/64
WITHDRAWN 5/64; Cashmores, Great Bridge 10/64

90434 8/50 3113 3/47
77474: Gorton 29/1/44; Bricklayers Arms 26/2/44; WD 11/44; Springhead 20/3/46; Heaton 28/5/47; Newport 12/2/49; Thornaby 14/6/58; Tyne Dock 15/6/63; West Hartlepool 19/6/65
WITHDRAWN 6/67; Drapers, Hull 10/67

90435 1/50 3114 3/47 63114 5/48
77486: Gorton then Stewarts Lane 26/2/44; Hither Green 25/3/44; WD 11/44; York 26/1/46; Heaton 28/5/47; Tweedmouth 29/11/47; Dairycoates 12/50; Newport 1/11/52; Thornaby 14/6/58; Goole 24/2/62; Dairycoates 12/5/62
WITHDRAWN 9/63; Darlington Works 9/63

90436 7/50 3115 3/47
77487: Gorton 29/1/44; Hither Green 25/3/44; WD 11/44; Aberdeen Ferryhill 26/1/46; St Margarets 1/3/47; Dunfermline 3/12/49; St Margarets 24/12/49; Dawsholm 1/11/52
WITHDRAWN 6/62; Darlington Works 11/63

90437 10/49 3116 3/47 63116 6/48
77491: Gorton 26/2/44; Feltham 25/3/44; Oxford 24/10/44; WD 11/44; Woodford Halse 26/1/46; Annesley 26/3/49; Colwick 18/6/49; Doncaster 4/12/65
WITHDRAWN 4/66; Drapers, Hull 9/66

90438 6/49 3117 4/47
77493: Gorton 26/2/44; Feltham 25/3/44; Oxford 24/10/44; WD 12/44; New England 1/47; March 23/10/48; New England 2/50; Immingham then Langwith Jct 5/10/57; Colwick 21/5/60
WITHDRAWN 10/65; Drapers, Hull 1/66

90439 1/51 3118 3/47 63118 8/48
77496: New England 26/2/44; Feltham 25/3/44; Reading 24/10/44; WD 12/44; New England 25/5/46; Frodingham 20/4/63
WITHDRAWN 11/65; W. George, Station Steel, Wath 3/66

90440 3/49 3119 3/47
77498: Longmoor 26/2/44; St Margarets 29/12/45; Eastfield 27/7/46; Dawsholm 12/8/50; Springs Branch 28/7/62
WITHDRAWN 9/63; Horwich Works 11/63

90441 6/49 3120 2/47 63120 4/48
77501: Longmoor 26/2/44; St Margarets 29/12/45; Eastfield 27/7/46; Thornton Jct 23/2/52
WITHDRAWN 10/66; Motherwell Machinery and Scrap Co, Wishaw 5/67

90442 12/50 3121 3/47
77502: Melbourne 26/2/44; March 29/12/45; New England 29/3/47; March 9/48; Colchester 23/10/48; Colwick 3/10/53; Plaistow 21/5/55; Tilbury 18/10/58; Doncaster 16/12/61; Langwith Jct 23/3/63
WITHDRAWN 4/65; Cashmores, Great Bridge 7/65

Newly outshopped 90428 at Darlington shed, 4 August 1953, waiting to return home to New England shed. It seems Darlington Works overhauled more of the workhorses of the ER/NER while the passenger classes (literally the racehorses) were more likely to be dealt with at Doncaster. This close up shows to good effect the balances on the driving wheels and the 'webbing' of the spokes, plus the whistle and its steam pipe disappearing through one of the ventilation holes by the cab roof. The sliding cab window is 'up'. Photograph J. Robertson, www.transporttreasury.co.uk

Another WD 'before and after'; 90428, by now profoundly filthy, at Colwick in May 1965. The WDs could obviously fall victim to priming, for we see them so often covered in the white running carbonate salt/sludge stains that have sploshed back on the boiler. This was often neglect (see *Eastern Region Memories*) but it looked worse because they were *never* cleaned. In this way only a few, perhaps widely separated instances of priming could make the engine look like it had been priming for years. Then again, it could have been! 90428 had arrived at Colwick in September 1964 and was withdrawn in January 1966. Photograph J. Davenport, Initial Photographics.

How enthusiasts remember the class, slogging with a long goods train to that accompanying and resoundingly diagnostic 'clank-bang-clank'. 90430, in reasonable external condition, is passing Marsden on 10 October 1953 on a train mainly consisting of wooden plank wagons. Photograph B.K.B. Green, Initial Photographics.

One 'in the landscape' for a change. Even at this fairly modest distance, there was little hope of getting a WD number. The photographer, however, had time to wade through that snow while the engine waited impatiently at the signals – it turns out to be 90435. Photograph Paul Chancellor Collection.

Dairycoates' 90435 in the yards near the shed on 13 August 1952 with a very mixed bag in tow. Photograph J. Robertson, www.transporttreasury.co.uk

A spectacularly filthy 90437 sags to a stand at Market Harborough shed on 13 April 1963. It was a Colwick engine and even amongst that shed's memorable collection this one would have been out in front in the (lack of) cleaning stakes. We affect to be amused by it all but it was disgusting really; almost a public demonstration of contempt. Nothing like this seemed to happen in France or Germany. Photograph Stephen Gradidge.

A very respectable looking 90441 at Eastfield shed, Glasgow on 31 March 1956; Thornton Junction shed plate. She would be newly out of works; Cowlairs presumably, just look at that buffer beam. A glance at those fire irons will bring home (recalling your levers and fulcrums from Second Form physics) the great strength needed to paddle out clinker at the end of that mighty iron. That's apart from the weight of the things themselves and the awkwardness of manoeuvring them in the cab. In the background one can note which football team is popular at the shed – the *gers*. 90441 survived at 62A until October 1966; 8F above number, RA6 centrally below it. Modification of the clacks had not yet got underway. Photograph J. Robertson, www.transporttreasury.co.uk

90444 at Thornton Junction, 17 May 1964; clacks duly modified. Photograph Peter Groom.

90443 2/51 3122 4/47 63122 4/48
77504: Melbourne 26/2/44; March 1/12/45; Colwick 9/48; March 10/51; Stratford 29/1/55; Plaistow 26/2/55; Immingham 21/5/55
WITHDRAWN 6/65 Arnott Young, Parkgate and Rawmarsh 10/65

90444 6/50 3123 2/47 63123 3/48
77505: Melbourne 26/2/44; Tay Bridge 29/12/45; Thornton Jct 6/7/63
WITHDRAWN 1/67; McWilliams, Shettleston 5/67

90445 8/50 3124 3/47
77506: Melbourne 26/2/44; Newport 8/12/45; Heaton 28/5/47; Tyne Dock 18/12/48; York 15/6/57; Wakefield 14/11/59; Darlington 18/6/60; Thornaby 25/1/64; West Hartlepool 16/5/64
WITHDRAWN 7/66; Thompsons, Stockton-on-Tees 10/66

90446 9/49 3125 2/47 63125 4/48
77507: Melbourne 26/2/44; March 1/12/45; Newport 26/4/47; Thornaby 14/6/58
WITHDRAWN 11/63; Darlington Works 1/64

90447 12/49 3126 2/47 63126 9/48
78625: WD 3/44; St Margarets 29/12/45; Carlisle Canal 4/48; Peterborough (LMR) 8/50; March 20/2/60; Doncaster 7/10/61
WITHDRAWN 11/63; Darlington Works 11/63

90448 1/51 3127 3/47 63127 6/48
78627: WD 3/44; Woodford Halse 26/1/46; Gorton 28/9/46; Woodford Halse 30/11/46; Annesley 26/3/49; Colwick 18/6/49; Woodford Halse 5/51; Agecroft 16/5/64; Rose Grove 31/10/64; Doncaster 19/6/65; Immingham 27/11/65
WITHDRAWN 12/65; Drapers, Hull 5/66

90449 4/49 3128 3/47
78628: WD 3/44; Colwick 1/12/45; York 23/10/48; Darlington 12/2/49; Dairycoates 8/9/51; Mold Jct 16/2/52; Colwick 17/5/52; Langwith Jct 22/6/54
WITHDRAWN 1/66; Drapers, Hull 5/66

90450 11/49 3129 4/47
78630: WD 3/44; Colwick 29/12/45; Gorton 28/9/46; Colwick 30/11/46; York 23/10/48; Dairycoates 14/5/49; York 10/49; Dairycoates 11/49; Darlington 1/51; Dairycoates 8/9/51
WITHDRAWN 6/67; Drapers, Hull 1/68

90451 5/50 3130 3/47 63130 4/48
4/48 78633: WD 4/44; Newport 29/12/45; Thornaby 14/6/58; Goole 7/9/63
WITHDRAWN 12/66; Drapers, Hull 3/67

90452 4/49 3131 3/47
78634: 4/44; March 29/12/45; Newport 26/4/47; Thornaby 14/6/58; Tyne Dock 15/6/63; Dairycoates 28/12/63
WITHDRAWN 6/65; Ellis Metals Ltd, Swalwell, Derwenthaugh 10/65

90453 3/49 3132 3/47
78635: WD 4/44; Colwick 1/12/45; New England 29/12/45; March 23/10/48; Colwick 3/10/53; March 6/10/56; Doncaster 23/3/57; Frodingham 16/12/61
WITHDRAWN 9/63; Doncaster Works 12/63

90454 8/51 3133 3/47 63133 10/48
78639: WD 4/44; March 1/12/45; New England 3/12/49; Retford 2/11/63
WITHDRAWN 6/65; Cox and Danks, Wadsley Bridge 2/66

90455 11/49 3134 2/47
78641: WD 4/44; Aberdeen Ferryhill 26/1/46
WITHDRAWN 9/62; Cowlairs Works 9/62

90456 10/50 3135 3/47
78642: WD 4/44; New England 1/12/45; Immingham 15/5/48; Frodingham 5/51
WITHDRAWN 2/66; Drapers, Hull 7/66

90457 5/50 3136 3/47
78645: WD 5/44; Colwick 1/12/45; Gorton 28/9/46; Colwick 30/11/46; York 23/10/48; Tyne Dock 12/48; Newport 12/2/49; Starbeck 23/2/57; Mirfield 3/10/59; Wakefield 25/1/64
WITHDRAWN 1/66; Drapers, Hull 5/66

90458 6/50 3137 2/47 63137 8/48
78646: WD 5/44; York 29/12/45; Heaton 28/9/46; Tyne Dock 18/12/48; Dairycoates 8/9/51; Goole 20/5/67
WITHDRAWN 6/67; Drapers, Hull 12/67

90459 5/50 3138 4/47
78648: WD 5/44; Colwick 1/12/45; Heaton then Gorton 28/9/46; Colwick 30/11/46; York 23/10/48; Newport 12/2/49; Thornaby 14/6/58; Tyne Dock 15/6/63; West Hartlepool 19/6/65
WITHDRAWN 6/67; Drapers, Hull 10/67

90460 4/49 3139 3/47
78649: WD 5/44; New England 1/47; Immingham 15/5/48; New England 4/51; Immingham 8/51; Staveley 29/12/51; Colwick 16/7/55; Immingham 20/9/58; Lincoln 24/12/60; Retford 5/10/63
WITHDRAWN 6/65; Cox and Danks, Wadsley Bridge 11/65

90461 3/49 3140 2/47 63140 4/48
78651: WD 5/44; March 1/12/45; Newport 26/4/47; Thornaby 14/6/58; Goole 24/2/62
WITHDRAWN 9/63; Darlington Works 9/63

90462 2/49 3141 3/47 63141 6/48
78653: WD 5/44; York 1/12/45; Heaton 28/9/46; Newport 12/2/49; Thornaby 14/6/58; Dairycoates 7/9/63
WITHDRAWN 1/67; Drapers, Hull 6/67

90463 9/50 3142 4/47 63142 4/48
78654: WD 5/44; Tay Bridge 29/12/45; Ayr 18/10/58; Ardrossan 21/1/61
WITHDRAWN 11/63; McLellans, Coatbridge 7/64

90464 4/50 3143 2/47
78655: WD 5/44; Thornton Jct 29/12/45; Kingmoor 16/6/49; St Margarets 3/10/53; Kingmoor 22/5/54; Sutton Oak 8/10/60
WITHDRAWN 3/64; Crewe Works 4/64

90465 6/50 3144 2/47 63144 6/48
78656: WD 5/44; Newport 26/1/46; Thornaby 14/6/58; Ardsley 30/6/62; Normanton 27/11/65
WITHDRAWN 1/67; Wards, Killamarsh 3/67

90466 12/50 3145 4/47 63145 6/48
78661: WD 5/44; Colwick 1/12/45; Woodford Halse 28/9/46; Annesley 23/8/47; Colwick 29/11/47; Chester (WR) 3/11/51; Shrewsbury 5/9/53; Leamington 3/10/53; Shrewsbury 27/3/54; Banbury 16/7/55; Southall 21/2/59; Warrington Dallam 8/9/62; Bolton 26/1/63; Colwick 3/10/64
WITHDRAWN 12/65; Drapers, Hull 4/66

90467 9/50 3146 3/47
78662: WD 5/44; Newport 29/12/45; Heaton 28/5/47; Newport 12/2/49; Darlington 17/6/50; Springhead 9/51; Neville Hill 10/9/55; York 11/7/59
WITHDRAWN 11/63; Darlington Works 1/64

90447, just arrived at its new home, former Midland shed Peterborough Spital Bridge, in 1950. It had acquired the painted front number in its earlier life as a Scottish engine. Photograph Paul Chancellor Collection.

A visitor from Woodford Halse, 90448 at Southall on 9 June 1963; it had been a 'GC' engine all its BR life, only going to the North West late on, in 1964. Photograph Peter Groom.

Scruffy and unkempt, 90454 stands in Retford (the old GC shed) yard on 9 September 1963; boiler with modified washout plugs, some of the boiler cladding sheets coming loose. Times were hard. Photograph Peter Groom.

An even more down-at-heel WD, Mirfield's 90457 under layers of priming deposit at Stockport Edgeley shed. Rearmost lubricator at 90 degrees to the others – see page 31 for instance. Photograph Paul Chancellor Collection.

A marvellous low angle look at 90459 but oh dear just look at the external condition of the loco. The BR totem on the tender has retreated into the grime but this shows how impressive the 'water carrier' of 5,000 gallons could be, topped off with nine tons of coal. A dint on the top edge has made a 'low point' for excess water to drain off, leaving streaking down the side. Perfect view of tender framing detail including the fashion in which the springs were connected in pairs and providing for once a look at the support brackets (linked to the internal baffles it is thought) under the tender running plate; the chalk marks note that one in the middle needs looking at. The tender springing was designed to make for easy running on the worn/hastily repaired/poorly ballasted track to be expected abroad. J.W.P. Rowledge in his book *Austerity 2-8-0s & 2-10-0s* relates that the rear pair of wheels in the first few tenders had a different flange profile, so that the axle was 'painted red and marked TRAILING AXLE to show that it was not interchangeable with the other three wheelsets.' This was discarded soon into the production series and the trailing wheelset made standard with the rest. Photograph www.transporttreasury.co.uk

A trio of WDs, headed by 90462, at the old Newport shed in April 1953. Photograph J. Davenport, Initial Photographics.

Western WD 90466, a Banbury and Southall engine for a while, at Oxford. Despite the 'tunnel' the original fire iron stowing point is being used; covered top feed. These feed pipes came from a pair of live steam injectors carried below the footplate, the pair of clacks having shut off valves to isolate a defective valve. Photograph B. Richardson, www.transporttreasury.co.uk

Early BR days and a partly renumbered 90467 (3146) with running number on front buffer beam, no smokebox number plate but shed code of 51B Newport. Nearing York on 3 June 1950. It was not officially renumbered until September 1950. Photograph A.G. Forsyth, Initial Photographics.

90468 10/49 3147 4/47
78663; WD 6/44; St Margarets 29/12/45; Motherwell 16/6/51; Hamilton 17/5/52; Motherwell 6/9/58; Thornton Jct 7/9/63
WITHDRAWN 4/67; Motherwell Machinery and Scrap Co, Wishaw 9/67

90469 10/49 3148 4/47
78664: WD 6/44; St Margarets 29/12/45; Doncaster 3/10/53; March 6/10/56; Frodingham 12/7/58
WITHDRAWN 11/64; Cox and Danks, Wadsley Bridge 3/65

90470 11/49 3149 2/47 63149 5/48
78665: WD 6/44; Gorton 28/9/46; Mexborough 28/5/47; Springhead 23/10/48; Dairycoates 2/50; Springhead 6/50; Wakefield 7/9/57; Sowerby Bridge 21/2/59; Wakefield 25/1/64
WITHDRAWN 12/66; Drapers, Hull 3/67

90471 4/49 3150 3/47
78667: WD 6/44; March 1/47; Colchester 20/3/48; March 10/51; Immingham 3/10/53; March 6/10/56; Canklow 5/9/59; Barrow Hill 19/6/65; Colwick 9/10/65; Frodingham 27/11/65; Doncaster 26/3/66;
WITHDRAWN 4/66; Drapers, Hull 9/66

90472 6/50 3151 2/47 63151 5/48
78668: WD 6/44; Thornton Jct 29/12/45
WITHDRAWN 12/63; Wards, Inverkeithing 6/64

90473 12/49 3152 3/47 63152 4/48
78670: WD 6/44; New England 29/12/45; Doncaster 1/3/47; March 26/7/47; Old Oak 20/3/48; March 11/48; Colwick 31/10/53
WITHDRAWN 9/62; Gorton Works 12/62

90474 10/50 3153 4/47
78673: WD 6/44; New England 29/12/45; Immingham 15/5/48; March 17/6/50; Woodford Halse 31/10/53; Aintree 16/5/64; Barrow Hill 3/10/64
WITHDRAWN 7/65; Wards, Killamarsh 10/65

90475 6/49 3154 3/47
78674: WD 6/44; Newport 29/12/45; York 15/6/57; Goole 18/6/60
WITHDRAWN 8/63; Darlington Works 9/63

90476 11/50 3155 2/47 63155 6/48
78676: WD 6/44; March 30/11/46; Colchester 20/3/48; March 15/5/48; Colwick 8/8/53; Doncaster 8/10/60
WITHDRAWN 7/65; Cox and Danks, Wadsley Bridge 2/66

90477 4/49 3156 3/47
78677: WD 6/44; Heaton 31/8/46; March 28/12/46; Colchester 20/3/48; March 10/51; Immingham 3/10/53; March 6/10/56; Doncaster 7/10/61; Immingham 27/11/65; Doncaster 26/2/66
WITHDRAWN 3/66; Arnott Young, Parkgate and Rawmarsh 6/66

90478 11/49 3157 4/47
78679: WD 6/44; Colwick 29/12/45; Gorton 28/9/46; Colwick 30/11/46; Annesley 20/2/48; Colwick 15/5/48; York 23/10/48; Dairycoates 15/5/49; York 8/10/49; Dairycoates 11/49; Springhead 6/50; Goole 15/11/58; Dairycoates 30/11/63; Goole 23/4/66; West Hartlepool 17/6/67
WITHDRAWN 9/67; Hughes Bolckows Ltd, North Blyth 11/67

90479 5/49 3158 4/47
78680: WD 6/44; York 1/12/45; Heaton 28/5/47; Tweedmouth 12/2/49; Dairycoates 4/51; Goole 17/5/58; Haverton Hill 14/6/58; Thornaby 11/7/59; West Hartlepool 1/6/63; Immingham 26/3/66
WITHDRAWN 10/66; Drapers, Hull 11/66

90480 3/49 3159 2/47 63159 3/48
78686: WD 7/44; York 1/12/45; Heaton 28/9/46; March 28/12/46; Stratford 4/4/59; Hornsey 26/3/60; Doncaster 15/7/61
WITHDRAWN 8/65; W George, Station Steel, Wath 9/65

90481 6/49 3160 3/47
78687: WD 7/44; Newport 26/1/46; Thornaby 14/6/58; Ardsley 14/7/62; Normanton 27/11/65; Royston 18/6/66
WITHDRAWN 10/66; Drapers, Hull 12/66

90482 11/50 3161 4/47
78690: WD 7/44; Newport 26/1/46; Heaton 28/5/47; Tyne Dock 18/12/48; Dairycoates 24/12/49; Springhead 15/12/56; Dairycoates 3/12/58; Wakefield 8/8/64; West Hartlepool 10/9/66
WITHDRAWN 7/67; Arnott Young, Dinsdale 11/67

90483 2/51 3162 3/47 63162 5/48
78691: WD 7/44; York 29/12/45; Heaton 28/5/47; Tweedmouth 12/2/49; Dairycoates 8/49; York 8/10/49; Immingham 8/51; Leamington 3/11/51; Shrewbury 3/10/53; Leamington 24/4/54; Banbury 5/9/59; Langwith Jct 29/12/62
WITHDRAWN 3/64; Darlington Works 3/64

90484 8/49 3163 4/47 63163 4/48
78692: WD 7/44; Woodford Halse 20/3/46; Annesley 23/8/47; Colwick 29/11/47; Woodford Halse 5/51; March 6/10/56; Stratford 24/12/60; Doncaster 15/7/61
WITHDRAWN 3/66; W. George, Station Steel, Wath 5/66

90485 11/50 3164 2/47 63164 6/48
78696: WD 8/44; York 29/12/45; Heaton 28/5/47; Tyne Dock 18/12/48; Malton 3/51; York 5/51; Immingham 8/51; Oxley 6/10/51; Banbury 29/12/51; Southall 1/11/52; Gloucester Horton Road 20/4/57; Worcester 13/7/57; Carmarthen 22/3/58; Reading 28/11/59; Southall 30/1/60; Gloucester Barnwood 3/4/60; Canton 18/6/60; Banbury 4/11/61; Mexborough 29/12/62; Canklow 21/3/64
WITHDRAWN 8/64; Wards, Killamarsh 11/64

90486 9/51 3165 3/47 63165 7/48
78697: WD 8/44; Woodford Halse 26/1/46; Staveley 29/11/52; Woodford Halse 8/1/53; Nottingham 22/2/64; Woodford Halse 18/4/64; Bolton 16/5/64; Aintree 3/10/64
WITHDRAWN 4/65; Wards, Killamarsh 7/65

90487 12/50 3166 3/47 63166 6/48
78698: WD 8/44; York 26/1/46; Heaton 28/5/47; Newport 12/2/49; York 15/6/57; Normanton 7/9/57
WITHDRAWN 8/63; Doncaster Works 10/63

90488 12/50 3167 4/47 63167 4/48
78699: WD 8/44; York 1/12/45; Heaton 28/5/47; Neville Hill 18/12/48; Newport 8/10/49; Thornaby 14/6/58; Royston 4/4/59
WITHDRAWN 12/64; Wards, Beighton, Sheffield 5/65

90489 2/50 3168 2/47 63168 4/48
78702: WD 8/44; Thornton Jct 29/12/45; Eastfield 6/11/54; Dawsholm 16/12/61; Grangemouth 30/11/63; Dunfermline 29/11/65; Grangemouth 30/11/63; Dunf'line 27/11/65
WITHDRAWN 4/67; Motherwell Machinery and Scrap Co, Wishaw, 9/67

90467 again but in full BR guise down to the totem on the tender side and looking reasonably clean. The location is Hull Springhead, now its home shed, on 10 April 1953. Photograph A.G. Forsyth, Initial Photographics.

A March WD, 90477, falls foul of the nets and snares in the rambling yard at Stratford shed, on 6 March 1958. It was running tender first of course and once again it was the tender that initially derailed; observe the bent tender brake stretcher bar just behind the screw coupling. From 'British Railways Illustrated,' Vol.16 No.5, February 2007: *Only the pony truck wheels and leading driving wheels remain on the rails, with the tread of the next driving wheels just on the rails. The driver would have applied the brakes just as soon as he felt the derailment, or noticed the strange behaviour of his tender. The breakdown boys ponder what would no doubt have been a fairly routine operation.* Photographs R.C. Riley, www.transporttreasury.co.uk

The GWR coal stage and water tank at Gloucester Horton Road is an unexpected backdrop for GC WD 90486, from Woodford Halse, on 10 May 1953. No doubt it is awaiting a duty back via Banbury and on to the GC route. Clack feeds outside boiler, 'by-passed' by the hand rail. Photograph A.R. Carpenter, www.transporttreasury.co.uk

90490 5/50 3169 2/47 63169 4/48
78703: WD 8/44; New England 29/12/45; Frodingham 6/51; New England 18/11/61; Immingham 22/9/62
WITHDRAWN 2/64; Doncaster Works 4/64

90491 9/49 3170 2/47 63170 6/48
78706: WD 8/44; Woodford Halse 20/3/46; Annesley 23/8/47; Colwick 29/11/47; New England then Colwick 23/10/48; Woodford Halse 11/2/56; March 6/10/56; Doncaster 23/3/57; Mexborough 14/6/58; Barrow Hill 21/3/64
WITHDRAWN 9/65; Drapers, Hull 12/65

90492 11/49 3171 2/47
78707: WD 8/44; Colwick 29/12/45; Gorton 29/8/46; Colwick 26/10/46; Annesley 1/51; Immingham 8/51; Langwith Jct 26/2/55; Colwick 21/5/60
WITHDRAWN 10/65; Drapers, Hull 2/66

90493 1/50 3172 2/47
78708: WD 8/44; St Margarets 29/12/45; Dunfermline 3/12/49; St Margarets 24/12/49; Motherwell 16/6/51; Dawsholm 1/12/51; Springs Branch 28/7/62; Frodingham 24/6/65
WITHDRAWN 2/66; Drapers, Hull 7/66

90494 8/50 3173 3/47 63173 3/48
78709: WD 8/44; New England 29/12/45; Tilbury 22/2/57; Doncaster 16/12/61
WITHDRAWN 9/62; Gorton Works 12/62

90495 7/50 3174 2/47 63174 4/48
78710: WD 8/44; New England 8/12/45; Colwick 27/11/48; New England 12/2/49; Mexborough 3/11/51
WITHDRAWN 12/62; Central Wagon Co, Ince, Wigan 1/64

90496 10/49 3175 2/47
78711: WD 8/44; St Margarets 29/12/45; Colwick 3/10/53; Doncaster 8/10/60; Barrow Hill 2/1/65
WITHDRAWN 4/65; Cashmores, Great Bridge 7/65

90497 9/50 3176 2/47 63176 6/48
78712: WD 8/44; Colwick 8/12/45; Gorton 28/9/46; Mexborough 28/5/47; Springhead 23/10/48; Wakefield 2/11/57
WITHDRAWN 3/63; Horwich Works 5/63

90498 6/49 3177 2/47 63177 4/48
78713: WD 9/44; Dunfermline 20/3/46; Thornton Jct 25/5/46; St Margarets 4/10/52; Doncaster 3/10/53; Mexborough 22/6/54; March 6/10/56; Stratford 23/2/57; March 15/11/58; Stratford 17/1/59; Doncaster 8/10/60; Frodingham 11/9/65
WITHDRAWN 2/66; W. George, Station Steel, Wath 8/66

90499 7/50 3178 2/47 63178 3/48
78716: WD 9/44; March 8/12/45; New England 1/3/47; Annesley 26/4/47; Colwick 29/11/47; Woodford Halse 10/51; Colwick 3/11/51; Mexborough 14/6/58
WITHDRAWN 12/63; Darlington Works 12/63

90500 8/49 3179 2/47 63179 3/48
78718: WD 9/44; Newport 8/12/45; York 18/4/53;
Newport 16/6/56; Thornaby 14/6/58;
Tyne Dock 23/3/63
WITHDRAWN 8/63; Darlington Works 9/63

90501 9/49 3180 2/47
79177: WD 9/44; St Margarets 29/12/45; Peterborough
(Spital Bridge) 12/8/50; March 20/2/60; Stratford
26/11/60; Cambridge 5/3/61; Tilbury 22/4/61; March
17/6/61; Doncaster 4/11/61; Retford 23/3/63;
Frodingham 19/6/65; Doncaster 27/11/65
WITHDRAWN 11/65; Wards, Beighton, Sheffield 1/66

90502 3/49 3181 3/47
79180: WD 9/44; New England 8/12/45; March 23/10/48;
Mexborough 21/4/51; New England 27/10/51; Langwith
Jct 31/12/54; Staveley (Central) 14/6/58;
Hornsey 30/1/60; New England 20/2/60
WITHDRAWN 5/63; Doncaster Works 10/63

90503 11/50 3182 2/47 63182 7/48
79185: WD 9/44; York 8/12/45; Heaton 28/5/47; Newport
18/12/48; York 15/6/57; Wakefield 7/9/57; Springhead
2/11/57; Dairycoates 13/12/58; Thornaby 20/2/60; Farnley
Jct 29/12/62; Royston 28/12/63; Normanton 8/10/66
WITHDRAWN 1/67; Wards, Killamarsh 4/67

90504 7/50 3183 3/47 63183 5/48
79187: WD 9/44; Woodford Halse 20/3/46
WITHDRAWN 5/63; Crewe Works 6/63

90505 11/49 3184 2/47
79191: WD 10/44; Colwick 29/12/45; Gorton 28/9/46;
Colwick 26/10/46; Annesley 20/2/48; Colwick 15/5/48;
Thornton Jct 12/2/49; Kingmoor 16/7/49; Motherwell
7/10/50; Kingmoor 4/11/50; Ayr 26/1/52;
Ardrossan 28/1/61
WITHDRAWN 6/62; Campbells, Shieldhall 2/64

90506 5/51 3185 2/47 63185 11/48
79192: WD 10/44; March 20/3/46; Colwick 31/10/53;
Mexborough 22/6/54; Doncaster 24/12/60; Immingham
27/11/65
WITHDRAWN 1/66; Drapers, Hull 5/66

90507 9/50 3186 2/47
79200: WD 10/44; Woodford Halse 1/46;
Springs Branch 21/3/59
WITHDRAWN 7/63; Crewe Works 9/63

90508 9/50 3187 2/47 63187 1/49
79211: WD 11/44; Eastfield then Thornton Jct 20/3/46;
Aberdeen Ferryhill 28/9/46; March 28/12/46; Colchester
20/3/48; March 27/10/51; Immingham 3/10/53; Langwith
Jct 26/2/55; Stratford 19/11/55; Mexborough 28/12/62
WITHDRAWN 12/62; Central Wagon Co, Ince, Wigan
1/64

90509 9/50 3188 3/47 63188 6/48
79216: WD 11/44; Woodford Halse 3/46; Springs Branch
21/3/59; Barrow Hill 3/10/64
WITHDRAWN 8/65; Garnham, Harris and Elton,
Chesterfield 10/65

90510 11/50 3189 2/47
79236: WD 12/44; New England 29/12/45;
March 23/10/48; Immingham 3/10/53; Colwick 5/11/60
WITHDRAWN 7/65; Cox and Danks,
Wadsley Bridge 4/66

90511 2/50 3190 2/47 63190 6/48
79240: WD 12/44; York 26/1/46; Heaton 28/5/47;
Tweedmouth 29/11/47; York 12/8/50; Springhead
18/4/53; Dairycoates 13/12/58; Royston 20/2/60;
Wakefield 2/11/63
WITHDRAWN 6/64; Cohens, Middlesbrough 10/64

90512 2/51 3191 2/47 63191 6/48
79241: WD 12/44; Woodford Halse 26/1/46; Annesley
23/8/47; Colwick 29/11/47; New England 13/12/49;
Frodingham 3/10/53
WITHDRAWN 9/62; Gorton Works 11/62

90513 9/50 3192 3/47 63192 7/48
79245: WD 1/45; Woodford Halse 20/4/46; Annesley
23/8/47; Colwick 29/11/47; Thornton Jct 12/2/49;
Kingmoor 16/7/49; Dunfermline Upper 19/11/49;
Thornton Jct 3/12/55
WITHDRAWN 7/62; Inverurie Works 9/62

90514 8/50 3193 3/47 63193 5/48
79247: WD 1/45; New England 5/46; Plaistow 19/4/58;
March 13/6/59; Plaistow 31/10/59; Tilbury 28/11/59; New
England 18/11/61; Retford 2/11/63; Colwick 19/6/65;
Frodingham 4/12/65
WITHDRAWN 1/66; Drapers, Hull 5/66

90515 10/49 3194 2/47 63194 4/48
79251: WD 1/45; Tay Bridge 29/12/45;
Dunfermline 26/1/63
WITHDRAWN 11/65; Campbells, Shieldhall 2/66

90516 12/49 3195 3/47 63195 6/48
79253: WD 1/45; Woodford Halse 20/3/46; Toton
23/11/63; Woodford Halse 18/4/64; Newton Heath
16/5/64; Aintree 3/10/64; Frodingham 24/6/65;
Doncaster 27/11/65
WITHDRAWN 11/65; Garnham, Harris and Elton,
Chesterfield 6/66

90517 10/50 3196 2/47 63196 9/48
79285: WD 3/45; Newport 12/45; York 20/8/54; Newport
16/6/56; Thornaby 14/6/58; York 29/12/62
WITHDRAWN 5/66; Drapers, Hull 8/66

90518 10/51 3197 2/47 63197 4/48
79288: WD 3/45; York 8/12/45; Newport 29/12/45;
Heaton 28/5/47; Neville Hill 18/12/48; York 8/10/49;
Starbeck 19/11/55; York 26/9/59
WITHDRAWN 2/66; Thompsons, Stockton on Tees 5/66

90519 2/51 3198 2/47 63198 1/49
79305: WD 4/45; New England 25/5/46; March 18/9/48;
Colwick 24/4/54; Barnsley 25/4/59; Mexborough
27/6/59; Canklow 7/3/64; Barrow Hill 21/3/64
WITHDRAWN 9/64; Drapers, Hull 5/65

90520 3/49 3199 3/47
79308: WD 5/45; Woodford Halse 20/3/46; Toton
23/11/63; Woodford Halse 18/4/64; Newton Heath
16/5/64; Aintree 3/10/64
WITHDRAWN 2/65; Wards, Beighton, Sheffield 8/65

90521 9/51
77050; Shrewsbury 6/43; Swansea Victoria 10/7/43; WD
16/9/44; Colwick 1/47; Barnsley 5/47; Neville Hill 11/47;
Mexborough 27/8/49; Canklow 7/3/64;
Barrow Hill 21/3/64
WITHDRAWN 10/64; Smiths, Ecclesfield 1/65

90502 and a pick-up at Hadley Wood in June 1960; one of the new tunnels to the left. Photograph Paul Chancellor Collection.

No doubt about the location... This is York, Holgate Platforms in fact, when a pride was taken in keeping lineside gardens tended. Local 50A WD 90517 (York was its last shed) is working south on 25 June 1964 on a short, mainly mineral train. This was one of Mr. Draper's '205'. Photograph B.W.L. Brooksbank, Initial Photographics.

90522 9/49
77051: Shrewsbury 6/43; Swansea Victoria 10/7/43; WD 27/1/45; Heaton 4/47; March 8/47; Colchester 15/5/48; March 27/10/51; Stratford 26/11/60; Cambridge 25/3/61; Tilbury 22/4/61; March 17/6/61; Doncaster 28/10/61; Retford 23/3/63
WITHDRAWN 5/65; Drapers, Hull 7/65

90523 10/49
77052: Shrewsbury 6/43; Swansea Victoria 10/7/43; WD 27/1/45; Feltham 2/11/46; Perth 11/2/50; Newton Heath 8/9/51
WITHDRAWN 12/62; Crewe Works 10/63

90524 2/49
77053: Shrewsbury 6/43; Swansea Victoria 10/7/43; Shrewsbury 11/11/44; WD 27/1/45; Canton 17/5/47; Pontypool Road 10/7/48; Hereford 27/11/48; Worcester 21/4/51; Gloucester Horton Road 8/9/51; Canton 21/2/53; Westhouses 11/7/59; Woodford Halse 31/10/59
WITHDRAWN 5/63; Crewe Works 9/63

90525 11/49
77054: Shrewsbury 6/43; Swansea Victoria 10/7/43; Shrewsbury 11/11/44; WD 27/1/45; Newton Heath 3/12/49; Lees 12/7/58; Newton Heath 18/4/64
WITHDRAWN 5/64; Slag Reduction Co, Rotherham 1/65

90526 11/49
77055: Shrewsbury 6/43; WD 27/1/45; Annesley 8/47; Tyne Dock 11/47; Dairycoates 12/2/49; Staveley 27/8/49; Huddersfield; 25/3/50; New England 30/3/52; Stratford 29/1/55; Plaistow 26/2/55; Mexborough 21/5/55
WITHDRAWN 12/62; Central Wagon Co, Ince, Wigan 1/64

90527 4/49
77056: Shrewsbury 6/43; WD 27/1/45; Feltham 2/11/46; Farnley Jct 31/12/51; Huddersfield 23/2/52; Farnley Jct 14/2/53; Shrewsbury 8/8/53; Farnley Jct 5/9/53; Aintree 21/4/56
WITHDRAWN 5/63; Horwich Works 6/63

90528 8/49
77057: Shrewsbury 19/6/43; WD 27/1/45; Immingham 5/47; Woodford Halse 11/47; Colwick 23/10/48; New England 3/12/49; Colwick 11/2/56; Peterborough (Spital Bridge) 5/10/57; March 20/2/60; Stratford 26/11/60; Doncaster 23/9/61; Retford 23/3/63; Colwick; 19/6/65
WITHDRAWN 9/65; Drapers, Hull 1/66

90529 2/49
77058: Shrewsbury 19/6/43; WD 30/12/44; Oxford 22/2/47; Newton Abbot 1/3/47; Southall 19/5/56; Carmarthen 22/3/58; Llanelly 18/6/60; Ebbw Jct 30/6/62; Mexborough 29/12/62; Canklow 7/3/64; Barrow Hill 21/3/64; Langwith Jct 9/10/65
WITHDRAWN 11/65; Drapers, Hull 2/66

90530 1/50
77059: Shrewsbury 19/6/43; WD 30/12/44; Feltham; 2/11/46; Perth 11/2/50; Newton Heath 8/9/51; Patricroft 20/2/60; Newton Heath 26/1/63
WITHDRAWN 5/63; Crewe Works 8/63

90531 6/50
77060: Shrewsbury 19/6/43; WD 27/1/45; Goole 12/8/50
WITHDRAWN 9/63; Darlington Works 9/63

90532 7/49
77061: Shrewsbury 19/6/43; WD 27/1/45; Colwick 1/47; Annesley 3/47; Woodford Halse 11/47; Colwick 23/10/48; Woodford Halse 11/8/51; Staveley 17/5/52; Colwick 9/8/52; Northampton 24/4/54; Mold Jct 20/4/57; Bidston 11/7/59; Mold Jct 8/8/59; Widnes 21/4/62
WITHDRAWN 11/62; Gorton Works 1/63

90533 2/49
77062: Shrewsbury 19/6/43; WD 27/1/45; Feltham 2/11/46; Bricklayers Arms 12/3/49; Newton Heath 11/8/51; Agecroft 22/2/64; Gorton 31/10/64; Aintree 27/2/65; Retford 24/6/65; Colwick 19/6/65
WITHDRAWN 2/66; Drapers, Hull 6/66

90534 10/49
77063: Shrewsbury 19/6/43; WD 30/12/44; Thornton Jct 3/47; Dunfermline 26/1/63
WITHDRAWN 10/66; Motherwell Machinery and Scrap Co, Wishaw 2/67

90535 8/51
77064: Shrewsbury 10/7/43; WD 30/12/44; Oxley 17/5/47; Shrewsbury 17/6/50; Newton Heath 16/12/50; Aintree 3/12/55; Springs Branch 13/7/63; Lostock Hall 5/10/63
WITHDRAWN 10/64; Wards, Beighton, Sheffield 3/65

90536 4/50
77066: Gorton 6/43; York 7/43; Springhead 4/44; Dairycoates 11/11/44; WD 1/45; Thornton Jct 8/47; Grangemouth 18/6/49; Polmadie 19/4/52; Aberdeen Ferryhill 24/3/62
WITHDRAWN 9/63; Inverurie Works 10/63

90537 7/50
77067: Gorton 6/43; York 8/43; Springhead 4/44; Dairycoates 11/11/44; Springhead 12//44; WD 1/45; York 3/47; Springhead 5/47; Mexborough 23/10/48; Doncaster 16/6/51; March 6/10/56; Doncaster 23/2/57; Frodingham 5/11/60; Doncaster 27/11/65
WITHDRAWN 2/66; Drapers, Hull 7/66

90538 8/49
77068: York 6/43; Severn Tunnel Jct 11/44; WD 1/45; Mexborough 11/47; March 6/10/56; Doncaster 23/2/57; Immingham 27/11/65; Doncaster 26/2/66
WITHDRAWN 4/66; Drapers, Hull 10/66

90539 12/50
77070: Gorton 7/43; York 8/43; Springhead 4/44; WD 1/45; Thornton Jct 1/47; Grangemouth 19/12/59
WITHDRAWN 11/63; McWilliams, Shettleston 6/64

90540 1/50
77071: York 7/43; Springhead 4/44; WD 12/44; March 9/47; Frodingham 21/4/51
WITHDRAWN 7/65; Cox and Danks, Wadsley Bridge 4/66

90541 4/49
77072: York 7/43; Springhead 4/44; WD 12/44; Lostock Hall 23/4/49; Rose Grove 28/11/64
WITHDRAWN 5/65; Cashmores, Great Bridge 8/65

90542 11/50
77073: York 7/43; WD 1/45; Dunfermline Upper 6/9/47
WITHDRAWN 7/63; Inverurie Works 9/63

A visitor to Cardiff on 14 March 1953, a rather clean 90520 from Woodford Halse; for years there had been mineral flows from the heart of England to South Wales in connection with the iron and steel industry. Photograph Stephen Gradidge.

Pairing at Lees (Oldham) shed with snowplough-fitted 90525 in front, September 1958. Smokebox clean after the inexplicable ways of the time; the reason seems to have been repairs to the box only. Thoroughly 'old time' boiler arrangements. Lees, presumably wary that it might be pinched, have taken the precaution of fixing a shed plate to the snow plough! Photograph J. Davenport, www.transporttreasury.co.uk

More ex-works finery, in the shape of 90525 at Crewe South shed; excellent detail always shows up in these 'fresh' views, particularly when the light is right. Photograph D. Forsyth, Paul Chancellor Collection.

The unique 90527, ex-works at Crewe on 27 February 1960, outside the Paint Shop; this was the one that was rebalanced to diminish the sometimes considerable 'fore-and-aft' movement and, though successful, no further engines were so altered. While the class worked on BR there were always complaints that the riding was unacceptably rough.

142

90543 9/50
77074: Gorton 7/43; York 8/43; Springhead 4/44; WD 2/45; Feltham 9/47; Mirfield 17/6/50; York 14/6/58; Wakefield 28/11/59
WITHDRAWN 2/65; Wards, Beighton, Sheffield 8/65

90544 5/51
77075: Stratford 7/43; March 9/43; Neasden 6/44; WD 1/45; Springhead 3/47; Colwick 23/10/48; Ebbw Jct 1/12/51; Southall 3/11/62; Frodingham 29/12/62; Mexborough 26/1/63; Canklow 7/3/64; Barrow Hill 21/3/64
WITHDRAWN 6/64; Wards, Killamarsh 10/64

90545 3/51
77076: Gorton then Stratford 7/43; March 10/43; Neasden 6/44; WD 12/44; Eastfield 8/47; St Margarets 23/2/52; Colwick 3/10/53; Langwith Jct 22/6/54; Colwick 21/5/60
WITHDRAWN 10/65; Drapers, Hull 1/66

90546 10/50
77077: Stratford 7/43; March 9/43; Neasden 6/44; WD 12/44; Oxley 17/5/47; Taunton 9/8/47; Swansea Victoria 20/5/50; Agecroft 16/12/50
WITHDRAWN 2/64; Crewe Works 3/64

90547 9/50
77078: Stratford 7/43; March 9/43; Neasden 6/44; WD 12/44; Thornton Jct 3/47; Dunfermline 4/10/52
WITHDRAWN 10/66; Motherwell Machinery and Scrap Co, Wishaw 2/67

90548 11/51
77079: Stratford 8/43; March 9/43; Neasden 6/44; WD 11/44; Oxley 19/4/47; Shrewsbury 15/7/50; Newton Heath 16/12/50; Patricroft 21/4/62; Newton Heath 26/1/63
WITHDRAWN 5/64; Slag Reduction Co, Ickles, Rotherham 1/65

90549 3/51
77080: Gorton then New England 8/43; WD 12/44; Eastfield 15/5/48; Motherwell 18/9/48; Eastfield 28/11/48; Dawsholm 12/8/50; Polmadie 9/8/58; Ayr 8/10/60; Ardrossan 25/2/61; Ayr 21/4/62
WITHDRAWN 12/62; Campbells, Shieldhall 12/63

90550 8/49
77081: Gorton then New England 8/43; WD 1/45; Neville Hill 6/47; Mexborough 27/8/49; March 27/10/51; Doncaster 23/3/57; Frodingham 20/2/60
WITHDRAWN 9/62; Crewe Works 12/62

90551 12/50
77085: Gorton then New England 8/43; WD 12/44; Annesley 4/47; Woodford Halse 29/11/47; Colwick 20/2/48; Annesley 27/11/48; Colwick 12/2/49; Staveley 27/10/51; New England 30/3/52; Stratford 29/1/55; Doncaster 8/10/60; Retford 1/6/63; Frodingham 19/6/65; Doncaster 27/11/65
WITHDRAWN 4/66; Drapers, Hull 10/66

90552 3/49
77086: Gorton then New England 8/43; WD 1/45; Bricklayers Arms 1/46; Newton Heath 8/9/51; Belle Vue 16/2/52; Aintree 13/12/58
WITHDRAWN 5/64; Central Wagon Co, Ince, Wigan 6/65

90553 5/50
77087: Gorton then New England 8/43; Ebbw Jct 11/44; WD 3/45; Dunfermline Upper 9/47; Grangemouth 1/12/62
WITHDRAWN 11/65; Campbells, Shieldhall 2/66

90554 3/49
77088: Gorton then New England 8/43; Severn Tunnel Jct 24/10/44; WD 1/45; March 10/47; New England 12/8/50; Langwith Jct 22/6/54; Colwick 21/5/60
WITHDRAWN 9/62; Crewe Works 11/62

90555 2/50
77089: Gorton then New England 8/43; WD 3/45; St Margarets 1/47; Canal 17/4/48; St Margarets 12/3/49; Accrington 8/9/51; Bury 31/12/51; Agecroft 15/6/63
WITHDRAWN 6/64; Central Wagon Co, Ince, Wigan 12/64

90556 12/50
77090: Gorton 8/43; New England 9/43; WD 1/45; Bricklayers Arms 1/46; Agecroft 11/8/51; Wakefield 8/9/51; Fleetwood 25/2/56; Lostock Hall 23/2/57; Lower Darwen 10/9/60
WITHDRAWN 3/65; Wards, Beighton, Sheffield 5/65

90557 10/49
77092: Gorton 8/43; New England 9/43; WD 1/45; Wakefield 8/10/49; Rose Grove 24/12/49; Canklow 3/10/64; Doncaster 19/6/65
WITHDRAWN 9/65; Wards, Beighton, Sheffield 11/65

90558 3/49
77094: Gorton then New England 9/43; Old Oak 11/44; WD 1/45; Bricklayers Arms 1/46; Newton Heath 11/8/51; Agecroft 13/12/58; Gorton 1/6/63; Canklow 3/10/64; Langwith Jct 19/6/65
WITHDRAWN 11/65; W. George, Station Steel, Wath 2/66

90559 9/50
77095: Gorton then March 9/43; WD 11/44; Heaton 1/47; Newport 5/47; New England 27/8/49; March 5/10/57; Ipswich 4/4/59; March 20/2/60; Stratford 5/11/60; March 17/6/61; Doncaster 7/10/61
WITHDRAWN 12/62; Central Wagon Co, Ince, Wigan 12/63

90560 11/50
77096: Gorton then March 9/43; WD 11/44; Dunfermline Upper 9/47; St Margarets 4/10/52; Dunfermline Upper 6/11/54; Grangemouth 1/12/62; Dunfermline 27/11/65; Sunderland 3/12/66; Dunfermline 18/2/67
WITHDRAWN 4/67; Motherwell Machinery and Scrap Co, Wishaw 9/67

90561 10/50
77097: Gorton then March 9/43; Neasden 6/44; WD 11/44; Oxley 17/5/47; Tyseley 12/7/47; Shrewsbury 15/7/50; Newton Heath 16/12/50; Wigan 17/1/59; Newton Heath 27/2/60; Aintree 27/6/64; Springs Branch 11/7/64
WITHDRAWN 3/65; Wards, Beighton, Sheffield 8/65

90562 4/50
77098: Gorton then March 9/43; Neasden 6/44; WD 12/44; Feltham 12/47; Mirfield 24/3/51; Farnley Jct 5/9/53
WITHDRAWN 10/62; Gorton Works 3/63

90563 11/52
77099: Gorton then March 9/43; Neasden 6/44; WD 11/44; Pontypool Road 14/6/47; Shrewsbury 21/2/53; Leamington Spa 3/10/53; Shrewsbury 24/4/54; St Philips Marsh 6/11/54; Westhouses 11/7/59; Woodford Halse 19/12/59; Nottingham 22/2/64; Aintree 16/5/64
WITHDRAWN 8/65; Cashmores, Newport 6/66

90564 11/50
77101: Gorton then March 9/43; WD 11/44; Bricklayers Arms 1/46; Agecroft 11/8/51; Lostock Hall 18/6/60; Agecroft 7/10/61; Gorton 1/6/63; Lees 5/10/63; Gorton 22/2/64
WITHDRAWN 5/64; Slag Reduction Co, Rotherham 1/65

Stratford's 90551 within sight of its home shed, clanking west through the station on 27 June 1956. It is only a short train, a mixed bag of battered wooden wagons; a pick-up coming home from Essex perhaps, though the lamp code is a mystery. 90551 ended up at Doncaster, conveniently placing it to become one of Mr Draper's 205. Photograph Stephen Gradidge.

90552 at Newton Heath shed early in BR days, in 1951, awaiting smokebox number plate; still with air pump and associated piping and fittings as well as the smokebox door irons from its days on the Southern. Absent as yet is the little curved grab iron on the smokebox rim. Photograph B.K.B. Green, Initial Photographics.

The working life cycle of the WD, illustrated in two very different views. Top, 90555 is fresh and shining in black after overhaul at Crewe; for every WD there now followed a descent into unending dirt and grime, and the plodding daily round of a blackened hulk like 90556, below. Then repairs again and a few weeks of respectability. Both have the 'old style' boiler arrangement but only 90555 has the little cinder guards on the cabside. Photographs Paul Chancellor Collection.

A seldom-recorded shed, Walton-on-the-Hill in Liverpool, 8 January 1961 finds 90563 in excellent condition by the look of it, a visitor from Woodford Halse shed. Once of the Western Region, it has the covered top feed and dual purpose lamp irons. Behind is O4 2-8-0 63573 a one-time Gorton loco. The shed was reduced from six to four roads in the 1950s and was the only one in the system to get the suffix R when it became 8R in September 1963.

90563 at Southall shed, 4 November 1962. Another 'visitor from Woodford Halse'; the phrase crops up all the time, so their WDs certainly got about a bit! It was getting due for shopping, and was ex-works at Crewe by June 1963. Photograph Peter Groom.

90565 8/52
77102: Gorton 9/43; March 10/43; WD 1/45; Oxley 14/6/47; Ebbw Jct 6/9/47; Canton 17/5/52; Gloucester Barnwood 28/11/59; Ebbw Jct 16/7/60; Southall 5/11/60; Didcot 25/3/61; Banbury 22/4/61; Southall 23/9/61
WITHDRAWN 10/62; Crewe Works 1/64

90566 1/50
77103: Gorton 9/43; March 10/43; WD 1/45; Hither Green 14/6/47; Mold Jct 3/11/51; Birkenhead 18/11/61; Warrington 29/9/62; Sutton Oak 26/1/63
WITHDRAWN 7/64; Central Wagon Co, Ince, Wigan 1/65

90567 5/51
77104: Gorton 9/43; March 10/43; WD 2/45; York 3/47; Springhead 5/47; Dairycoates 25/2/50; Mold Jct 16/2/52; Colchester 17/5/52; Langwith Jct 22/6/54; March 14/7/56; Doncaster 23/3/57; Mexborough 14/6/58; Canklow 7/3/64; Barrow Hill 14/3/64
WITHDRAWN 11/64; Smiths, Ecclesfield 3/65

90568 4/49
77106: Gorton 9/43; March 10/43; WD 11/44; Severn Tunnel Jct 19/4/47; Canton 12/7/47; Ebbw Jct 5/3/50; Swansea Victoria 3/6/50; Bury 2/10/53; Patricroft 21/1/61; Newton Heath 26/1/63
WITHDRAWN 1/64; Crewe Works 3/64

90569 5/50
77107: Gorton 9/43; Colwick 10/43; WD 1/45; Dunfermline Upper 9/43; St Margarets 18/11/50; Doncaster 23/3/57; Immingham 31/7/65
WITHDRAWN 10/65; Drapers, Hull 3/66

90570 9/50
77108: Gorton 9/43; Colwick 10/43; WD 12/44; Feltham 5/47; York 12/8/50; Aintree 16/6/51; Wigan (Central) 28/11/53; Newton Heath 27/2/60; Patricroft 26/3/60; Woodford Halse 23/2/63; Kirkby-in-Ashfield 22/2/64; Woodford Halse 18/4/64
WITHDRAWN 5/64; Cashmores, Great Bridge 10/64

90571 3/49
77111: Gorton then Colwick 10/43; Pontypool Road 9/44; WD 3/45; York 9/47; Dairycoates 3/12/49; Springhead 17/6/50; Dairycoates 15/11/58; York 23/9/61
WITHDRAWN 11/63; Darlington Works 12/63

90572 10/50
77115: Gorton then Colwick 10/43; WD 11/44; Oxley 17/5/47; Chester (WR) 14/6/47; Banbury 14/6/52; Canton 12/7/52; Southall 13/6/59; Canton 11/7/59; Southall 22/9/62; Mexborough 29/12/62; Barrow Hill 25/1/64; Langwith Jct 9/10/65
WITHDRAWN 2/66; Drapers, Hull 6/66

90573 9/51
77116: Gorton then Colwick 10/43; Canton 9/44; WD 1/45; St Philips Marsh 11/46; Ebbw Jct 6/10/51; Aberdare 1/11/52; Oxford 21/3/53; Gloucester Horton Road 16/5/53; Canton 4/10/58; Southall 23/9/62; Frodingham 29/12/62; Mexborough 26/1/63; Canklow 7/3/64; Barrow Hill 14/3/64
WITHDRAWN 8/65; Garnham, Harris and Elton, Chesterfield 10/65

90574 10/50
77118: Gorton then March 10/43; WD 1/45; Woodford Halse 5/47; Annesley 8/47; Woodford Halse 11/47; Colwick 18/12/48; Woodford Halse 16/6/51; Springs Branch 21/3/59
WITHDRAWN 2/64; Central Wagon Co, Ince, Wigan 1/65

90575 11/49
77119: Gorton then March 10/43; WD 2/45; Dunfermline Upper 9/47
WITHDRAWN 7/62; Cowlairs Works, 3/63

90576 11/51
77120: Gorton then March 10/43; WD 11/44; Newport 3/47; Rose Grove 29/1/49; Newton Heath 28/11/53; Aintree 23/4/60; Rose Grove 14/7/62
WITHDRAWN 3/63; Crewe Works 3/63

90577 8/51
77121: Gorton then March 10/43; WD 11/44; New England 3/47; Langwith Jct 3/12/54; Colwick 21/5/60; Lincoln 5/11/60; Retford 7/9/63
WITHDRAWN 5/65; Drapers, Hull 7/65

90578 11/50
77122: Gorton then March 11/43; WD 11/44; Feltham 12/47; Mirfield 15/7/50; York 14/6/58
WITHDRAWN 12/63; Darlington Works 1/64

90579 2/49
77123: Gorton then March 10/43; WD 11/44; Newport 17/5/47; Canton 12/7/47; Ebbw Jct 25/3/50; Swansea Victoria 3/6/50; Swindon 27/1/51; Banbury 21/4/51; Canton 5/10/55; Southall 29/9/62; Mexborough 29/12/62; Canklow 7/3/64; Barrow Hill 14/3/64
WITHDRAWN 2/65; Arnott Young, Parkgate and Rawmarsh 7/65

90580 9/51
77124: Gorton then March 10/43; WD 11/44; March 4/47; Mexborough 7/3/52; Canklow 7/3/64; Barrow Hill 14/3/64; Doncaster 8/8/64
WITHDRAWN 8/65; Wards, Beighton Sheffield 11/65

90581 6/49
77126: Gorton then March 10/43; WD 11/44; Wakefield 11/6/49; Sowerby Bridge 14/2/53; Wakefield 8/8/53
WITHDRAWN 11/64; Wards, Beighton, Sheffield 4/65

90582 4/49
77127: Gorton then March 11/43; WD 11/44; March 8/47; Mexborough 21/4/51; Doncaster 16/6/51; Mexborough 4/10/52
WITHDRAWN 3/64; Wards, Beighton, Sheffield 6/64

90583 2/51
77128: Gorton then March 11/43; WD 11/44; York 3/47; Springhead 5/47; Mexborough 23/10/48; Immingham 29/12/51; Retford 5/10/63
WITHDRAWN 4/64; Smiths, Ecclesfield 7/64

90584 3/51
77129: Longmoor 11/43; Newport 3/47; Rose Grove 29/1/49; Wigan (Central) 2/10/54; Newton Heath 25/1/58; Hellifield 12/7/58; Lostock Hall 13/12/58; Rose Grove 11/8/62; Bolton 25/1/64; Aintree 21/3/64
WITHDRAWN 8/64; Cashmores, Great Bridge 2/65

90585 2/49
77130: Gorton then March 11/43; WD 11/44; Old Oak 19/4/47; Motherwell 11/2/50; Kingmoor 4/11/50; Old Oak 8/9/51; Ebbw Jct 6/10/51; Banbury 21/5/55; Springs Branch 11/8/62; Gorton 20/4/63; Springs Branch 1/6/63
WITHDRAWN 4/65; Wards, Beighton, Sheffield 7/65

90586 8/49
77135: Gorton then Newport 11/43; Severn Tunnel Jct 24/10/44; WD 2/45; Neville Hill 9/47; Springhead 15/5/48; Dairycoates 25/2/50; Springhead 17/6/50; Dairycoates 13/12/58
WITHDRAWN 2/66; Drapers, Hull 6/66

Lot of clanking going on at York on 24 March 1963 as 90566 works past York Racecourse Platform with Holgate bridge in the background. It was a Sutton Oak engine at the time. AWS-fitted and as usual thoroughly begrimed, so much so that it appears to be WD 'No.6'. Photograph A.G. Forsyth, Initial Photographics.

90568 rolling through Cheadle Hulme on a rather long and mixed goods, 15 September 1951. An ex-Western loco, it carries the by-now obsolete fire iron 'tunnel' and the residual lamp irons, together with the faded buffer beam painted number; the clack cover has disappeared and is probably serving some useful storage purpose back in the Wakefield workshop. Photograph B.K.B. Green, Initial Photographics.

90569, once a Scottish engine, on the GN with coal, at Walton, 22 June 1960. Modified washout plugs and hand rail, projecting filler for rearmost 'gravity' sander instead of 'flush' one. Photograph Paul Chancellor Collection.

Patricroft's 90570, approaching Manchester Victoria under that splendid signal gantry, probably about 1960, with the East box in the background; 108 levers now reduced to 96. The WD is one that had a little 'cinder guard' strip of glass. Photograph J. Davenport, Initial Photographics.

WDs in one of the York roundhouses; this would be about 1961, when both 90571 and 90518 were residents. Photograph Paul Chancellor Collection.

A Western Region 'crate', 90572 left in 1962 to eke out its days on the coal of Nottinghamshire and Yorkshire. On 22 April 1955 it was (sort of) fresh out of repair/painting at Crewe (note dual purpose lamp irons) inexplicably carrying a 26A Newton Heath shed plate. This could have been an error in the works, for if it was sent to Manchester, the move is not recorded. Photograph Peter Groom.

The usual catastrophic decline in cleanliness has ensued as we find 90572 on the Eastern Region in its latter years. The top lamp iron at least, has reverted to 'normal'. Photograph Paul Chancellor Collection.

That's more like it. Smooth lines and shiny paint on 90574, in an unusual view at Crewe, by the traverser. Some sort of plate, with instructions perhaps, hangs from the running plate; the window is 'up'. Photograph D. Forsyth, Paul Chancellor Collection.

That familiar WD backdrop, Cheadle Heath, provides for a fine view of 90576 as it waits the 'away'. Modified washout plugs, hand rail, etc. A schoolboy, agog, has been invited onto the footplate from the platform. He still remembers it, no doubt. Photograph D. Forsyth, Paul Chancellor Collection.

A splendid 90579, of Canton shed, passes through Cardiff station on 30 August 1956. Good view of the WR ATC conduit and the collector shoe behind the buffer beam. It did not require the protecting plate of the BR AWS arrangement. Like most WR WDs it ended life on another Region, in this case the Eastern, at Barrow Hill. The pace of WR dieselisation allowed the Region to rapidly offload its WDs. Photograph Stephen Gradidge.

90581 in peculiar state at Crewe, at an unknown date. Plain black engines like WDs did not warrant a spell in the Paint Shop so presumably in the middle of painting, poor old 90581 has been dragged out to make way for something more urgent in Ten Shop. Will it be finished here or taken back inside? Photograph J. Davenport, Initial Photographics.

Darlington Works on 7 July 1956 with 90587 awaiting return to Mexborough, a shed that in 1950 had nearly sixty of them. In front is class L1 67729, from Stratford. Oval Vulcan builder's plate on expansion link bracket. Photograph A.R. Carpenter, www.transporttreasury.co.uk

90587 6/51
77138: Gorton then Newport 11/43; Swindon 11/44; WD 1/45; Springhead; 3/47; Mexborough 23/10/48; Canklow 7/3/64; Barrow Hill 14/3/64; Langwith Jct 9/10/65
WITHDRAWN 11/65; W. George, Station Steel, Wath 2/66

90588 6/50
77141: Gorton 11/43; Severn Tunnel Jct 11/44; WD 3/45; Farnley Jct 15/7/50; Huddersfield 20/4/63; Thornaby 28/12/63; West Hartlepool 31/10/64
WITHDRAWN 2/67; Drapers, Hull 10/67

90589 2/49
77142: Gorton 11/43; Pontypool Road 11/44; WD 1/45; St Philips Marsh 19/4/47; Swindon 28/1/50; Shrewsbury 12/8/50; Newton Heath 30/12/50; Agecroft 5/10/57; Lees 28/12/57; Newton Heath 12/7/58; Toton 21/4/62; Woodford Halse 26/1/63; Kirkby-in-Ashfield 22/2/64; Woodford Halse 18/4/64
WITHDRAWN 5/64; Crewe Works 6/64

90590 9/51
77144: Gorton 12/43; Newport 12/43; Banbury 11/44; WD 2/45; Mexborough 10/47
WITHDRAWN 3/64; Wards, Beighton, Sheffield 5/64

90591 4/50
77145: Gorton then Newport 12/43; WD 1/45; Farnley Jct 25/3/50; Huddersfield 25/2/61; Royston 24/3/62
WITHDRAWN 10/62; Darlington Works 8/63

90592 10/50
77147: Gorton then Newport 12/43; WD 12/44; St Margarets 6/47; Kingmoor 18/9/48; Rose Grove 29/1/49; Lower Darwen 17/6/61
WITHDRAWN 6/64; Central Wagon Co, Ince, Wigan 9/64

90593 6/50
77148: Gorton then Newport 12/43; Worcester 11/44; WD 2/45; Mirfield 12/8/50; Darlington 14/6/58; Thornaby 5/9/59; West Hartlepool 16/5/64
WITHDRAWN 7/66; Thompsons, Stockton 10/66

90594 4/51
77149: Gorton then Newport 12/43; New England 9/44; WD 11/44; York 3/47 Springhead; 5/47; Mexborough 23/10/48; Immingham 29/12/51; Langwith Jct 13/8/55; Colwick 22/9/62
WITHDRAWN 9/62; Gorton Works 11/62

90595 3/49
77451: Newport 12/43; WD 1/45; Lostock Hall 26/3/49; Hellifield 13/12/58; Lancaster (Green Ayre) 7/9/63
WITHDRAWN 2/64; Central Wagon Co, Ince, Wigan 1/65

90596 3/49
77452: March 29/12/43; Mexborough 26/2/44; Colwick 2/12/44; WD 12/44; Mexborough 25/10/47; Frodingham 18/4/53; Dawsholm 23/3/57; Polmadie 19/4/58; Aberdeen Ferryhill 7/9/63; Immingham 27/11/65; Thornton Jct 23/4/66
WITHDRAWN 4/67; Motherwell Machinery and Scrap Co, Wishaw 9/67

90597 6/49
77453: March 29/12/43; Mexborough 29/1/44; Bath Road 23/11/44; WD 12/44; Colwick 25/1/47; Annesley 29/3/47; Mexborough 29/11/47; Frodingham 19/11/55
WITHDRAWN 7/63; Doncaster Works 7/63

90598 3/49
77454: March 29/12/43; Mexborough 26/2/44; Neath 24/10/44; WD 11/44; Colwick 25/1/47; Annesley 29/3/47; Mexborough 29/11/47; Frodingham 19/11/55
WITHDRAWN 2/64; Doncaster Works 3/64

90599 5/50
77455: March 29/12/43; Mexborough 29/1/44; Bath Road 23/11/44; WD 11/44; Eastfield 23/8/47; Dawsholm 23/10/48; Motherwell 18/12/48; Wigan (Central) 2/10/54; Agecroft 27/2/60; Aintree 26/3/60
WITHDRAWN 8/64; Central Wagon Co, Wigan 12/64

One in the landscape again. 90089 (the number sequence is not important for our purpose) takes a mixed freight round the curve and on to a straight section at Oakenshaw Junction, Wakefield, in July 1965. It's interesting to reflect that WDs *alone* could have been moving a quarter of a million tons or more every working day at one point, before 9Fs took some of the best of the work that is. Possibly a lot more; I'd be pleased to hear from any reader who cares to estimate it, and how it might compare with the total daily tonnage in Britain today. Photograph M. Mitchell.

In profile the WDs had a businesslike, no-nonsense look, pleasing to the eye even when filthy (almost) and even the squat chimney does not detract from their outline. 90595 (it has the little cinder guard 'window') is at Crewe South, probably after repair at the nearby works, if its condition is anything to go by, in June 1961; it was always based in the North West and was broken up in a Wigan scrapyard. Photograph D. Forsyth, Paul Chancellor Collection.

Cheadle Heath again. 90599 is a perfectly standard WD, almost respectable in fact, compared to many of its brethren. Photograph D. Forsyth, Paul Chancellor Collection.

90600 7/50
77456: March 29/12/43; Mexborough 26/2/44; Bath Road 23/11/44; WD 12/44; Eastfield 17/4/48; Dunfermline 20/4/57; Grangemouth 1/12/62; Dunfermline 27/11/65; Thornton Jct 4/12/65
WITHDRAWN 8/66; Mcwilliams, Shettleston 11/66

90601 3/50
77457: Mexborough 29/1/44; Swindon 23/11/44; WD 11/44; March 4/10/47; Doncaster 31/12/54; Frodingham 29/1/55
WITHDRAWN 6/65;Cox and Danks, Wadsley Bridge 12/65

90602 4/49
77458: March 29/1/44; Mexborough 26/2/44; Worcester 23/11/44; WD 11/44; March 25/1/47; Doncaster 23/3/57; Frodingham 5/11/60
WITHDRAWN 1/65; Drapers, Hull 3/65

90603 3/51
77459: March 29/1/44; Mexborough 25/2/44; WD 11/44; York 26/4/47; Stockton on Tees 23/8/47; York 20/8/54; Newport 16/6/56; Thornaby 14/6/58
WITHDRAWN 2/62; Darlington Works 2/62

90604 5/50
77460: Mexborough 29/1/44; Neath 23/11/44; WD 11/44; Feltham 8/47; Aintree 16/6/51; Wakefield 24/11/51
WITHDRAWN 12/63; Darlington Works 3/64

90605 1/51
77461: March 29/1/44; Mexborough 26/2/44; Worcester 23/11/44; WD 11/44; Newport 26/4/47; Thornaby 14/6/58; Royston 11/7/59; Normanton 28/1/67
WITHDRAWN 9/67; Drapers, Hull 4/68

90606 3/49
77462: Colwick 29/1/44; WD 12/44; York 23/8/47; Staveley 8/49; Colwick 4/51; Mold Jct 17/5/52; Birkenhead 18/6/60; Sutton Oak 22/9/62; Colwick 3/10/64
WITHDRAWN 2/66; Drapers, Hull 6/66

90607 10/49
77463: Colwick 29/1/44; WD 11/44; Wakefield 5/11/49; Normanton 15/6/57; Wakefield 5/10/57
WITHDRAWN 10/62; Darlington Works 12/62

90608 8/50
77464: Colwick 29/1/44; WD 12/44; March 27/12/47; Doncaster 23/3/57; Mexborough 14/6/58
WITHDRAWN 12/62; Central Wagon Co, Ince, Wigan 12/63

90609 6/49
77465: Gorton then Colwick 29/1/44; WD 11/44; Colwick 25/1/47; Barnsley 26/4/47; Neville Hill 29/11/47; York 9/49; Dairycoates 9/51
WITHDRAWN 8/63 Darlington Works 10/63

90610 5/49
77466: Gorton then Colwick 29/1/44; WD 11/44; Accrington 14/5/49; Bolton 11/8/51; Agecroft 24/11/51; Accrington 19/4/52; Wakefield 17/10/53; Normanton 15/6/57; Royston 21/1/61; Wakefield 2/11/63
WITHDRAWN 5/67; Arnott Young, Parkgate and Rawmarsh 9/67

90611 7/51
77467: Gorton then Colwick 29/1/44; WD 11/44; Annesley 1/3/47; Tyne Dock 29/11/47; York 15/6/57; Royston 4/4/59; Wakefield 2/11/63; Normanton 17/6/67
WITHDRAWN 7/67; Drapers, Hull 6/68

90612 9/51
77468: Gorton then Colwick 29/1/44; WD 12/44; Annesley 25/1/47; Barnsley 26/4/47; Neville Hill 29/11/47; Springhead 5/48; Mexborough 10/48
WITHDRAWN 3/64; Wards, Killamarsh 8/64

90613 2/49
77469: Gorton then Colwick 29/1/44; WD 11/44; New England 3/47; Frodingham 20/4/63
WITHDRAWN 5/65; Arnott Young, Parkgate and Rawmarsh 8/65

90614 4/49
77470: Gorton then Colwick 29/1/44; WD 12/44; Thornton Jct 29/3/47; Grangemouth 1/12/62
WITHDRAWN 11/63; McWilliams, Shettleston 6/64

90615 9/49
77471: Gorton then Colwick 29/1/44; WD 11/44; Wakefield 8/10/49; Royston 18/6/66; Normanton 28/1/67
WITHDRAWN 9/67; Arnott Young, Parkgate and Rawmarsh 1/68

90616 7/49
77476: Gorton 29/1/44; Stewarts Lane 26/2/44; Bricklayers Arms 25/3/44; WD 12/44; Thornton Jct 23/8/47; Grangemouth 18/6/49; Polmadie 23/2/52
WITHDRAWN 6/62; Cowlairs Works 11/62

90617 8/49
77479: Gorton 29/1/44; Bricklayers Arms 26/2/44; WD 11/44; Wakefield 13/8/49; Normanton 15/6/57
WITHDRAWN 6/67; Arnott Young, Parkgate and Rawmarsh 11/67

90618 6/51
77480: Gorton then Stewarts Lane 26/2/44; Bricklayers Arms 25/3/44; WD 12/44; Neville Hill 6/47; Colwick 8/49; Mexborough 2/50; Colwick 17/5/52; New England 21/5/60; Immingham 22/9/62
WITHDRAWN 5/64; Slag Reduction Co, Rotherham 1/65

90619 11/50
77481: Gorton then Stewarts Lane 26/2/44; Hither Green 25/3/44; WD 11/44; March 20/3/46; Bricklayers Arms 3/46; Huddersfield 3/6/50; Wakefield 9/10/65
WITHDRAWN 10/65; Drapers, Hull 3/66

90620 8/49
77482: Gorton 26/2/44; Stewarts Lane 26/2/44; Hither Green 25/3/44; Old Oak 23/11/44; WD 12/44; Wakefield 8/49; Mirfield 4/11/50; Wakefield 4/11/50
WITHDRAWN 6/67; Drapers, Hull 3/68

90621 10/51
77484: Gorton then Bricklayers Arms 26/2/44; Hither Green 25/3/44; WD 11/44; Colwick 25/1/47; Annesley 29/3/47; Barnsley 14/5/47; Neville Hill 29/11/47; Rose Grove 29/1/49; Sowerby Bridge 16/6/51; Rose Grove 8/8/53; Huddersfield 3/10/53; West Hartlepool 14/11/64
WITHDRAWN 12/65; Ellis Metals Ltd, Swalwell, Derwenthaugh 5/66

90622 11/49
77485: Gorton then Stewarts Lane 26/2/44; Hither Green 25/3/44; WD 11/44; March 20/3/46; Bricklayers Arms 3/46; Ashford 30/6/49; Mirfield 17/6/50; Immingham 22/9/62; Wakefield 25/1/64
WITHDRAWN 9/66; Cashmores, Great Bridge 1/67

Mexborough and a very clean 90601 on 1 July 1962; in this condition it could only be running in after an overhaul, presumably at nearby Doncaster. The overhead wire warning flashes would gradually disappear under layers of grime over the next few months. Photograph Stephen Gradidge.

90606, from Mold Junction, as presentable as the average resident, at Edge Hill shed on 2 June 1957. Once again, if you are modelling a locomotive and it has to be 'just so', you have to have a dated photograph; as this picture of 90606, along with so many others demonstrates, WD smokebox rivet patterns could be a law unto themselves. For once, the steam pipe to the blower is actually straight. And what is that GW-style buffer beam lamp iron doing on a WD that never spent (recorded) time on that line? You can never be sure... Photograph J. Robertson, www.transporttreasury.co.uk

At Cheadle Heath, 90606 still has those relict GW irons... Photograph D. Forsyth, Paul Chancellor Collection.

The phrase 'down at heel' could have been invented for the WD. Flaking, peeling and rusting is 90611 in store at Wakefield shed in April 1966. It had been transferred here in November 1963 but came out of store, surprisingly, to make a move (officially) to Normanton in June 1967. It was withdrawn only the next month to become one of 'the 205', so you'd suspect one of those 'paper transfers', with poor old 90611 remaining at Wakefield. Photograph J. Davenport, Initial Photographics.

90623 2/49
77488: Gorton 26/2/44; Feltham 25/4/44; WD 12/44; Retford 26/7/47; Stockton on Tees 29/11/47; Springhead 17/5/52; Dairycoates 13/12/58; York 23/9/61
WITHDRAWN 12/63; Darlington Works 3/64

90624 3/49
77489: Gorton 26/2/44; Feltham 25/3/44; Severn Tunnel Jct 24/10/44; WD 11/44; Neath 17/5/47; Llanelly 14/6/47; Wakefield 13/8/49; Huddersfield 16/6/56
WITHDRAWN 12/63; Darlington Works 3/64

90625 2/51
77492: Gorton 26/2/44; Feltham 25/3/44; Old Oak 24/10/44; WD 12/44; Heaton 25/1/47; Newport 26/4/47; York 15/6/57; Wakefield 7/9/57; Ardsley 14/7/62; Wakefield 9/10/65
WITHDRAWN 5/67; Drapers, Hull 12/67

90626 6/50
77494: Gorton 26/2/44; Feltham 25/3/44; Reading 24/10/44; WD 11/44; St Margarets 29/3/47; Lostock Hall 23/4/49; Bury 14/6/52; Agecroft 5/1/60; Gorton 8/6/63; Lower Darwen 28/11/64
WITHDRAWN 3/65; Wards, Beighton, Sheffield 8/65

90627 12/51
77497: New England 26/2/44; Feltham 25/3/44; Oxford 23/11/44; WD 11/44; Immingham 1/3/47; Tyne Dock 29/11/47; Dairycoates 9/51; West Hartlepool 17/6/67
WITHDRAWN 9/67; Hughes Bolckows Ltd, North Blyth 11/67

90628 4/49
77499: Longmoor 26/2/44; Neville Hill 10/47; Colwick 10/48; Dalry Road 11/2/50; Motherwell 17/6/50; Dunfermline 7/9/63; Thornton Jct. 26/6/64
WITHDRAWN 1/67; McWilliams, Shettleston 5/67

90629 8/49
77503: Melbourne 26/2/44; York 25/10/47; Colwick 8/49
WITHDRAWN 9/65; Drapers, Hull 12/65

90630 2/49
77508: Melbourne 26/2/44; Longmoor 25/3/44; St Philips Marsh 30/11/46; Westbury 3/12/49; Pontypool Road 24/3/51; Ebbw Jct 16/6/51; Aintree 11/8/51; Southall 19/5/56
WITHDRAWN 10/62; Crewe Works 11/63

90631 5/49
78626: WD 3/44; Wakefield 14/5/49
WITHDRAWN 1/67; Arnott Young, Parkgate and Rawmarsh 4/67

90632 5/49
78629: WD 3/44; Lostock Hall then to Accrington 14/5/49; Agecroft 24/11/51; Springs Branch 31/10/64; Aintree 2/1/65
WITHDRAWN 5/65; Cashmores, Great Bridge 8/65

90633 3/49
78632: WD 4/44; Old Oak 22/3/47; Canton 10/7/48; Wakefield 8/10/49; Bolton 14/7/51; Goole 16/6/56; Bank Hall 8/9/56; Low Moor 28/1/67 WITHDRAWN 7/67; Drapers, Hull 1/68

90634 2/51
78637: WD 4/44; Annesley 26/7/47; Staveley Central 29/11/47; Colwick 5/51; Staveley 1/12/51; Colwick 29/12/51 WITHDRAWN 12/62; Arnott Young, Bilston 4/63

90635 5/49
78638: WD 4/44; Wakefield 14/5/49
WITHDRAWN 1/64; Darlington Works 3/64

90636 4/49
78643: WD 4/44; York 25/10/47; Colwick 10/48; Annesley 11/48; Colwick 6/49; Doncaster 6/11/54; March 6/10/56; Doncaster 23/2/57
WITHDRAWN 4/66; Drapers, Hull 10/66

90637 5/49
78644: WD 4/44; Wakefield 21/5/49; Normanton 15/6/57
WITHDRAWN 10/62; Darlington Works 8/63

90638 8/49
78650: WD 5/44; York 25/10/47; Colwick 10/48; Woodford Halse 10/50; Colwick 4/11/50; Woodford Halse 4/51
WITHDRAWN 12/62; Crewe Works 6/63

90639 5/49
78652: WD 5/44; Wakefield 11/6/49; Goole 17/10/53; Wakefield 27/2/54
WITHDRAWN 1/67; Cox and Danks, Wadsley Bridge 5/67

90640 3/49
78658: WD 5/44; Lostock Hall 26/3/49; CME Rugby 23/4/49; Lostock Hall 14/5/49; Polmadie 20/4/57; Dawsholm 13/7/57; Polmadie 9/8/58; Grangemouth 11/8/62; Ferryhill 29/9/62; Thornton Jct 23/4/66
WITHDRAWN 8/66; Motherwell Machinery and Scrap Co, Wishaw 1/67

90641 5/50
78666: WD 6/44; Ashford 23/8/47; Redhill 31/7/48; Newton Heath 11/8/51; Bolton 18/4/53; Aintree 3/10/64
WITHDRAWN 8/65; Cashmores, Newport 6/66

90642 3/49
78671: WD 6/44; Laira 19/4/47; Wakefield 8/10/49; Mirfield 11/2/50; Huddersfield 17/6/50; Mirfield 15/7/50; Wakefield 21/1/61; Newport 23/9/61; Wakefield 11/9/65; Royston 18/6/66; Normanton 28/1/67
WITHDRAWN 9/67; Drapers, Hull 5/68

90643 6/49
78672: WD 6/44; Wakefield 18/6/49; Aintree 11/9/54
WITHDRAWN 2/64; J. Routledge, Bootle, Liverpool 8/64

90644 9/49
78675: WD 6/44; Wakefield 18/6/49; Ardsley 18/6/60; Normanton 27/11/65
WITHDRAWN 6/67; Arnott Young, Parkgate and Rawmarsh 11/67

90645 2/50
78681: Wd 6/44; Farnley Jct 11/2/50; Royston 28/12/63
WITHDRAWN 1/67; Wards, Killamarsh 4/67

90646 6/50
78682: WD 7/44; Annesley 4/10/47; Colwick 29/11/47; Immingham 5/48; Frodingham 5/51
WITHDRAWN 5/64; Slag Reduction Co. Rotherham 1/65

90647 9/49
78683: WD 7/44; Annesley 4/10/47; Staveley Central then Colwick 29/11/47; Immingham 5/48; New England 4/51; Frodingham 6/51 WITHDRAWN 3/65; Drapers, Hull 7/65

A WD hard at work; even the ever-present clanking might be obscured with one of them in this mood. Colwick's 90618 is near Kings Langley on 18 September 1952. Photograph Stephen Gradidge.

I like the arch supports in the background bridge – necessary because of mining subsidence, no doubt. 90627 takes to the colliery siding at Horden before bringing out a load of coal on 7 August 1967. More and more in the last years the WDs were reduced to coal trip work; 90627 had gone to West Hartlepool shed in June 1967, surviving until September, amongst the last of the class to be withdrawn. Photograph Paul Cotterell.

A Western WD, 90630 at Southall shed with 'tunnel', clack cover and proper array of lamp irons, 22 August 1959. Naturally the irons are stowed on the tender inset, not in the 'tunnel'. She has the 'Doncaster/Darlington/Crewe' boiler with amended washout plugs, presumably fitted during its time off the WR, at Aintree; it went there from Ebbw Junction in 1951 and returned home, to Slough, in 1956. Photograph N. Nicolson, www.transporttreasury.co.uk

90633 at its last shed, Low Moor, in 1967; it's intact apart from front number plate, but it's doubtful that it ever steamed again. Photograph Paul Chancellor Collection.

A WD on the Met, 90638 going about its business amid the third and fourth rails, safety valves blowing, at Rickmansworth on 23 February 1954. Photograph Stephen Gradidge.

Tired and wheezing, Wakefield's 90639 looks relieved to reach the haven of Mirfield shed in 1966.

90643 tucked in a yard somewhere; starting off at Wakefield, it soon moved to Aintree and spent more or less its entire BR life there. Photograph Paul Chancellor Collection.

A derelict WD, 90644 amid the weeds at Normanton shed on 31 July 1967; chalked 'nameplate' (it reads THE NORMANTON REGIMENT) and STEAM FOR EVER on the smokebox, daubed front number, dome pinched for another WD, or for someone's allotment. Photograph M. Mitchell.

Frodingham shed, home to 90646 for thirteen years. There were about twenty WDs here for the coal and steel traffic of the district, with 90646 withdrawn in May 1964. Photograph J. Davenport, Initial Photographics.

90648 with a train of wooden sided wagons passing through Grantham, a station notable for its chimneys! The date is 2 September 1950; 90648, a Colwick engine, was to be one of twelve broken up at Gorton Works, in September 1962. Photograph R.J. Buckley, Initial Photographics.

90648 8/50
78684: WD 7/44; Neville Hill 25/10/47; York 5/48; Colwick 10/48; Woodford Halse 4/51; Colwick 18/4/53; Immingham 16/7/60; Frodingham 8/10/60
WITHDRAWN 8/62; Gorton Works 9/62

90649 2/50
78685: WD 7/44; Farnley Jct 25/2/50; Huddersfield 11/7/59; Royston 28/1/67
WITHDRAWN 1/67; Drapers, Hull 5/67

90650 4/49
78688: WD 7/44; Bricklayers Arms 20/3/46; Ashford 30/6/49; Huddersfield 17/6/50; Mirfield 14/2/53; Farnley Jct 5/9/53; Royston 5/11/60; Normanton 22/2/64; Royston 27/3/65; Normanton 28/1/67
WITHDRAWN 6/67; Arnott Young, Parkgate and Rawmarsh 11/67

90651 6/49
78689: WD 7/44; Wakefield 18/6/49
WITHDRAWN 10/66; Drapers, Hull 12/66

90652 3/49
78695: WD 7/44; Oxley 17/5/47; Chester (WR) 7/8/48; Wakefield 8/10/49; Huddersfield 31/12/55; Wakefield 28/1/56; Normanton 15/6/57
WITHDRAWN 9/66; Drapers, Hull 11/66

90653 12/49
78700: WD 8/44; Mexborough 13/12/47; Mexborough 3/51; Plaistow 21/5/55; Tilbury 14/11/59
WITHDRAWN 9/62; Stratford Works 3/63

90654 5/49
78704: WD 8/44; Wakefield 14/5/49
WITHDRAWN 6/67; Cox and Danks, Wadsley Bridge 11/67

90655 2/51
78705: WD 8/44; Ashford 6/47; Hither Green 1/4/48; Huddersfield 3/6/50; Mirfield 10/11/56; Wakefield 21/1/61; Mirfield 15/7/61; Wakefield 28/1/67
WITHDRAWN 4/67; Drapers, Hull 9/67

90656 3/49
78714: WD 9/44; Oxley 17/4/47; Croes Newydd 4/10/47; Wakefield 8/10/49
WITHDRAWN 2/65; Thompsons, Stockton on Tees 3/65

90657 1/50
78715: WD 9/44; Mexborough 25/10/47; New England 8/50; Immingham then Langwith Jct 5/10/57
WITHDRAWN 9/62; Gorton Works 10/62

90658 3/49
78717: WD 9/44; Laira 14/5/47; Lostock Hall 8/10/49; Fleetwood 22/9/62; Rose Grove 28/12/63; Canklow 3/10/64; Langwith Jct 19/6/65
WITHDRAWN 11/65; W. George, Station Steel, Wath 2/66

90659 12/49
79178: WD 9/44; Mexborough 25/10/47; New England 2/50; Colwick 5/11/55; New England 28/1/56
WITHDRAWN 5/63; Doncaster Works 7/63

90660 1/50
79181: WD 9/44; March 14/6/47; Immingham 3/10/53; Langwith Jct 13/8/55; Stratford 19/11/55; Hornsey 26/3/60; New England 15/7/61; Immingham 22/9/62
WITHDRAWN 7/65; Drapers, Hull 11/65

90661 9/49
79182: WD 9/44; Immingham 26/4/46; Tyne Dock 29/11/47; Dairycoates 2/49: York 10/49; Dairycoates 11/49; Springhead 6/50; Haverton Hill 14/6/58; Royston 4/4/59; Normanton 3/10/59
WITHDRAWN 12/63; Darlington Works 2/64

90662 6/49
79184: WD 9/44; Mexborough 23/8/47; Annesley 4/10/47; Staveley Central then Colwick 29/11/47; New England 21/5/60; Immingham 22/9/62
WITHDRAWN 8/65; Drapers, Hull 1/66

90663 1/51
79186: WD 9/44; Dairycoates 23/8/47; York 10/49; Dairycoates 11/49; Springhead 6/51; York 11/7/59
WITHDRAWN 4/64; Darlington Works 5/64

90664 2/50
79190: WD 10/44; Farnley Jct 11/2/50; Royston 11/7/59; Normanton 3/10/59; Wakefield 9/10/65
WITHDRAWN 10/66; Drapers, Hull 2/67

90665 1/50
79194: WD 10/44; Mexborough 25/10/47; New England 2/50; Frodingham 22/9/62; Colwick 31/7/65
WITHDRAWN 12/65; Drapers, Hull 4/66

90666 2/50
79195: WD 10/44; Farnley Jct 25/2/50; Huddersfield 11/7/59
WITHDRAWN 10/62; Darlington Works 8/63

90667 6/49
79196: WD 10/44; Wakefield 18/6/49; Birkenhead 17/10/53; Mold Jct 13/2/54; Woodford Halse 22/3/58; Springs Branch 21/3/59
WITHDRAWN 5/64; Central Wagon Co, Ince, Wigan 9/65

90668 11/50
79198: WD 10/44; March 14/6/47; Stratford 29/1/55; Plaistow 26/2/55; Mexborough 21/5/55; Barrow Hill 21/3/64
WITHDRAWN 4/65; Cashmores, Great Bridge 7/65

90669 12/49
79199: WD 10/44; Hither Green 23/8/47; Newton Heath 11/8/51; Patricroft 16/1/60; Woodford Halse 26/1/63; Kirkby in Ashfield 22/2/64; Woodford Halse 18/4/64; Springs Branch 16/5/64; Retford 24/6/65; Frodingham 19/6/65; Colwick 31/7/65
WITHDRAWN 2/66; Drapers, Hull 6/66

90670 4/49
79202: WD 10/44; Retford 26/7/47; Tweedmouth 29/11/47; Selby 24/4/54; Goole 20/5/67
WITHDRAWN 6/67; Drapers, Hull 1/68

90671 3/50
79203: WD 10/44; Bricklayers Arms 20/3/47; Hither Green 28/12/46; Aintree 11/8/51; Wigan (LYR) 28/11/53; Lees 18/5/57
WITHDRAWN 9/63; Crewe Works 12/63

90672 5/49
79204: WD 10/44; Annesley 4/10/47; Colwick 29/11/47; Nottingham 28/12/63; Woodford Halse 18/4/64
WITHDRAWN 5/64; Crewe Works 7/64

90673 9/49
79205: WD 10/44; Wakefield 8/10/49; Normanton 15/6/57
WITHDRAWN 3/64; Looms, Spondon 9/64

Huddersfield WD 90649 earning its keep on a typical coal train, passing Beighton Junction on 13 July 1963; AWS fitted. Photograph B.W.L. Brooksbank, Initial Photographics.

The crumbling (it would have crumbled without those wooden supports at the front) four road former Midland shed at Normanton late in the day; 90650 came to the shed in February 1964, moved to Royston in March 1965 and back to Normanton in January 1967. This picture dates from those dog days of 1967, before 90650 was withdrawn in June that year. The shed itself then closed in October. This provides, unexpectedly, a good view of the looping connecting pipework to the BR AWS, unlike that found on any other class; compare with 43043 for instance. It would be interesting to know what is chalked on the tender of the WD alongside... Photograph Paul Cotterell.

Normanton again, and a line of 'standard issue' WDs (90652 in front) alongside the surviving bases for the old post-war oil fuel tanks. Photograph Paul Chancellor Collection.

90656 jollying along past Mirfield shed, 25 July 1963 on a coal train (actually it looks like the infamous 'cobbles') on 25 July 1963. AWS and some remnant WR lamp irons. Photograph A.G. Forsyth, Initial Photographics.

90658 at Crewe Works, 28 September 1957, during its long stay at Lostock Hall; exotic irons still there from its days at Laira long before. Oval Vulcan plate. Photograph D. Forsyth, Paul Chancellor Collection.

Abbots Ripton and 90660 on 18 July 1961; these were the last days of the WDs on the GN, with the coal trains largely gone over to the 9Fs. Photograph Paul Chancellor Collection.

The overhead gantries are going up on the Crewe-Manchester section alongside Stockport Edgeley shed; in the yard is a WD from Lees – much of that shed's work was getting freight round the east side of Manchester and this is where they handed over. The WDs carried on the time-honoured tradition of the British 0-6-0; they could haul more but the patterns of working were traditional to a fault. Photograph D. Forsyth, Paul Chancellor Collection.

Wagons everywhere. 90673 blasting over some impossible localised incline, by one of our long-vanished goods yards. A problem with any book of this sort is not illustrating the locomotives but knowing where they all are, in the not-infrequent event of the photograph having no details attached. You do your best but, what a wonderful sight; pity the poor Dutch! Photograph Paul Chancellor Collection.

90674 5/49
79206: WD 11/44; Retford 26/7/47; Tweedmouth
29/11/47; Dairycoates 4/51; Mold Jct 16/2/52; Colwick
17/5/52; Doncaster 6/11/54; Colwick 11/2/56;
Immingham 23/2/57; Colwick 8/10/60
WITHDRAWN 8/65; Arnott Young, Parkgate and
Rawmarsh 11/65

90675 8/50
79207: WD 11/44; Fratton 14/5/47; Feltham 12/47;
Perth 11/2/50; Newton Heath 8/9/51; Aintree
3/12/55; Newton Heath 25/1/58;
Lostock Hall 7/2/59; Doncaster 5/9/64
WITHDRAWN 4/66; Drapers, Hull 10/66

90676 5/51
79208: WD 11/44; Immingham 19/4/47; Annesley
23/8/47; Colwick 29/11/47; Ebbw Jct 1/12/51; Newton
Abbot 1/11/52; Ebbw Jct 22/5/54; Llanelly 7/10/61;
Gorton 16/6/62
WITHDRAWN 1/64; Crewe Works 3/64

90677 9/49
79209: WD 11/44; Dairycoates 23/8/47; Springhead
10/49; Dairycoates 11/49; Springhead 6/50;
Dairycoates 11/1/58; Springhead 19/4/58; Dairycoates
13/12/58; West Hartlepool 17/6/67
WITHDRAWN 9/67; Hughes Bolckows Ltd, North
Blyth 11/67

90678 7/49
79210: WD 11/44; Bricklayers Arms 20/3/46; Hither
Green 28/12/46; Mirfield 21/4/51; Wakefield 5/11/60;
Mirfield 15/7/61; Wakefield 25/1/64
WITHDRAWN 6/67; Cox and Danks,
Wadsley Bridge 9/67

90679 6/49
79213: WD 11/44; Wakefield 11/6/49; Goole 17/10/53;
Wakefield 27/2/54; Goole 28/1/56; Wakefield
25/2/56; Mirfield 26/2/66
WITHDRAWN 9/66; Cashmores, Great Bridge 3/67

90680 10/49
79214: WD 11/44; Huddersfield 5/11/49;
Royston 28/1/67
WITHDRAWN 1/67; Wards, Killamarsh 5/67

90681 4/49
79215: WD 11/44; Lostock Hall 23/4/49; Fleetwood
10/2/62; Rose Grove 28/12/63
WITHDRAWN 7/65; Wards, Killamarsh 10/65

90682 3/49
79219: WD 11/44; Oxley 14/5/47; Wakefield 13/8/49;
Normanton 2/11/57
WITHDRAWN 9/67; Arnott Young, Parkgate and
Rawmarsh 1/68

90683 9/51
79220: WD 11/44; Gorton 1/3/47; Annesley 26/4/47;
Neville Hill 29/11/47; New England 8/49;
March 2/11/57; Doncaster 24/12/60
WITHDRAWN 2/66; W. George, Station Steel, Wath
8/66

90684 2/50
79221: WD 11/44; Farnley Jct 11/2/50; Royston
7/10/61; Wakefield 2/11/63
WITHDRAWN 1/67; Cox and Danks, Wadsley Bridge
5/67

90685 2/49
79224: WD 11/44; Oxley 19/4/47; Tyseley 23/8/47;
Leamington 15/7/50; Chester (WR) 2/12/50;
Leamington Spa 27/1/51; Ebbw Jct 16/6/51;
Gloucester Horton Road 21/3/53; Canton 4/10/58;
Ebbw Jct 18/6/60; Southall 5/11/60;
Doncaster 29/12/62; Canklow 26/1/63
WITHDRAWN 11/64; Smiths, Ecclesfield 3/65

90686 12/51
79225: WD 12/44; Oxley 19/4/47; Chester (WR)
7/8/48; Gorton 20/4/63; Springs Branch 1/6/63
WITHDRAWN 4/65; Wards, Beighton, Sheffield 7/65

90677 outside the Erecting Shop, after overhaul at Darlington. It still needs some minor attention, a hose at the front and the right-hand steam pipe. Photograph Paul Chancellor Collection.

From this angle 90677 does not seem so well, its smokebox door looking like it has been rescued from the scrap line. This must have been one of the last WD overhauls, in September 1965. Brush Type 4 D1582 in the background was one of the batch that had gone new to Gateshead the previous year. A Dairycoates engine, 90677 returned there and outlasted the Works, which closed the following year. The WD survived until September 1967, when it was withdrawn from West Hartlepool. Photograph J. Davenport, Initial Photographics.

More landscape. 90680 readies its wagons before finding a brake and heading off. Photograph Paul Chancellor Collection.

90684 glides (can a WD glide? 'gently clanks' might be better) past the 'coal hole' at Stockport Edgeley. Photograph D. Forsyth, Paul Chancellor Collection.

Westernised 90685 at Southall, 2 September 1962. Fire irons, of course, stowed on the tender inset, not in the 'tunnel' provided for them. The latter serves only for the chalked message BUD IS A with the noun fortunately erased. Something rather different about that snifting valve behind the chimney; perhaps BUD was the culprit. Photograph Peter Groom.

90687 1/52
79226: WD 12/44; Oxley 17/5/47; Bath Road 14/6/47;
Rose Grove 4/11/50; Aintree 24/3/51;
Springs Branch 11/7/64; Doncaster 5/9/64
WITHDRAWN 1/66; Drapers, Hull 4/66

90688 10/51
79227: WD 12/44; Immingham 26/4/47; Tyne Dock
26/11/47; Dairycoates 2/49; York 10/49; Dairycoates
11/49; Springhead 6/50; Dairycoates 13/12/58;
Goole 20/5/67
WITHDRAWN 6/67; Drapers, Hull 1/68

90689 5/51
79228: WD 12/44; Ebbw Jct 5/48; Lostock Hall 23/4/49;
Fleetwood 10/2/62; Bolton 28/12/63; Aintree 3/10/64;
Retford 22/5/65; Frodingham 19/6/65; Colwick
31/7/65
WITHDRAWN 2/66; Drapers, Hull 6/66

90690 3/49
79229: WD 12/44; Thornton Jct 29/3/47;
Polmadie 16/1/60; Motherwell 16/6/62
WITHDRAWN 9/62; Darlington Works 10/63

90691 5/51
79232: WD 12/44; Worcester 19/4/47; Gloucester Horton
Road 14/5/47; Worcester 7/10/50; Gloucester Horton
Road 8/9/51; Pontypool Road 18/4/53; Gloucester
Horton Road 16/5/53; Canton 4/10/58;
Banbury 5/11/60
WITHDRAWN 7/62; Crewe Works 7/62

90692 9/49
79233: WD 12/44; Wakefield 8/49; Ardsley 5/11/60;
Sowerby Bridge 15/7/61
WITHDRAWN 12/63; Darlington Works 1/64

90693 6/51
79234: WD 12/44; Old Oak 19/4/47; Motherwell
11/2/50; St Philips Marsh 8/9/51; Llanelly 9/8/52; Neath
1/11/52; Canton 9/10/54; Banbury 28/1/61; Southall
7/10/61
WITHDRAWN 10/62; Crewe Works 11/63

90694 3/49
79235: WD 12/44; Pontypool Road 12/7/47; Wakefield
8/10/49; Huddersfield 24/12/49; Royston 28/1/67
WITHDRAWN 1/67; Wards, Killamarsh 5/67

90695 3/49
79239: WD 12/44; Dairycoates 23/8/47; York 10/49;
Dairycoates 11/49; Haverton Hill 10/50;
Dairycoates 9/51; West Hartlepool 17/6/67
WITHDRAWN 9/67; Hughes Bolckows Ltd, North Blyth
11/67

90696 2/51
79242: WD 12/44; Mexborough 29/3/47; March 10/51;
Doncaster 26/1/52; March 1/11/52; Doncaster 29/11/52;
March 6/10/56; Frodingham 20/2/60
WITHDRAWN 8/63; Doncaster Works 8/63

90697 9/49
79243: WD 1/45; Dairycoates 23/8/47; Colwick 10/48;
Woodford Halse 8/51; Toton 23/1/63; Canklow 3/10/64;
Woodford Halse 18/4/64; Springs Branch 16/5/64;
Canklow; 3/10/64; Barrow Hill 19/6/65;
Langwith Jct 9/10/65
WITHDRAWN 11/65; Arnott Young, Parkgate and
Rawmarsh 4/66

90698 4/50
79244: WD 1/45; Farnley Jct 3/6/50; Ardsley 5/10/57;
Bradford then Low Moor 11/1/58; Darlington 14/6/58;
Thornaby 8/8/59; Mirfield 14/11/59;
Low Moor 29/12/62; Wakefield 25/1/64;
Sunderland 3/12/66
WITHDRAWN 7/67; Drapers, Hull 10/67

90699 4/50
79254: WD 1/45; Farnley Jct 22/4/50; Royston 28/12/63;
Normanton 18/4/64
WITHDRAWN 9/67; Drapers, Hull 4/68

90690 at Eastfield shed; the place saw a great many WDs of course as they were delivered from North British nearby but it only ever had a few of its own. It continued to use them ex-works, like this one, on 13 September 1959 destined for its home at Thornton Junction. Its Scottish associations can be discerned in the larger cabside numerals, the outlined smokebox numberplate and the shed painted on the front buffer beam. And of course, the clacks.

An unusual place for a WD, Old Oak Common, and one in good nick, too. 90691spent all its life on the WR, withdrawn quite early before its last shed, Banbury, was transferred to the LMR. Photograph Paul Chancellor Collection.

Another doomed WD at Southall shed; I came across a few of them at 81C including this one, 90693. This is 15 September 1962 and 90693's official withdrawal came the following month, as a 'period ending', like so much else. The chalk marks (the writer in his haste missing out a 'D') afford us a little more precise insight for a change, however; on the tender it says CONDEMED DO NOT COAL 8/9/62. Inexplicably, the Vulcan (oval) building plate remains in place on the expansion link bracket. This was another one from Southall broken up at Crewe Works, which unlike Swindon would still be interested in WD parts. An enormous amount of material was taken off engines being broken up, for re-use. All the bearings were sent to the brass shop to have the while metal melted off, before they in turn went into the melting pot, or were recovered for further use. Often boilers were used again too. It might well have been the boiler on this occasion Crewe were after. Photograph Stephen Gradidge.

Sunderland was one of the final sheds and it's a surprise to find that its first WDs didn't come on the complement until August 1966. 90698, outside the shed on 12 May 1967, had arrived late the previous year and had only two months to go before withdrawal. Cylinder casing bashed, AWS probably of little use on the sort of colliery jobs it now found itself on and lamp irons rearranged in the light of OHL hazard; there are electrification flashes under the grime. Photograph Stephen Gradidge.

90699, anonymous under the filth. It was hardly morale boosting as a 'place of work'... Photograph Paul Chancellor Collection.

175

90700 3/49
79259: WD 1/45; Mexborough 26/4/47; Canklow
29/12/62
WITHDRAWN 2/64; Wards, Killamarsh 5/64

90701 2/49
79261: WD 1/45; St Philips Marsh 1/3/47; Westbury
3/12/49; Ebbw Jct 16/6/51; Canton 11/8/51; Neath
21/2/53; Shrewsbury 18/4/53; Pontypool Road
28/12/57; Westhouses 8/8/59;
Woodford Halse 3/10/59;
WITHDRAWN 11/62; Crewe Works 6/63

90702 3/50
79262: WD 2/45; Bricklayers Arms 20/3/46; Hither Green
28/12/46; Colwick 10/48; Warrington 8/9/51; Mold Jct
31/12/51; Sutton Oak 10/9/60; Aintree 2/11/63;
Frodingham 22/5/65
WITHDRAWN 8/65; Arnott Young, Parkgate and
Rawmarsh 9/65

90703 6/49
79263: WD 2/45; Retford 26/7/47; Neville Hill
29/11/47; New England 21/5/60; Colwick 30/6/62
WITHDRAWN 7/65; Cox and Danks, Wadsley Bridge 4/66

90704 8/51
79264: WD 2/45; Heaton 26/4/47; Tweedmouth
29/11/47; Dairycoates 12/50; Goole 14/11/59;
Dairycoates 30/11/63; Goole 3/12/66
WITHDRAWN 6/67; Drapers, Hull 12/67

90705 11/49
79265: WD 2/45; Dunfermline 4/10/47; Thornton Jct
22/12/56; Polmadie 16/1/60; Motherwell 16/6/62;
Aberdeen Ferryhill 5/10/63; Thorton Jct 30/11/63
WITHDRAWN 7/64; Arnott Young, Old Kilpatrick
10/64

90706 11/49
79266: WD 2/45; Newton Heath 3/12/49; Hellifield
12/7/58; Lancaster 17/1/59; Aintree 16/5/64;
Barrow Hill 19/6/65; Colwick 9/10/65
WITHDRAWN 2/66; Drapers, Hull 6/66

90707 7/50
79268: WD 2/45; Sowerby Bridge 12/8/50; Mirfield
7/10/50; Wakefield 24/12/60; Mirfield 15/7/61;
Wakefield 25/1/64
WITHDRAWN 1/67; Cox and Danks, Wadsley Bridge 5/67

90708 11/49
79269: WD 2/45; Newton Heath 3/12/49; Lees
14/6/58; Newton Heath 18/4/64
WITHDRAWN 5/64; Slag Reduction Co. Ickles, Rotherham
1/65

90709 5/50
79271: WD 2/45; Mexborough 25/10/47; March
10/51; Mexborough 3/51; New England 10/51; Plaistow
26/2/55; New England 21/5/55; March 5/10/57;
Doncaster 24/12/60
WITHDRAWN 4/66; Drapers, Hull 10/66

90710 6/49
79272: WD 2/45; Wakefield 18/6/49
WITHDRAWN 2/65; Darlington Works 3/65

90711 6/50
79273: WD 2/45; Farnley Jct 17/6/50; Ardsley 5/10/57;
Low Moor 14/6/58; Wakefield 10/9/66;
Low Moor 8/10/66
WITHDRAWN 1/67; Cox and Danks, Wadsley Bridge 7/67

90712 4/49
79274: WD 2/45; Severn Tunnel Jct 4/10/47;
Bolton 16/12/50; Aintree 14/7/56
WITHDRAWN 8/64; Central Wagon Co, Wigan 5/65

90713 3/49
79275: WD 2/45; Rose Grove 26/3/49; Accrington
24/12/49; Agecroft 24/11/51; Lostock Hall 18/6/60
WITHDRAWN 11/63; Crewe Works 2/64

90714 5/50
79276: WD 2/45; Mexborough 25/10/47; Doncaster
10/51; Frodingam 22/3/52
WITHDRAWN 12/64; Wards, Beighton, Sheffield 4/65

90715 4/49
79278: WD 3/45; Gloucester Horton Road 29/11/47;
Worcester 27/11/48; Newton Heath 16/12/50
WITHDRAWN 5/64; Slag Reduction Co, Rotherham
1/65

90716 2/49
79279: WD 3/45; Severn Tunnel Jct 20/3/48;
Shrewsbury 21/3/53; Banbury 23/4/55; Shrewsbury
2/11/57; Westhouses 8/8/59; Gorton 30/6/62
WITHDRAWN 11/63; Crewe Works 1/64

90717 3/49
79280: WD 3/45; Neville Hill 25/10/47; Springhead
5/48; Colwick 10/48; New England 21/5/60; Colwick
30/6/62; Retford 5/10/63
WITHDRAWN 3/64; Cox and Danks, Wadsley Bridge
1/65

90718 7/49
79281: WD 3/45; Bricklayers Arms 20/3/46; Hither
Green 28/12/46; Accrington 6/10/51; Bury 31/12/51;
Lees 28/11/59; Newton Heath 18/4/64; Aintree
3/10/64; Retford 24/6/65; Doncaster 19/6/65
WITHDRAWN 2/66; Drapers, Hull 7/66

90719 9/49
79282: WD 3/45; Wakefield 8/10/49; Canklow 5/9/59;
Staveley Central 24/6/65; Langwith Jct 19/6/65
WITHDRAWN 2/66; Drapers, Hull 6/66

90720 8/50
79283: WD 3/45; Old Oak 5/48; Lostock Hall 23/4/49
WITHDRAWN 7/65; Cashmores, Great Bridge 11/65

90721 8/50
79294: WD 3/45; Sowerby Bridge 9/9/50;
Mirfield 7/10/50; Wakefield 25/1/64; Royston 18/6/
66; Normanton 8/10/66
WITHDRAWN 9/67; Drapers, Hull 4/68

90722 9/49
79298: WD 4/45; Wakefield 8/10/49;
Normanton 15/6/57
WITHDRAWN 6/67; Arnott Young, Parkgate and
Rawmarsh 11/67

90723 2/49
79301: WD 4/45; St Philips Marsh 5/10/46; Wakefield
14/5/49; Mirfield 11/2/50; Wakefield 17/6/50; Mirfield
15/7/50; Tyne Dock 31/10/64; Low Moor 2/1/65;
Wakefield 10/9/66
WITHDRAWN 11/66; Drapers, Hull 4/67

Another visiting WD on one of my favourite sheds, Willesden, 90703 of Colwick on 19 May 1963. They were definitely turning up in London by now and some changes in working were obviously afoot further north (Colwick passed to the LMR in 1966) which brought its engines to the LNW – this would of course had been unthinkable if the WDs had not not been rapidly reducing the ranks of the O1s and O4s. Photograph Stephen Gradidge.

90708 at home at on Lees (Oldham) in August 1958, having arrived just a month or so before; oddly the guard irons at the front have been removed – note the bolt holes immediately in front of the pony wheels. Maybe a snowplough had been removed - even if it was August! 90708 moved, as Lees engines usually did, to Newton Heath in 1964. Photograph J. Davenport, Initial Photographics.

A Frodingham based WD on a different job, 90714 banking a goods train 'near Scunthorpe' which suggests to me the bank from Gunhouse Junction up to Scunthorpe. It's the same train as the one shown on page 39. It is working hard with a clean white exhaust, the safety valves joining in; it will drop away at the top and switch to the down line to return to Gunhouse Junction, where it lived in a siding with a water column. The fireman appears to be taking it easy enough. This loco stayed at Frodingham for over twelve years before withdrawal at the end of 1964. Photograph Stephen Gradidge.

As fine a WD as you'll see, at Gorton I'd suspect, from the L1 tank alongside. Photograph Paul Chancellor Collection.

Splendidly scruffy 90721 at Newton Heath on 4 April 1965. At the time it was a Wakefield engine with further moves in 1966 to Royston and Normanton before withdrawal in September 1967 and yes, it was one of Mr Draper's '205'. Photograph J. Davenport, Initial Photographics.

90724 7/50
79302: WD 4/45; Sowerby Bridge 12/8/50; Wakefield 4/11/50; Aintree 3/12/55; Rose Grove 22/9/62; Bolton 25/1/64; Aintree 2/1/65
WITHDRAWN 6/65; Central Wagon Co, Ince, Wigan 10/65

90725 3/49
79303: WD 4/45; Didcot 4/10/47; Wakefield 14/5/49; Bolton 18/4/53; Fleetwood 22/9/62; Agecroft 21/3/64; Springs Branch 31/10/64; Rose Grove 28/11/64
WITHDRAWN 8/65; Cashmores, Newport 1/66

90726 8/50
79304: WD 4/45; Sowerby Bridge 9/9/50; Farnley Jct 4/11/50
WITHDRAWN 1/63; Darlington Works 2/64

90727 12/49
79306: WD 4/45; Dunfermline 4/10/47; Tay Bridge 8/10/49; St Margarets 4/10/52; Dunfermline 6/11/54; Ayr 1/12/62; Thorton Jct 30/11/63
WITHDRAWN 9/65; Motherwell Machinery and Scrap Co, Wishaw 11/65

90728 8/50
79307: WD 4/45; Sowerby Bridge 12/8/50; Farnley Jct 4/11/50
WITHDRAWN 12/63; Darlington Works 1/64

90729 3/49
79309: WD 5/45; St Philips Marsh 25/1/47; Wakefield 14/5/49; Bolton 18/4/53
WITHDRAWN 4/63; Horwich Works 5/63

90730 3/50
79310: WD 5/45; York 4/10/47; New England 8/49; Frodingham 22/9/62; Barrow Hill 25/1/64
WITHDRAWN 10/65; Drapers, Hull 1/66

90731 8/50
79311: WD 5/45; Sowerby Bridge 12/8/50; Mirfield 7/10/50; Ardsley 21/3/64; Low Moor 19/6/65; Wakefield 8/10/66
WITHDRAWN 11/66; Drapers, Hull 4/67

90732 5/50
79312: WD 5/45; March 29/11/47; Colchester 5/48; Doncaster 23/3/57; Frodingham 20/2/60
WITHDRAWN 9/62; Gorton Works 12/62

79303, delivered to the GWR in August 1947, awaiting attention at Swindon. As 90725 it moved to Didcot shed in the autumn of 1947 after 'treatment' here. It did not remain a Western loco for long and spent the rest of its days on the LMR, though it was broken up in South Wales.

Its latter days as 90725, at Bolton shed. Photograph D. Forsyth, Paul Chancellor Collection.

The highest numbered and only (BR) named WD 2-8-0, 90732 VULCAN (after its place of birth) at March shed, 4 OCTOBER 1953. Photograph B.K.B. Green, Initial Photographics. *Below*. Nameplate helpfully picked out. Photograph Paul Chancellor Collection.

90093 (New England) on 31 May 1956 southbound, approaching the Sandy bottleneck with a Class H goods.

90096 (New England) on 25 March 1953, southbound near Biggleswade with a Class F goods.

Eastern Region Memories

Notes by Brian C. Bailey

It was probably on the Eastern Region that the WDs were used to best effect, in the sense of running an important long distance coal service with concentrations of them at major sheds. Tellingly, they were replaced only by a similar concentration of 9Fs when the 2-10-0s became available. On other Regions they tended to operate in a more 'diffuse' manner, and while more useful than the biggest 0-6-0s, say, might not be regarded, often, as quite up to the level of the 'local' eight-coupled top-notch power, 28XXs on the WR, 8Fs on the LMR and so on. *British Railways Illustrated* regular contributor Brian C. Bailey knew their work well on the Eastern Region and recollects some of this most fascinating period of 'Austerity' effort, on the GN from 1946 onwards. 'My first memories of WD 2-8-0s are of those that either were returned from the Continent as surplus during 1946 or, because of the end of the war in Europe, were never sent abroad. These were very quickly absorbed by the LNER as they were almost new and did not require much maintenance and were simpler to service than the types they replaced. Also, the LMSR were keen to have the Stanier 8Fs (classified O6 on the LNER) sent to them so by the end of 1947 the LNER owned 200 WDs classified O7, with many more on loan. Once the LNER renumbering scheme was complete the WDs they owned were numbered 3000-3199 and the remainder carried WD numbers from 70801 upwards. In BR days they were all numbered in one batch 90000-90732, and ex-3000-3100 became 90000-100 and ex-3101-99, 90422-90520.

'I can remember that in the period 1946-47 the engines that had been used by the WD had large running numbers painted on the smokebox door, and in the general scruffiness and dirt of the time were much more easily identified than the LNER owned engines which quickly became anonymous under the grime. Also the engines on loan from the government usually had Westinghouse brake pumps fitted on the running plate on the right-hand side of the smokebox.

'By 1947 the WDs monopolised the freights on the southern end of the GN, but they had also become dominant at Colwick, Woodford Halse and Frodingham. However, it was at New England and Woodford Halse that they entirely replaced other classes on the coal trains to London and on to the WR. 90504 of Woodford Halse which was originally LNER 3183 is interesting as it is probably the only WD that was stationed at only one shed during its working life. I have a photo of this engine taken at Princes Risborough on 12 May 1951 leaving with a southbound coal train for Neasden, a job it must have done hundreds upon hundreds of times.

'I will conclude these short notes with a complete list of the WDs working from New England in January 1954, before their monopoly was broken by the 9F 2-10-0s 92030-93042, that were all working regularly between Peterborough and Ferme Park, Hornsey by March 1956. There is no doubt this group of engines transformed the service, both from an operating point of view and in working conditions for the crews. However, they did not completely replace the WDs and *British Railways Illustrated* (Vol. 16.10 July 2007) has an interesting photo taken by Andrew Forsyth at Welwyn Garden City in March 1962, showing 90000 making good speed on the down main with a Class H freight which was the main duty of the class throughout the system, along with the Class J duties in the industrial areas. The WD 2-8-0 allocation at Peterborough New England at 1 January 1954 was:

90028, 90034, 90062, 90063, 90088, 90093, 90096, 90106, 90151, 90156, 90158, 90162, 90165, 90169, 90180, 90191, 90208, 90239, 90244, 90246, 90253, 90256, 90259, 90279, 90349, 90428, 90438, 90454, 90494, 90501, 90502, 90514, 90526, 90528, 90551, 90554, 90559, 90577, 90613, 90657, 90659, 90665, 90683, 90709, 90730, total 45.

'Some of these were at New England for many years and became very familiar; from memory these included 90028, 90034, 90088, 90093, 90151, 90156, 90158, 90180, 90191, 90244, 90246, 90253 90256 90259, 90428, 90438, 90494, 90514, 90559, 90657, 90659, 90665, 90683, 90709 and 90730.

'Over the years there were some sheds that kept their WDs in respectable condition and from my first-hand experience these seemed to be ex-LNER establishments in Scotland; Thornton, Dundee and Ferryhill. Even as late as 1960 I have clear memories of 90004, 90019, 90020, 90513 of 62A, 90041, 90097, 90455 of 61B and 90441, 90444, 90463, 90472 and 90513 of 62B in reasonably clean condition months after having been overhauled. In August 1960 I took a photo of 60161 standing at Dundee shed, and next to it was 90444 just cleaned and comparing very favourably with the Haymarket Pacific.'

90151 (New England) about to run up the Harringay flyover, to get to Ferme Park northbound marshalling yard.

90256 (New England) on 17 May 1952, southbound near Hatfield with a Class F goods.

90400 of Mexborough with a Class H goods on 9 August 1956, transferring from the up main to the slow in Doncaster station.

90526 (New England) on 24 March 1953, northbound at Biggleswade with a Class F goods.

90528 (Colwick) on 31 May 1956 slowing at Sandy with an up Class H goods; it is easing up to the signal to wait for a gap on the main line, in order to get on to the two line section through the station.

90554 (New England) on 21 May 1951, climbing past Brookmans Park with yet another Class F coal train for Ferme Park.

90613 (New England) on 15 August 1955, easing past Red Hall signal box, Hatfield, with an up Class H goods.

90613 (New England) on 31 May 1956 passing under the Oxford-Cambridge branch north of Sandy station with the Class K pick-up goods from Peterborough to Hitchin.

90665 (New England) running light on 16 April 1952, after bringing a freight in to the reception sidings at Hornsey.

90096 of New England (now coded 34E) on 25 July 1959 slowing for the Sandy stop with an up Class H goods.

90130 (New England) on 4 March 1961 climbing out of Hatfield at Red Hall with an up pick up goods. This engine was one of the newcomers to New England, having been at Mexborough and Colwick.

And on 11 March 1961. The identical engine in the same spot one week later, with the same staining from the water deposits on the smokebox, but with an altogether much heavier load, of ballast for the next weekend relaying job.

90154 (New England) hauling a southbound Class F goods on 4 March 1961 with Red Hall box in the background; the first six wagons have sufficiently valuable cargoes to warrant tarpaulin covers. 90154 is another former Colwick engine.

90165 (New England) on 31 December 1960 at Red Hall, opening up for the climb to Potters Bar with yet another train of coal for the capital. 90165 was one of the long-term residents of New England and regular spotters saw it two or three times a week, week after week.

90269 (New England) on 4 November 1961. A good portrait of a WD in its final years and in a reasonable condition. It has all the modifications that most of the GN WD fleet had in later years; AWS, raised hand rails above the hand holds for the wash plug accesses, which were set lower (as we presumed) on either replacement boilers or renewed fireboxes. Like several other WDs 'down here' 90269 came from the GC section.

90270 on 4 November 1961 at Hatfield. A stranger in the camp as a Mexborough engine passes with a ballast train for the engineering department.

90428 (New England) on 4 November 1961 at Hatfield. An old faithful, today in charge of a local pick-up freight.

90659 (New England) on 3 October 1959 turned out on to the up main at Hatfield with a Class H, but running under caution as the section ahead is not yet clear.

90717 (New England) on 4 March 1961 at Red Hall with the up local pick-up goods for Hornsey. Like 90662 this engine had joined the New England club from Colwick.

90730 (New England) on 4 March 1961 at Hatfield running light southbound. A well lit picture showing a WD in all its 'glory'! In truth sheds on the GN (and almost certainly elsewhere) didn't bother to wash out the poor old WDs properly. The late and fondly remembered Bert Collins, once of the famous Ian Allan Bookshop in London, recollected that at Hornsey for instance when the water got 'a bit milky' the tender was filled up, the injectors put on and the water drained through the blow down valve – the grandly named 'scum cock' – until clean(ish) water came through. Ill treated they may have been but this is how they are remembered and the condition in which they worked most of the time. They rarely failed and they delivered the coals, but at a cost to the crews in rough riding on the main line, with only the steam brake on the engine and the guard in the brake van to control the train.

2-10-0s
90750 - 90774

90750 3/51
73774: March 21/7/45; WD 9/46; Hornsey 6/48; Dawsholm 23/10/48; Grangemouth 2/49; Motherwell 8/10/49
WITHDRAWN 5/62; Cowlairs Works 6/62

90751 1/50
73775: March 21/7/45; WD 10/46; Kingmoor 3/12/48; Polmadie 17/5/52; Motherwell 7/10/61
WITHDRAWN 12/62; Darlington Works 12/63

90752 6/51
73776: March 21/7/45; WD 9/46; Hornsey 12/6/48; Grangemouth 2/49; Motherwell 8/10/49
WITHDRAWN 12/61; Cowlairs Works 6/62

90753 2/51
73777: March 21/7/45; WD 10/46; Carstairs 2/49
WITHDRAWN 7/61; Cowlairs Works 8/61

90754 4/50
73778: March 21/7/45; WD 10/46; Motherwell 20/5/50
WITHDRAWN 7/61; Cowlairs Works 6/62

90755 4/49
73779: March 21/7/45; WD 10/46; Grangemouth 12/48
WITHDRAWN 12/62; Campbells, Shieldhall 1/64

90756 6/50
73780: March 21/7/45; WD 9/46; Motherwell 17/6/50
WITHDRAWN 12/62; Darlington Works 11/63

90757 4/50
73781: March 21/7/45; WD 10/46; Carstairs 2/49; Grangemouth 19/11/49; Doncaster 9/8/52; Grangemouth 1/11/52
WITHDRAWN 12/62; Campbells, Shieldhall 11/63

90758 6/50
73782: March 21/7/45; WD 9/46; Motherwell 2/49
WITHDRAWN 12/62; Darlington Works 12/63

90759 11/50
73783: March 21/7/45; WD 11/46; Carstairs 2/49; Grangemouth 19/11/49
WITHDRAWN 12/62; Cowlairs Works 6/63

90760 11/51
73784: March 21/7/45; WD 9/46; Motherwell 26/3/49
WITHDRAWN 5/62; Cowlairs Works 7/62

90761 5/49
73785: March 21/7/45; WD 11/46; Motherwell 23/4/49
WITHDRAWN 11/62; Darlington Works 11/63

90762 6/50
73786: March 21/7/45; WD 10/46; Motherwell 2/49
WITHDRAWN 12/62; Darlington Works 11/63

90763 4/50
73787: March 21/7/45; WD 10/46; Kingmoor 20/5/50; Doncaster 17/5/52; Grangemouth 6/9/52; Kingmoor 1/11/52; Bidston 5/9/59; Kingmoor 16/7/60
WITHDRAWN 12/62; Darlington Works 11/63

90764 9/52
73788: March 21/7/45; WD 10/46; CME Rugby 4/49; Grangemouth 12/49; Hamilton 6/9/58; Motherwell 3/10/59
WITHDRAWN 5/62; Cowlairs Works 6/62

90765 12/51
73789: March 21/7/45; WD 11/46; Grangemouth 2/49
WITHDRAWN 12/62; Campbells, Shieldhall 1/64

90766 7/49
73790: March 21/7/45; WD 10/46; Motherwell 16/7/49; Grangemouth 17/1/59
WITHDRAWN 12/62; Campbells, Shieldhall 11/63

90767 8/50
73791: March 21/7/45; WD 9/46; Kingmoor 12/8/50; Polmadie 17/5/52; Motherwell 7/10/61
WITHDRAWN 12/62; Darlington Works 12/63

90768 6/50
73792: March 22/8/45; WD 11/46; Carstairs 2/49
WITHDRAWN 7/62; Darlington Works 12/63

90769 12/49
73793: March 22/8/45; WD 9/46; Kingmoor 3/12/49; Grangemouth 23/4/55
WITHDRAWN 12/62; Darlington Works 12/63

90770 7/52
73794: WD 8/45; Motherwell 26/3/49
WITHDRAWN 12/62; Darlington Works 11/63

90771 9/51
73795: WD 8/45; Motherwell 26/3/49; Hamilton 6/9/58; Motherwell 3/10/59
WITHDRAWN 12/62; Darlington Works 12/63

90772 10/49
73796: WD 8/45; Motherwell 5/11/49; Hamilton 6/9/58; Motherwell 3/11/62
WITHDRAWN 12/62; Darlington Works 12/63

90773 10/50
73798: WD 8/45; Kingmoor 29/3/47; Grangemouth 6/9/52
WITHDRAWN 12/62; Campbells, Shieldhall 12/63

90774 9/52
73799: WD 8/45; Kingmoor 29/3/47; CME Rugby 7/8/48; Kingmoor 4/49; Grangemouth 23/4/55
WITHDRAWN 12/62; Campbells, Airdrie 12/63

On show at Ayr station in 1951. It would never look this good again! Photograph J. L. Stevenson, courtesy Hamish Stevenson.

90753 (former 73777) at Haymarket shed on 23 March 1958; this was the one that remained at Carstairs shed all its working life. This view indicates well the sheer size of the engine; from buffer to buffer they were 67ft 6¼in long; an overall wheelbase of 57ft 1in and 12ft 10in at chimney height. Photograph J. Robertson, www.transporttreasury.co.uk

90753 at home at Carstairs on 22 September 1951, minus top feed cover. A clean loco in full BR regalia including 'cycling' BR totem and larger cabside numbers typical of the Scottish Region. Photograph R.H. Fullagar, www.transporttreasury.co.uk

At first glance the smokebox door seems rather flat but it is just the lighting on 90754, at Motherwell shed in September 1955. This was always home to a number of the class in BR days, until withdrawal by the end of 1962. 90754 had been here for over five years, remaining until the end. Photograph W. Hermiston, www.transporttreasury.co.uk

90756 at Motherwell shed in a line-up of 2-10-0s, probably derelict. Photograph Paul Chancellor Collection.

90756 at Motherwell shed. It's quite late and the loco may even be withdrawn; it spent most of its time in Scotland at Motherwell and 90751 behind came there in October 1961. BR AWS (battery box on running plate) and electrification flashes. Diagaonal works place still on expansion link bracket. Both came south to be cut up at Darlington Works. Photograph Stephen Gradidge.

90757 ex-works at Eastfield shed, 6 April 1957, with highlighted smokebox number plate, larger cabside numerals and still with BR cycling totem. This engine went south in August 1952 first to Doncaster (as did 90763) then Banbury and in October was working out of Ashford shed. This was to acquaint Regional authorities destined to get 9Fs with the 2-10-0 type and then to explore the notion of using 9F 2-10-0s for SR continental workings. The WDs soon returned to Scotland and though some 9Fs did eventually work on the Southern it was in a later, very different sphere of operations. Photograph J. Robertson, www.transporttreasury.co.uk

Of the 150 2-10-0s constructed only 25 were taken into BR service. This is an unusual view, of one at Feltham shed in the early days of BR, 73784 (later 90760) on 20 March 1948 The boiler had three rings with the dome on the middle one and the covered feeds forward of that. Photograph R.J. Buckley, Initial Photographics.

90760 with painted on smokebox number in the bleak surrounds of Beattock with a typical long goods train. The signalbox was certainly built to withstand the elements. 90760 was another of the WD 2-10-0s confined to a single shed throughout its life, in this case Motherwell. Photograph W. Hermiston, www.transporttreasury.co.uk

Some Trip! Motherwell Trip 'M24' with 90760 in charge, passing Polmadie. Photograph W.S. Sellar.

These locos did look exceptionally smart when ex-works and they were withdrawn before the period of truly appalling filth and neglect descended upon the 2-8-0s so 90761 makes for a fine sight at Eastfield shed on 18 May 1959. Typical ScR numerals and the later type of BR totem; still no side windows, leading to the suspicion they were never fitted. As in other locomotive types a new coat of paint shows up the slight distortions in the tender side caused by the internal baffle arrangement; modellers could note, never worry if any plating looks slightly wobbly! This effect disappeared as the grime layers were deposited. Photograph R.J. Buckley, Initial Photographics.

Beattock again this time with 90762, always a Motherwell loco and another without a smokebox numberplate. That '7' does not look too good... The engine has halted for water (see the fireman on the tender) while the train is a splendid British 'mixed bag', about 1951 at a guess. On the left can only be that remarkable institution, the 'siege', at rest with a carriage door open. Many staff lived in inaccessible communities such as Auchencastle, Greskine and Hartrope between the Summit and Beattock itself (some ten miles away). The 'siege' consisted of one of the bankers and a single carriage for the convenience of staff either going on shift or taking the chance for some shopping. Photograph J. Patterson, www.transporttreasury.co.uk

Motherwell based all its BR life, 90761 looking a little along the way to becoming a hulk. Section of cladding removed and stuffed between frames at front, steam pipe to blower removed and the smokebox dart partly dismantled; a real oddity is the Scottish 'star' background in the centre of the smokebox door. Such a scene *could* indicate a partly stripped loco (it looks like Eastfield) ready for works but it's a bit late for that really, with that electrification flash. Diagonal works plate still in place. Photograph Stephen Gradidge.

90763, said to be at Eastleigh - which would make the occasion the trials of 1952.

90763 had borne a painted (and half-obscured) front number and a 68A Kingmoor shed plate until at least the summer of 1955 but now has **CARLISLE KINGMOOR** on the buffer beam and no shed plate, but a proper if dirty smokebox number plate. A partly or fully fitted goods train consisting of nothing but vans, it is coming south past Beattock shed on the left, home of the bankers. The cover has been removed from the top feed; again, up to the summer of 1955 at least, this had been in place. Photograph T.G. Hepburn, Rail Archive Stephenson.

Kingmoor on 13 August 1962, cover back on top feed. Photograph Peter Groom.

73788, later 90764, at St.Rollox on 5 August 1951 with the beginnings of its BR guise; it carries its shed code 66B Motherwell but has yet to be renumbered or get the totem on the tender. Then of course it is awaiting the removal of the air pump so might well be waiting a visit to the nearby works. Photograph B.K.B. Green, Initial Photographics.

Kingmoor, and 90764 from Motherwell shed (according to both plate and buffer beam) seems to dwarf the 4Fs behind. Alongside is Black Five 44706 from Corkerhill. Photograph E. Blakey, www.transporttreasury.co.uk

90765 at Grangemouth, 13 February 1955. Photograph W. S. Sellar.

90766 at home at Grangemouth on 17 May 1959 with 90773 behind. Both went in the mass withdrawals of December 1962 and ended their days at Campbells, Shieldhall. Photograph R.J. Buckley, Initial Photographics.

Motherwell's 90766 begins the clunking climb southwards to Beattock, at Elvanfoot on 2 May 1953, exiting the loop with a really mixed bag of stock in tow. The wagons over on the left are stabled on the track of the former Wanlockhead branch. Photograph J. Robertson, www.transporttreasury.co.uk

90767 pounds over the troughs at Strawfrank (which it couldn't use) on 7 June 1952. It had become a Polmadie engine the previous month. Without a scoop it is not taking water of course; even if one could have been fitted in amongst all those wheels! The reason that some 8Fs ran around with Austerity tenders during the 1948 exchanges, was that Southern locomotives could have tenders, *with* scoops, borrowed from the 8Fs. Photograph J. Robertson, www.transporttreasury.co.uk

Ex-works at Eastfield, 19 October 1951. Photograph J. L. Stevenson, courtesy Hamish Stevenson.

A WD 2-10-0 feeling sorry for itself, 90769 at home on Kingmoor shed in September 1955; once again a fading smokebox number. What was it about the Scottish Region and these smokebox number plates? Photograph J. Davenport, Initial Photographics.

AWS-equipped 90769 (battery box this side) at Eastfield. Photograph Paul Chancellor Collection.

These 2-10-0s spent their short BR working lives in Scotland and were of course frequently to be seen at Carlisle; indeed some had brief spells at Kingmoor shed when it was 68A in the Scottish Region. 73794, later 90770, is at Balornock shed, better known as St Rollox and has yet to lose the air pump and acquire new numbers but has been issued with a shed plate. A decent illustration of the middle, flangeless, pair of driving wheels though impossible to see is the reduced thickness of the flanges on the wheels either side. In this way the engines could negotiate chains down to curvatures of 4½ chains. One curiosity to be observed on these 2-10-0s is the lever emerging from the cab front on this right-hand side to a winding linkage on the running plate by the firebox. This worked the blow-down valve located in the firebox throat plate. They were not a normal fitting for locos in this country and their survival is a surprise. Photograph J. Davenport, Initial Photographics.

The vast shed at Eastfield was long host to the 2-10-0s even if none of them were actually on the books. They could often be seen there ex-works or like 90770, visiting in this case from its home shed, Motherwell, on 23 June 1957. Even though they were only based in the Scottish Region twelve were scrapped at Darlington Works. Photograph R. Wilson, www.transporttreasury.co.uk

90772, still with air pump, at Kingmoor shed in June, 1950; lamps awaiting disposition at the front. Photograph J. Davenport, Initial Photographics.